Before You Leap... Again

Preparing Yourself for the Adventures and Challenges of Remarriage

Jeff Parziale Ph.D. and Judi Babcock Parziale Ph.D.

In reading Jeff and Judi's book, "*Looking Before You Leap...Again,*" I was excited about how much this could benefit those hurting from divorce and needing hope and help in the remarriage process. I wish every divorced person would read and work this manual before leaping again. It gives grace, guidance and wisdom in many practical areas. Hidden in the book are jewels like the Dr. P. rules, "forgiveness takes one, reconciliation and trust takes two." Taking the time to work on your life by working this manual will bring emotional and spiritual blessings I am sure.
Randy Reynolds, Executive Director, Renewal Centers

Looking Before You Leap...Again is a comprehensive and practical resource for anyone interested in building a strong, spiritually based stepfamily. With inventories and questions, participants are encouraged to realistically look at their journeys of life which have gotten them to where they are today and enabling them to have realistic expectations for the future. This resource challenges individuals to know that creating a strong stepfamily is not a matter of chance but of accepting roles and responsibilities which will help them discover ways of listening and communicating in a new relationship.
Dr. Lee Sankey, Executive Presbyter, Presbytery de Cristo

I found this book insightful, practical, and extremely well organized. I wish it would have been available when I started my stepfamily.
Rick Kern MA, Learning & Development Specialist, Center for Learning & Staff Development, Tucson Medical Center

"Looking Before You Leap...Again" is a resource to help persons considering (or who will one day consider) remarriage. It will help these persons to figure out what remarriage really means and how to do it most effectively. It is a well-written book that gives a thoughtful perspective on the questions that need to be asked before remarriage.
Rev. Dr. Frank Williams, Director of Education and Training, Family Counseling Agency

Dr. Parziale's books, *Looking Before You Leap...Again* and *Building Healthy Relationships* have been great assets to the members and the staff of Equally Yoked Christian Singles. We are truly blessed to have this valuable information available to us.
Tearle Wysockie, Owner and Director of Equally Yoked Christian Singles, Tucson and Phoenix

Looking Before You Leap… Again

Preparing Yourself for the Adventures and Challenges of Remarriage

Jeff Parziale Ph.D. and Judi Babcock Parziale Ph.D.

Looking Before You Leap...Again:
Preparing Yourself for the Adventures and Challenges of Remarriage

International Standard Book Number: 1-893-757-35-8

Published by InStep Ministries
1181 N. El Dorado Place, Suite 312, Tucson, AZ 85715
520 721-0800
www.instepministries.com

Cover Design by Aztec Publishing

Table of Contents

In Loving Memory

Susan Marie (Thrasher) Esham
1951 - 2002

Acknowledgments

Most books are a team effort; this book is no different. We would like to thank three people who made substantial contributions to this workbook. First, Don Esham, who lived through many of the aspects of this workbook and whose contributions to clarity were very useful. Next, Rev. Bill Evans, good friend and colleague, who consistently challenged us to continue our work and ministry. Finally, Linda King, who thoroughly reviewed the manuscript and made invaluable suggestions.

The individuals who graciously reviewed our book deserve special mention. Randy Reynolds is a good friend, gifted counselor and one of the most articulate spokespersons for the needs of others in our community. Rick Kern has been a good friend for many years. Talking through various parts of this book with him has been especially helpful. Rev. Lee Sankey is a kind and compassionate clergymen and leader. His encouragement and wisdom was extremely helpful. Tearle Wysocki is a man of great integrity, who really cares about singles. Finally, Dr. Frank Williams, a true pioneer in the areas of divorce recovery and remarriage, has been teaching and doing the principles outlined in this book for many years. It was a true honor to talk through this book with him.

Our lives have been enriched and our spirits continually lifted by our six children, Jennifer, Chad, Wes, Jaimie, Jenna and Julie, and our two incredible grandsons, Jeffrey and Jason. God has truly blessed us. Finally, we would like to thank the hundreds of singles, singles parents and remarrying and remarried individuals who graciously shared their lives and stores with us. They are the real heroes because they demonstrated to us over and over again the incredible vitality of the human spirit and the unlimited grace of the God of second chances.

Preface

Divorce continues to be a major fact of our society. Likewise is remarriage. Nearly eighty percent of those who divorce will remarry. Of those who remarry, it is likely that more than half will divorce a second time. Most of those who remarry will do so without adequately thinking through the transition that they have experienced through their divorce.

For twenty-five years, the *Divorce Recovery Program* of Tucson, Arizona has provided help for persons going through the transition at the end of a relationship. In order to assist people going through this transition, we continually have sought resources that will help them in this task. Providing useful resources for these persons, especially as they begin to develop new relationships and consider remarriage, has been difficult because there have not been many such resources. Jeff and Judi Parziale have written a significant and helpful workbook for these persons.

"Looking Before You Leap...Again" is a tremendous resource to help persons considering (or who will one day consider) remarriage. It will assist these persons in determining what remarriage really means and how to do it most effectively. It is a well-written book that gives a thoughtful perspective on the questions that need to be asked before remarriage.

Additionally, as a Pastor for many years, I can recommend this as an important resource for the Christian who is considering remarriage. The author has provided helpful biblical references that will assist in answering difficult questions about divorce and remarriage.

The Rev. Dr. Frank R. Williams
Director, Education and Training
Family Counseling Agency
Tucson, Arizona

Foreword

Our prayers are answered not when we are given what we ask, but when we are challenged to be what we can be. Morris Adler

You are considering remarriage. Congratulations. The remarriage divorce rate is over **60%.** If that does not get your attention, check your pulse! Now that we have your attention, thank you for obtaining a copy of our workbook, ***Looking Before You Leap…Again.*** We wrote this workbook for one express purpose—to help you prepare for the challenges of remarriage and stepfamily life. It might amaze you to know that less than 25% of those who remarry ever read a book about divorce and remarriage or seek any form of premarital counseling. **Most remarrying individuals are totally unprepared for remarriage.** We certainly were unprepared when we remarried and became a stepfamily. The issues covered in this book are the result of our professional experience as well as the lessons we have learned on our journey.

We felt impressed by God to share the lessons we have learned (and are still learning) with others. One result has been the forming of InStep Ministries and the development of a series of materials for singles and remarried adults and their children. Three books have been written so far, including the one you are reading. The first book is entitled *Developing Healthy Relationships*. This book helps singles develop a healthy Christian lifestyle and a Biblical approach to building relationships. Our second book is *The Journey: A Travelguide for Christian Stepfamilies*. In this book we address every major topic involved in building a successful stepfamily.

Over the past 25 years, Jeff has counseled hundreds of remarrying individuals. In each case, they started their new marriage with high hopes for a long and fulfilling relationship. Some marriages survived, some did not. The question we asked was why do so many remarriages fail? As we researched this question and interviewed both singles and remarried couples, ***we discovered some very important answers.*** We also discovered how to significantly improve your chances of having a successful remarriage. This is a success workbook, and if you will follow the steps outlined in this book, you can have a successful remarriage. We are convinced that God stands for marriage, including remarriage. Less than 40% of remarriages succeed; the choice is yours.

What will I learn from this workbook?

- How to take great care of yourself and your children
- How to build a healthy single lifestyle that really works
- How to identify and grieve your losses
- How to deal with loneliness, anger, guilt and depression
- How to build healthy relationships
- How to prepare yourself and your children for remarriage
- How to know when you are ready to remarry
- How to create a great stepfamily right from the start
- How to identify unrealistic expectations that can sabotage your relationships
- How to spot "red flags" in a potential partner
- How to change unsuccessful relationship patterns

- How to radically change the statistics of remarriage success—in your favor

Many individuals approach marriage, even remarriage, with a "let's get married and work out the details later" attitude. In fact, most remarrying couples have known each other less than *nine months.* Couples remarry long before they have finished grieving their losses, worked through their issues or developed a healthy single lifestyle. The high divorce rate for remarriage suggests that this approach will not work. Successful remarriages and stepfamilies result when individuals take the time to work out the details first.

Remarriage is like an uncharted jungle, foreboding and dangerous, and yet, with the right guide, exciting and gratifying. Use the material in this book as your guide. However, this workbook, or any book for that matter, is not intended to take the place of qualified assistance. Please do not hesitate to consult a pastor or counselor if needed. Before remarrying, attend at least four to six premarital education sessions. We suggest you find a pastor or counselor familiar with remarriage and stepfamily dynamics.

Make an investment in yourself and your future. Have your pen and Bible handy as you read through this material. Answer the questions as candidly as possible and begin to build a future for yourself and your children. Please take your time reading through this workbook. This is not a race. Some things in life are like cooking with a crock pot, others are like cooking with a microwave. This is definitely crock pot territory. It takes time to make changes and to assimilate new information. It takes time to grieve your losses and to determine the kind of life you want in the future. Keep in mind that God is a God of second chances (read Jonah 3:1; Hosea 3:1; Joel 2:12-13; Romans 8:1; I Cor. 6:9-11; I John 2:1; II Tim. 2:21). His timing is perfect; He wants to change you from the inside out through the work of His Spirit. The ultimate trademark of remarriage readiness is grace and humility. These lead to tolerance, flexibility, love, compassion, respect, and acceptance. However, it is the depth of your commitment to God and to yourself and your children that will give you the strength and will to persevere no matter what. In *Failing Forward*, John Maxwell writes, "People change when they hurt enough that they have to, learn enough that they want to, and receive enough that they are able to" (p. 146). Our prayer is that this material will assist you on your journey. God bless you, may happiness and fulfillment lie ahead.

Jeff and Judi Parziale
Tucson, Arizona
II Corinthians 1:3-7

Introduction

If you are divorced or widowed and have children, this workbook is for you. If you are single and currently dating someone with children, this workbook is for you. If you have children and are contemplating marrying someone who also has children, this workbook is especially for you. Remarriage, when children are involved, represents an incredible challenge and a tremendous opportunity. The statistics on remarriage success are quite grim. Grab a pencil and your Bible, because you are going to explore a number of concepts and principles that can radically improve your chances for a successful remarriage.

The questions we have been asked over the years have guided the development of this workbook. Some of them are listed below. Perhaps you have asked many of these questions yourself (we did). Perhaps you are asking them right now.

> "How do I keep from making the same mistakes in relationships?"
> "How do I find someone who will love me and accept my children?"
> "How will I know when I am "ready" to get remarried?"
> "How will I know if he/she is the right one?
> "What if he/she doesn't like my kids?"
> "What about my children; what's best for them?"
> "How tough is it to "blend" a family?
> "How do I know if I can trust him/her with my kids?"
> "What does God have to say about divorce and remarriage?"
> "How long does the pain of death/divorce last?"
> "What about my needs?"
> "How will I know if we both want the same things?"
> "What do I need to know about stepfamilies?"

The answer to these and other questions are addressed in the pages ahead. For now, let us tackle some key questions we have been asked as we interviewed singles contemplating remarriage.

What is the first step in remarriage readiness?
The first step to a healthy remarriage is you. Is this a surprise? Life wounds all of us. The losses, disappointments and hurts of life will not heal themselves—you must choose to heal. In fact, you will not grow until healing has taken place—and this takes time. You will determine the success of your next relationship by the investment you make in becoming a healthy single. Your friendships, habits, spiritual disciplines, attitudes, expectations, doubts and fears—everything that defines who you are and what you will need in a relationship—will all play a role in the success or failure of your next relationship. The healthier you are, the better your chances of success. So the question is, will you take the time to invest in your own healing and growth? You may be wondering, what exactly does that mean. The list below highlights some things you need to bring to a healthy relationship (and we will talk about every one of these). How many of these do you have right now?

- A healthy single lifestyle
- A good relationship with your children
- A meaningful connection to a community of believers
- Adequate grieving of past losses
- Resolution of any emotional issues such as guilt, anger or bitterness
- Realistic expectations about future relationships
- A handle on any abuse issues, addictions or self-sabotaging behaviors
- Effective communication and problem solving skills
- A willingness to change and learn
- A willingness to repent and forgive
- An ability to know and articulate your needs
- A healthy release of the past
- A willingness to understand and respond adequately to the needs of a partner
- Accurate, realistic information about remarriage and stepfamily life
- A well thought out sense of what you want in a partner and what you have to give
- A committed relationship to God

However, if instead you bring unrealistic expectations, underdeveloped relationship skills, unresolved issues from the past, and inaccurate information into your next relationship, you will repeat unhealthy patterns and behaviors that will sabotage every one of your relationships. Becoming emotionally, spiritually and relationally prepared for the challenges of remarriage is far more critical than fine-tuning your list of qualities in a potential partner. The healthier you are, the better relationship choices you will make. By taking the time to read this material, complete the exercises and look honestly at yourself, you can determine your own personal remarriage readiness and ultimately that of a partner. What we ask is that you make an investment in yourself. ***Do not consider remarriage until you are spiritually, relationally and emotionally healthy.*** In fact, restrict your dating until you have addressed the issues presented in the next few chapters. Please keep an open heart and mind about this. In Philippians 1, God promises to complete the good work He has started in us. It will take that kind of personal commitment. God wants to partner with you in both your personal growth and healing as well as in your remarriage. Only when Christ becomes your true source of intimacy will you be able to establish healthy relationships that are driven not by fear or loneliness but by your fullness in Christ and a desire to share life with another.

Action Step: **Your story-part one: Where have you been and where are you now?** We all begin this process somewhere. How did your story start? Where are you now on your journey? Take a few moments and jot down some thoughts. Use extra paper if need be. When you are done with this workbook, you will have written your story—a chronicle of your journey.

How do I get healthy?

Becoming a healthy single is a promise you make to yourself. The steps will vary from person to person. However, the first step is to grieve and mourn your losses. Divorce or the death of a spouse is a huge loss; actually it is many losses. Understanding and grieving these losses is critical to your growth. The next step is to understand and resolve your past. This could include confession and repentance for poor choices and harm brought to others, dealing with destructive personal habits, working through your role in a divorce, or letting go of the painful results of losses in past relationships. Becoming healthy also involves dealing with loneliness and getting connected to a support network. Whether it is a church group, support group or close friends, we grow best when we have support, encouragement and accountability. Another critical aspect of health is your vocational and financial life. This means that career goals are solid and finances are under control. Finally, learn how to take great care of yourself (and your children). This means learning new skills, unlearning some old bad habits and taking responsibility for your spiritual and emotional well-being.

When can I start dating?

Most experts seem to agree that you should wait at least one year after a divorce or death of a spouse. Our maxim is no dating until you have some things in place. My friend, Don Esham, reminded me recently that you must be healthy spiritually, emotionally, socially, vocationally and financially before you are ready to begin dating. You must be developing a healthy single lifestyle that includes adequately grieving, taking great care of yourself and your children, letting go of the past, resolving past relationships, and involving yourself in some form of community. Also, you need to have the right attitude toward dating. We do not support dating that is superficial or exploitive. Healthy dating is about making friends, being real and sharing yourself (goals, values, passions, dreams, etc.) with another. Healthy dating is being clear about who you are, what you need and what you can give to another. Unhealthy dating is like panning for gold, keeping the nuggets and discarding the rest. Healthy dating is God-honoring and involves your group of supporters. Breaking away from your support group once you start dating or compromising your values is not healthy. Before you date, be clear about dating others with children. Single parents (even non-custodial parents) and their children always come as a package.

How do I find the right person?

That's a great question. Actually, in our experience, it is really about being the right person and finding the right relationship. This distinction is critical to understand. Focusing on the "right person" means looking for a partner who possesses certain qualities. People who think this way have a long "laundry list" of expectations. Focusing on the right relationship means involving someone in your life who "fits" with your lifestyle and your needs, passions and values. Focusing on the right person often leads us to amend our expectations to "fit" the other person. It is amazing how many people throw out their laundry lists when they meet someone to whom they are attracted. "Being the right person" means committing to being emotionally and spiritually healthy and being clear about who you are and what you are willing to give in a relationship.

Selecting a healthy partner is more about developing a healthy single lifestyle than fine-tuning your mate selection skills. The clearer you are about becoming the person God is calling you to be, the better your ability to discern a partner who represents a great "fit." The more we "need" another person to fulfill us or make us whole, the more demanding or dependent we will be and the less discerning. Not every great person will be a great fit. God wants to partner with you in this area. He has given you incredible relationship tools—He loves you and accepts you for who you are, He made you in His image (a relational being), He provided the Church (fellow journey takers) and He gave you His Spirit.

What about the Internet?

Meeting via the Internet is controversial. In principle, we would prefer couples meet and develop relationships in person. However, the Internet can provide a means to meet other singles. We do, however, have many concerns. First, most Internet services do very little screening of members. Second, Internet "dating" is vulnerable to "false-self dating" which means people can be less than candid about their circumstances or who they are. Third, Internet "daters" tend to isolate themselves. Feedback from others who know and love us is a critical part of building healthy relationships. Fourth, Internet relationships tend to develop much too quickly. Internet contacts tend to be intense for a short period of time. This can give the illusion of closeness and intimacy. Finally, Internet relationships "slip" into "cyber-sex" too often. Cyber-sex is incredibly unhealthy and is a total distortion of God's view of healthy sexuality. Please be careful about meeting people over the Internet. Keep your support group informed and involved. Be discreet but totally honest when sending pictures or personal information. Let the relationship evolve slowly. If you arrange to meet, consider taking a friend along or meeting in a group setting. Please consult your pastor or accountability before making any commitments to fly somewhere to meet.

What about singles groups or dating services?

These can be good ways to meet people and make friends—not just "troll" for possible marriage partners. Many churches have effective singles groups. If your church has a singles ministry, please join if possible. Larger organizations, like Equally Yoked Christian Singles, can also provide opportunities to meet people and develop relationships. Whatever type of organization or group you chose, please keep a few simple dating rules—take your time, be real, make friends, stay connected to your support group, honor God and respect the other person.

Dating rules? I'm an adult, why do I need rules?

You may not need rules, but you could certainly benefit from some healthy guidelines. Most of us are painfully unaware of why we have struggled in relationships. Denial or an unwillingness to look at our unhealthy relationship patterns can yield a high price—a continuing series of relationship failures. God takes relationships very seriously. From the beginning, He said that we were relational beings, made in His image. His rules for relationships can be found in the Bible. See Matthew 5 and 6, I Corinthians 13, Romans 12, Ephesians 5 and 6, Philippians 2 and I Thessalonians 5.

What about my children?

After a death or divorce, many parents become so absorbed in their own grief and loss that they can miss the fact that their children are grieving losses and adjusting to huge changes over which they have no control. Some parents minimize the impact of loss and change on their children. Children struggle with loss and change as much or more than adults. Allow your children time to grieve. Talk to them and/or let them talk to your pastor or counselor. When you start to date, be sensitive to their needs. Most adults begin dating before their children are emotionally ready. Do not introduce them to everyone you date. Some children will instantly bond to a new adult or act out if they feel you are trying to replace an absent parent. Involve your children in your support group. Some children feel abandoned when their parent begins to date. Introduce them to a potential partner only if both of you have agreed to move your relationship toward marriage. Be sensitive to the fact that your children, like many others, are not looking for a new parent and may be resistant to meeting this new person.

How do I prepare for remarriage?

The most important aspect of preparing for remarriage is accepting the fact that preparation is necessary. How important is it for you to have a successful remarriage? What are you willing to do to ensure that your next marriage will be healthy? Many individuals we have counseled assumed that "time" was all that really mattered. More couples than ever are remarrying less than one year after meeting. We feel this is very unwise and the statistics bear this out. Preparing for remarriage means going through a series of emotional steps that begin with the ending of your relationship, whether by death or divorce, and end with your actual remarriage. There are critical readiness principles to learn to assist you in determining if you and/or your potential spouse are truly "ready" to remarry. This is some of the most important work you will do.

What if I find "Mr. or Ms. Right?"

Congratulations. Spend time together. Go to church and pray together. Introduce him or her to your pastor, family, friends, support group and accountability partner. Be as real as humanly possible. Ask and answer a million questions. Be candid about your expectations and your needs. Schedule some time for premarital counseling. Remember our main adage, you are not looking for the "right" person but for the "right" relationship.

Are marriage and remarriage really that different?

Yes. Even if there are no children involved, and there usually are, remarriage is very different from a first time marriage. For starters, remarrying couples often carry wounds and hurts from past relationships. This "baggage" can create invisible barriers to intimacy in a new relationship. The age differences in remarriage are much larger than first-time marriages. Remarriages often create stepfamilies, which means that each individual is connected to children and other family members that will tend to compete with the couple relationship. Most remarriages begin because of some form of loss, suggesting that individuals may still be grieving those losses. Also, images of past relationships will have an impact on expectations for future relationships.

What is a stepfamily?

Any family, where at least one partner has children, even grown children, from a previous relationship, constitutes a stepfamily. Most stepfamilies result from divorce or the death of a spouse. Typically one partner, most often the mom, brings children into the new marriage. While stepfamilies may come in all shapes and sizes, they share some common traits. Stepfamilies always begin because of some form of loss. Stepfamilies tend to develop through a series of stages, lasting from five to seven years. The early stages are marked by tremendous turbulence and stress as the new family attempts to sort out new rules, roles and relationships, often with virtual strangers. Communication and problem solving are difficult because the family has many competing needs and little history together. Loyalty conflicts and power struggles threaten to pull the family apart. It is no surprise that the first few years of stepfamily life yield the highest rate of divorce. Couples whose marriages do not survive are forced to re-live the trauma and loss associated with yet another divorce.

Why the term "stepfamily?"

Stepfamilies have been given many names—by the media, by various agencies and by family professionals. These names include: blended, binuclear, integrated, complicated, merged, reconstituted or combined. The Stepfamily Association of America suggests that the word stepfamily is the most appropriate name.

Many struggle with the term stepfamily because it has such a negative connotation. The word "step" is actually derived from the old English word "Steop," which means orphaned. Indeed, society, the media and even the church have often viewed stepfamilies as "second-class." It's refreshing to know that in God's kingdom we are all "first-class." Blended is the term commonly used by the church, particularly because it is a softer word than "step." The difficulty with the term blended is that families do not actually blend, they really combine or integrate. Using the term "blending" may put undue pressure on a family. Family members in stepfamilies maintain their individual identities for several years before becoming something that looks and acts like a family. Our recommendation is that you use the word stepfamily.

How does one create a healthy stepfamily?

Very carefully! Combining families can be tough, but it is an important process for you to understand if you plan to remarry. **Creating a healthy stepfamily means taking a group of strangers with very different preferences, routines, traditions, loyalties and expectations and combining them over time to form something that looks and works like a family**. Let's unpack this definition. ***First,*** the group of strangers represents you and all your family and friends, including your ex-spouse as well as a new spouse and his or her family, friends and former spouse. This group of strangers is in no way bonded; some may not even like each other at first or want to be a part of the new family. ***Second,*** each of these groups, called mini-families, has very different ways of looking at and doing everything. This means that even the smallest detail or event can provoke a conflict. Holidays, for example, which are normally joyous times, can be very stressful because everyone has different expectations about how they should be celebrated. Of course, as you may have expected, everyone feels his/her way is right. "Different" in a stepfamily often translates into "wrong." ***Third,*** "combining" is an intentional process, which means time alone will not necessarily create a healthy stepfamily. It takes from five to seven years of caring, sharing, listing and adjusting. During this time, mini-families (groups such as a Mom and her children) can remain fairly separate. Some family members do not want to combine and may resist all efforts to do so. The first few years of stepfamily life are normally extremely turbulent as all these differences are resolved. ***Finally***, the definition of family must be expanded to include children who may not live with you all the time. In fact, in the average stepfamily, children are continually moving between households, which plays havoc with such concepts as family identity, consistent discipline, parenting schedules, vacations and family loyalty. Stepfamilies and nuclear families are not the same, nor do very many stepfamilies ever become exactly like nuclear families. However, a stepfamily can become a place of love, safety and acceptance. A wonderful metaphor for stepfamilies is the Body of Christ, incredible diversity yet great unity.

Sounds tough—why would anyone want to remarry?

Great question. Please do not remarry until you can say with complete confidence, "I draw my value and worth from God." "I have worked through my issues to the best of my ability." "I and my friends/pastor/counselor/support group consider me ready to remarry." "I am committed to my ongoing health in these five critical areas: spiritual, emotional, relational, financial and vocational." "I completely understand my new partner's circumstances and I am ready to remarry this person and his or her children now." "I am ready to put my new marriage first and to nurture my spouse." "I am ready to co-parent my children/stepchildren with all the other parental figures involved."

God made you and I relational beings. We long for relationships. Relationships are where our needs are met. Further, God is a God of second chances. Perhaps you are looking for a second chance. In the next chapter, we will examine some of the challenges of remarriage. Remarriage is challenging, but it can also be very fulfilling. God stands for marriages, including remarriages.

Action Step: No matter where you are in the remarriage process, take a moment and promise yourself that you will not remarry until you have worked through the issues outlined in this workbook. Sign and date this promise.

On ________________, I ______________________________ make this promise.
Date Name

If you are currently dating, have that person sign and date the same pledge.

On________________, I______________________________ make this promise.
Date Name

The Remarriage Challenge

If you work these words into your life, you are like a smart carpenter who built his house on solid rock. Rain poured down, the river flooded, a tornado hit—but nothing moved that house. It was fixed to the rock (Matt 7:24 The Message)

A client asked recently, "Is remarriage *really* that different from first-time marriage? I have been married before, why the need to spend so much time preparing for remarriage?" Another client commented, "It's been years since my divorce, I think I'm ready to remarry." Still another client suggested, "My spouse died recently, we had a great marriage, do I need remarriage preparation?" Yes, you need remarriage preparation, and yes, there are many differences between a remarriage and a first-time marriage. Time alone does not prepare you for remarriage. There is a direct correlation between your preparation for remarriage and the success of your remarriage. A divorce or the death of a spouse can be a devastating experience, both to you and to your children. Healing from such tragedies takes time. *Jane was marrying for the fifth time. All the men she married were alcoholics, although at the time she claimed she didn't know they were. Interestingly, the man she is now (re)marrying was her first husband.*

What makes remarriage so challenging? Listed below are some of the key reasons remarriage can be challenging as well as some ways that marriage and remarriage differ. Take some time and review (re-read) these factors—they are about you!

- Humans have a tendency to not learn from their mistakes. Most individuals, for example, learn nothing from their divorce and are therefore primed to enter a new relationship without a clue as to why their last relationship failed. They seldom develop any new skills or insights, so they are destined to repeat the same behaviors or choose the same type of partners—over and over.

- Our culture, including the church, has only one predominant image of the family, the nuclear family. Consequently all others family forms have no set of established norms. This results in "alternative" families feeling shamed or inferior or at best confused and directionless.

- Divorced individuals are extremely wounded, both emotionally and spiritually. This woundedness has many consequences: guilt, shame, fear, distrust, self-protection, reality distortions, difficulty bonding with others, and an inability to communicate or solve problems effectively. Many divorced individuals feel like a failure. Wounded individuals have difficulty discerning the essential qualities of a potential partner. Fear and loneliness often guide partner choices. Wounded individuals are self-absorbed and therefore unable to effectively meet the needs of a partner.

- Remarrying adults bring a host of unresolved issues, inaccurate beliefs and unrealistic expectations to a new stepfamily. The mental picture they have of remarriage and stepfamily life does not reflect reality.

- Loyalty binds are common in stepfamilies. The bonding between individuals seen in nuclear families does not generally exist in stepfamilies. Children and stepparents do not understand each other and parents often feel pulled between children and a new spouse. Most children do not want their parent to remarry; in fact, many children never give up hope that their divorced parents will re-unite.

- First-time marriages, in general, receive far more emotional and physical support from church, family and friends than remarriages.

- Most individuals remarry too soon, often less than two years after a death or divorce. Many individuals remarry before they or their children have completed the grieving process. Further, the time between meeting someone and remarrying is less than half that of first-time marriages. The average remarrying adult has known their partner less than nine months.

- Remarriage is not about "picking" the right person but about finding the right relationship, being the right person and picking the right "people."

- Stepfamilies live in a constant state of "relational overload." Step-relationships are far more numerous and complex than first-time families. For example, stepfamilies often include former spouses and all their relatives. These relationships can range from cordial to openly hostile and can exert unwanted control over the family. Children move back and forth between households that are very different from one another, challenging the definition of "family" and making "blending" all the more difficult. Co-parenting and discipline issues are complex and can create a great deal of conflict.

- Children of divorce experience a great many changes and losses. They do not adjust to these changes or grieve these losses quickly. Many adults remarry long before their children are ready to adjust to another change. Many children are still emotionally wounded when their parents remarry. Consequently, they often have difficulty adjusting to a new family structure. This difficulty can manifest itself as depression, withdrawal, or acting out. These problems can become then focus of remarrying parents, potentially causing additional stress to an already fragile new marriage.

- First time marriages involve the church far more frequently than remarriages. Most individuals do not seek spiritual guidance prior to remarriage. Few remarriages occur in a church setting. The church does a great job of preparing couples for marriage, but it is almost silent in its preparation of couples for remarriage. Most pastors have virtually no knowledge of the demands and complexities of stepfamilies. In many churches, single and/or divorced individuals are marginalized and remain on the periphery. Few churches provide support for singles (many of whom are divorced and likely to remarry) or existing stepfamilies.

- Accountability is often absent in the life of remarrying individuals. Spiritual maturity is a great hedge against divorce. Accountability with other believers in the context of Christian community is a wonderful way to grow and heal. Unfortunately, many divorced individuals have difficulty working though their guilt and shame and therefore stay isolated. Many perceive the church as a place they are not welcome. Further, their strong feelings of loneliness often propel them into new relationships much too soon. Spiritual maturity allows us to draw on God as a source of our "Ok-ness." Many remarrying individuals are looking for affirmation from a new partner. However, a wounded partner is looking for much the same and both are unable to give what the other needs.

- New relationships create very different power distributions in families. Children, for example, who perhaps had some role in the single-parent family, now find themselves on the periphery of the new family. Power struggles are common in stepfamilies, making new relationships even more difficult to develop.

- Remarrying couples have a much wider disparity in age than first-time couples—often ten years of more. This means that their children may have different needs and be at very different places socially, educationally and developmentally. Age disparity can also impact such issues as discipline, lifestyle, vocation or retirement.

- Sexual boundaries are far more ambiguous in remarriages. Due to emotional wounds, pain and loneliness, premarital sex is far more prevalent among remarrying couples. Unfortunately, sexual relationships often give the illusion of closeness, prompting couples to remarry too soon.

- Remarrying couples generally display a much lower commitment to marriage than first-time couples.

The result is that remarrying singles like yourself have difficulty making good partner choices and, once married, often find themselves overwhelmed, disillusioned and poorly equipped to handle all the decisions and adjustments that must be made—immediately. In telling their story, too many remarried couples have shared that the best times they had together were before their marriage.

Preparing ***yourself*** emotionally, socially, vocationally and spiritually is the most important thing you can do to insure the success of a potential remarriage. The majority of remarried couples we have counseled or interviewed readily admitted that, after looking back, they were not prepared for the challenges of remarriage. Many candidly discussed the "red flags" they either missed or simply chose to ignore. Most remarrying individuals have *far more* emotional woundedness and *far less* understanding of the challenges of creating a stepfamily than they realize. What they do know is that they are in love and want to be together—they want a second chance. What they *do not* know is the inherent difficulties of remarriage and stepfamily life and the tendency they have, due to their own woundedness, to sabotage their relationships.

This does not look promising!

You may be thinking, "I thought you said this was a success workbook?" This is a success book; but let's get this clear upfront: **The main cause of remarriage failure is that most individuals are <u>totally</u> unprepared for remarriage and stepfamily life.** We will unpack this as we move through the workbook, but it is a truth you must accept. Most of the individuals we have counseled or interviewed truly thought they were ready for remarriage—they were not. The good news is that you can be and we will show you how. Remarriage and stepfamily life can be the greatest spiritual adventure you will ever undertake. If you allow Him, God will stretch you in areas like flexibility, servanthood, love, community and accountability.

"OK, I'm convinced. How do I prepare for remarriage?" There are several steps to the answer.

- Commit to not remarry until you are ready—emotionally and spiritually.
- Get yourself and your children ready by working through any unresolved issues and being clear about what you need in a healthy relationship.
- Stay connected to a supportive community that can provide spiritual direction, accountability and encouragement.
- Read this workbook thoroughly—the steps presented will help prepare you for remarriage.

How do I get ready to remarry? Readiness simply means being mentally, relationally and spiritually prepared. You can become ready to remarry if you will follow the steps outlined in this workbook. Preparing for remarriage is a personal process that begins with your divorce from or the death of your spouse and ends after your remarriage. Every relationship, event, attitude, belief and feeling that occurs during this time period is included in the process. There are several critical aspects of this process and it is absolutely imperative that you deal with each one, since each aspect builds on the one before.

The **first** is recovery and growth, both for yourself and your children. Divorce or the death of a spouse involves both loss and change. Change is difficult for most of us; it is particularly tough on children. Losses must be embraced and grieved. Most remarrying individuals have not adequately grieved their losses. This first stage is a time for addressing your spiritual life and assessing who you are. It is a time for learning from and resolving the past, for rebuilding, for taking great care of yourself and for preparing yourself to risk getting re-involved in relationships. If you get involved in an intimate relationship during this phase, that relationship will more than likely be unhealthy and will, in fact, prevent you from becoming healthy yourself.

The **second** aspect is remarriage preparation. Everything you do (or don't do) after your spouse dies or leaves is preparing you for remarriage. Few people ever think about this at the time and we are certainly not suggesting that remarriage is a necessity. However, the person you will become and the type of person you will choose to remarry is being shaped from that moment on. Long before there is someone else, there is you and your children. This is also a time of spiritual preparation. Remarriage that involves combining two families can be extremely stressful and challenge our deep beliefs. Developing a successful stepfamily requires our ability to adopt a servant mindset. The needs of others, perhaps even those who do not particularly like you, must, at times, take precedence over you own needs. The ability to be tolerant and patient with others can only come through your own spiritual fullness—being okay in Christ and therefore not needing to be in control or have everything your way. The ability to love those who do not reciprocate your love can only come from a deep awareness of being loved by the great Lover.

The **third** critical aspect of this process is stepfamily awareness. There is a body of knowledge you must understand, and more importantly, accept. Stepfamilies are unique, with their own set of rules and characteristics. They are unlike nuclear families in many important ways. Most individuals attempt to recreate a nuclear family when they remarry—this seldom works. Understanding the unique qualities of stepfamilies is critical to success. Having a thorough working knowledge of stepfamilies and how to make them work is particularly important during the first year of remarriage. If you remarry with unrealistic expectations based on a limited or inaccurate understanding of stepfamily dynamics, your new marriage will be in trouble—instantly.

Second chances

Valerie came in for counseling. She had been remarried for just six months. She explained that John, her new husband, was acting just like her former husband. "How can this be, I looked for someone just the opposite of Bill. Now I feel exactly the same. It's like I remarried my ex-husband."

In *Second Chances*, Judith Wallerstein and Sandra Blakeslee discuss some of the hopes and fears individuals face after a divorce. They review some of the questions and challenges a divorce poses, and conclude that, "People want to believe that divorce will relieve all their stresses—back we go to square one and begin our lives anew. But divorce does not wipe the slate clean. Some second chances come with three small children, a low-paying job, and the ghosts of a failed marriage. Some come with a sense of having been torn away from one's children and not knowing how to reestablish a home. Some second chances begin with loneliness and a feeling of being unloved and unlovable. Some bring on acute problems that turn into chronic problems (p. 4)."

Second chances come with consequences, according to Wallerstein and Blakeslee. How many of these consequences fit your circumstances?

- Lack of trust in the reliability of relationships?
- Relationships infused with anxiety?
- Rising levels of shame, guilt, anger, fear or doubt?
- Children assuming responsibilities well beyond their years?
- Single parents struggling to raise their children?
- Noncustodial parents trying to make the best of an ambiguous role?
- Remarrying adults struggling with deep loss and unresolved pain?
- Parents desperately trying to find some semblance of family?
- Children who seldom see a successful marriage or family?
- Struggles to make your faith relevant.

Few adults accurately anticipate what lies ahead after a divorce or the death of a spouse. Few adults are prepared for the incredible wounds a divorce causes or the broken trust that must be repaired. Few adults appreciate the tasks involved in recovering from a partner's death or a divorce. According to Wallerstsein and Blakeslee divorce is unique among family crises because it is the only one in which the social supports fall away. "When there is a death in the family, people come running to help. After a natural disaster, neighbors rally to assist those who have been hurt. After most crises, clergymen may call on the family to console adults or speak with children who are badly shaken. But not so with divorce. Friends are afraid that they will have to take sides, neighbors think it is none of their business. Although half the families in our study belong to churches or synagogues, not one clergyman came to call on the adults or children during divorce. When a man and woman divorce, many people tend to act as if they believe it might be contagious. The divorced person is seen as a loose cannon" (pp. 7-8). How tragic.

Divorce or the death of a spouse is a devastating experience that can leave us with many emotional wounds and many intense emotions—depression, anger, fear, bitterness, guilt or shame. There must be a time of grieving and healing. ***Successfully addressing these feelings and emotional wounds is one of the most important factors in remarriage success.*** Few individuals understand or successfully complete the process of becoming a healthy single. Most adults do absolutely nothing to prepare for remarriage. The unrealistic expectations and inaccurate information individuals carry into their next marriage are vestiges of unresolved issues from past relationships. "I want to do it right this time," many have told us. "I want to find a better father for my children." "Maybe this time I'll find my true soulmate." "I want to find someone who won't abuse me or be unfaithful to me." "I want someone who will talk to me." Perhaps one of these statements reflects your feelings.

Emotional wounds

We have discovered that in addition to the wounds caused by divorce, many divorced and remarried individuals have wounds dating back to childhood. Perhaps you grew up in a family that provided extremely low levels of emotional nurturing. While families vary widely, there are some characteristic traits that most low-nurturing families share: addictions, lack of affection, violence or abuse, unclear rules and roles, lack of boundaries, unrealistic expectations, poor communication and not being allowed to express one's thoughts and/or feelings safely. The unfortunate consequences of growing up in a family that did not provide healthy nurturing include fear, shame, trust issues, impaired communication and problem-solving skills and difficulty bonding with others. Unless these traits are resolved, healthy relationships are almost impossible to maintain.

Poisonous Needs!

David Thompson suggests that such traits produce "poisonous needs." In *Counseling and Divorce,* he observes that some individuals develop poisonous needs after a divorce that often drive them toward remarriage. He maintains that such needs are unhealthy reasons to remarry. What are these poisonous needs? "I'm lonely." "I can't manage these kids anymore." "I can't support myself." "Please take care of me." "I'll show her" "I need a partner to be complete." "Other men find me attractive." or "I'm afraid to be alone." While not all individuals contemplating remarriage are motivated by such poisonous needs, the *vast majority* have not worked through their past issues or anticipated the challenges of a new marriage and family. In fact, nearly **80%** of remarrying individuals bring a high degree of emotional woundedness into their new marriage. As a result, many remarried individuals soon find themselves so overwhelmed by negative situations and emotions that the only solution is to leave. Then hopefulness gives way to despair and a growing fear that this marriage, like the last, will not survive. That's the bad news.

The good news is that many remarriages are surviving. We believe with a strong commitment to God and to one another and a willingness to invest in your own personal growth and healing, that you can be one of the success stories. The task of remarriage and/or starting a stepfamily is not easy, but it can be incredibly satisfying and rewarding. Taking the time to be prepared is one of the most important gifts you can give yourself.

<u>Action Step:</u> How prepared are you?

- **What are your personal remarriage challenges?**

- **Personalize the three critical aspects of the remarriage process. What do they mean to you?**

- **Write down any of your "poisonous" needs. How will they impact your future relationships?**

- **What will it take before you are ready to remarry?**

- **What does this chapter add to your story?**

Part One
Between Goodbye and Hello

Most people are more comfortable with old problems than new solutions. John Maxwell

"Goodbye" is our way of identifying the time when a relationship has ended. "Hello" is when you find someone you may want to marry. The interim period is a critical time for you and your children. This time period is called a transition, and, as we shall see, it is a time of incredible adjustment and change. What you do during this time will determine, to a large degree, what kind of future relationships you will have. Life has changed. For both you and your children, things will never be the same.

Everyone reading this book will have his or her own definition of goodbye. For some, goodbye is still very fresh. You still carry the hurt and pain of being abandoned or rejected. You still see the hurt, disappointment or loneliness in your children's eyes. Goodbye may symbolize the ending of a marriage that has been rocked by divorce. Goodbye could be a funeral for a dear partner. Trying to fill the emptiness of that loss can be overwhelming. Goodbye may include doubts of never marrying or finding the right person. It may include grieving over many failed relationships or bearing the scars of an abusive or unfaithful partner. Goodbye might even represent immense guilt over leaving your family for less than honorable or Biblical reasons. Whatever your circumstance, goodbye is about letting go of the past (and all that it represents) and partnering with God and a few other traveling companions on a journey to a new beginning. How do you define Goodbye?

"Hello" is about meeting someone you may want to marry. Hello encompasses understanding your needs, identifying what you are looking for in a potential partner and, here is that awful word—dating. Based on our research and experience, "hello" should last awhile.

The time between "Goodbye and Hello" may well seem like a lifetime—it is not. However, it is a time to repent, forgive, learn, reflect, change and grow. We have identified a number of emotional and spiritual tasks and growth activities that will help you make sense out of this time and use it more effectively. The partner choices you will make in the future are directly related to your work here. Use these tasks and activities as guidelines; they can help you weave your way through some of the confusion that a transition can bring.

I withdrew to a higher vantage to start anew...The anger had passed, now only remains a calm. Confusion replaced with conviction that transitions are made ...pain with memories...fear with understanding ...loneliness with vision ...old joys with new beginnings.
Anonymous

After Goodbye: Transitions

Between who you were and might yet be, a vacuum, nothing at all except a chance to begin again.
Sam Keen

I'm not sure of anything right now. I don't know what to do and I don't feel like doing anything. Mostly I feel numb. A recently divorced client spoke these words. While this is not a divorce recovery workbook, it is important to address the key issues that you will face after a divorce or the death of a spouse. "**After Goodbye**" can mean different things to different people; what does it mean for you?

- ❑ A time of overwhelming pain and despair
- ❑ Struggling with letting go
- ❑ A time to sort things out and find a new direction
- ❑ Strong feelings of guilt and shame
- ❑ Hard questions about poor choices
- ❑ Deep feelings of anger and resentment
- ❑ Deep feelings of rejection and abandonment
- ❑ Fear of what the future may hold
- ❑ Intense loneliness; feeling disconnected
- ❑ Self-doubt
- ❑ Hope for a better future

Perhaps many of these apply to you or have in the recent past. Whatever your current state, the time after the death of a spouse or a divorce is a critical time. Long before thoughts turn to dating and remarriage, the focus needs to be on taking great care of yourself and becoming emotionally and spiritually healthy. "After Goodbye" is a time period referred to as a **transition,** and, as we shall soon see, it is a time of unparalleled change and loss and an incredible opportunity for growth. Coping with these changes and grieving these losses is your primary assignment during this period. In *For Better or Worse*, Mavis Hetherington echoes these sentiments. "I often describe the challenges of the early psotdivorce period as the raw material of personal change. Thc rcason: How these stresses are managed helps to determine whether a person's postdivorce future is better and happier, the same or worse than her redivorce past" (p. 45).

What choices will you make? Better still, will you see yourself as having choices or as the victim of circumstances that are beyond your control? The time after a death or divorce represents a window of opportunity, but it also represents a loss of control. Things are changing and many will never be the same. In *Why Change Doesn't Work,* authors Robbins and Finley report that most people can embrace change if they perceive that the change has a positive meaning for them. If, however, change represents something very negative and stressful, fear sets in and people tend to resist change or deny the process. Life after a divorce or the death of a spouse is rarely seen as a positive event. Psychiatrist Victor Frankl, writing from the perspective of having survived the horrors of a Nazi prison camp, concluded that the ultimate freedom and thus the ultimate choice, when everything else is taken away, is to choose one's attitude in any given set of circumstances; to choose one's own way. You obviously have choices, particularly how you will cope with unwanted change such as a death or divorce. The question remains, what choices will you make? Can you—will you—embrace the changes that have occurred (are occurring) in your life?

This transition period is not just happening to you, but to your children as well. Both you and your children may be coping with huge changes and deep losses. Children feel very out of control during transitions and may act out or withdraw. Be sensitive to your own and your children's reactions to the changes taking place. Name them, acknowledge them and face them together. Even a change that seems minor to you, such as the loss of pet, changing schools or neighborhoods, or a different bedroom, could be devastating to a child.

The time between a divorce or the death of spouse and remarriage could actually involve several transition periods. For example, becoming single again or a single-parent, a shift from being a homemaker to working outside the home, dating again after many years, remarrying or possibly having more children. Each transition has its own set of challenges. To serve as an example, let's briefly examine the transition from being a married partner to being a single parent.

This transition can be extremely challenging and even overwhelming. Suddenly you are the only adult caretaker. You may have to deal with loneliness or guilt or abandonment. Perhaps you must return to work (or get a job for the first time) to support your family. Changes may include friendships, lifestyle, downsizing a home, moving to a different neighborhood or arranging for fulltime childcare. Losses could include security, your support network, free time, quality time with your children or sharing life with a partner. For children, this transition may mean a loss of security, best friends and play areas, a change in schools and neighborhoods and a loss of both parents, one that is gone and the other that is now at work. The question is, how does one cope with a transition?

Dr. P. Rule: People fear and resist change by nature. First we try ignoring the problem. Then we try pretending to change. Next we try placating the person "pushing" us to change. Only when all else has failed do we really begin the change process. God is in the transformation (change) business (Rom. 12: 1-2; II Cor. 3:18; James 1:2-4). Real change can only happen in community with other believers.

Action Step: List the transitions in your life. How are they impacting you right now?

Coping with transitions

In 1980, William Bridges published his groundbreaking book *Transitions* to share with others the discoveries he had made while coping with his own life transitions. He soon found himself teaching a seminar called "Being in Transition." Out of his own experience and that of his many seminar participants, Bridges discovered that all transitions have some things in common. In a booklet entitled *Personal Transition*, Bridges writes,

> "Change is usually an event, but it is the experience of that event that provides (or doesn't provide) us with meaning. The pattern that the change creates in our experience is what we call transition. Transition is made up of three parts: the experience of an ending, the experience of a confusing in-between time called the "Neutral Zone," and the experience of a new beginning. Whenever things change outside of us, inside us a sequence of experiences is triggered off:
>
> First we feel as though we have lost something, as though something is over and that we have to give something up.
> Then we become disoriented, we feel lost, we feel anxious—but, at the same time, we also feel excited at the prospect of a fresh start.
> Finally, we catch a new wind, start off in a new direction, feel a surge of new energy, feel a new sense of purpose.
>
> It is important to our well-being that we recognize and respect this three-part process, for transition is the bridge which we cross over to enter the next chapter of our lives and to renew ourselves" (p. 3).

Bridges has identified several "rules" to illustrate the transition process.

Rule #1, "You find yourself coming back in new ways to old activities when you're in transition" (Transitions, p. 8). There is a tendency to want to return to what is safe and familiar. Most transitions are unwanted and force us to make changes we neither want nor feel able to make. Many of us hold on to the past with clenched fists, refusing to move on. Some do this out of fear, others, out of anger.

Rule # 2, "Every transition begins with an ending. We have to let go of the old thing before we can pick up the new—not just outwardly, but inwardly, where we keep our connections to the people and places that act as definitions of who we are" (Transitions, p. 11). Change cannot happen unless we accept the "ending." This involves letting go and grieving our losses. Letting go is so hard because it forces us to look at who we were, who we are and who we will become at a time when we are not sure of any of those answers. It also forces us to accept the finality of an "ending," something very difficult for many of us. You cannot have a new beginning without bringing closure to the ending.

Rule #3, "Although it is very advantageous to understand your own style of endings, there is some part of you that will resist that understanding as though your life depended on it" (Transitions p. 16). Most people find endings difficult. Although we each have our own style, Bridges believes endings are hard on all of us. Fear often keeps us from venturing forth. Endings mean finality—a door that is closed and locked. Rarely, however, does God shut doors without opening others.

Rule #4, "First, there is an ending, *then* a beginning, with an important empty or fallow time in between" (Transitions p. 18). Bridges incredible insight was that a new beginning cannot and will not happen until one has accepted the reality of an ending and endured the "neutral zone." There is no healthy short cut, no other way to gain healing, wisdom, strength and resolve.

How does this apply to divorce, the death of a spouse or remarriage? By Bridges' definition, these are all transitions. Every transition begins with an ending and ends with a new beginning. Whether your marriage ended due to death or divorce, you begin the transition process with an "ending."

We begin with an "ending" (Revelation 21:6)
Most stories begin with beginnings and end with endings; but not most life stories about death or divorce. In *The Healthy Divorce*, Craig Everett and Sandy Volgy suggest that there are three critical divorce tasks: letting go, developing new social ties and redefining parental roles. They maintain that the letting go task is the most critical if one is to have a successful divorce. Some divorce experts assert that the divorce process can go on long after the legal divorce has been obtained. They distinguish between a legal divorce and a psychological divorce, suggesting that the two seldom happen simultaneously. Before a person can begin again, he or she must bring closure to the past chapters of his or her life. Endings always involve losses and cause us to question who we are. Endings are often traumatic, even terrifying for some. Endings cause us to deal with the meaning of things. This is a period of uncertainty, of reluctance to leave old roles and surroundings and of great pain. This is the time of the most intense feelings. Energy is focused on the past, on the person or relationship lost or on what might have been

Bridges suggests that "endings" involve four distinct phases: disengagement, disidentification, disenchantment and disorientation. These phases have direct application to the remarriage process.

Disengagement is about separating oneself from the past. Events such as deaths, divorces or job changes can "disengage" us from what is familiar. It is in these familiar settings that we draw our identity and understand our roles. Disengagement begins the process of change. One cannot adopt a new system as long as the old one is in place.

Disidentification is the inner work of disengagement. This is the "letting go" process in which we slowly become less and less identified with the past, especially past relationships. These bonds with the past must loosen if one is to develop a new identity. This is a very painful process, made worse by the fact that most of us do not really want to let go of the past.

Disenchantment signals a shift in thinking. The notion that things were not as they seemed is part of this phase. We are in limbo. We begin to come to grips with the *un*reality of our beliefs and ideas. Things are in flux. We challenge our old ideas of how life should be and begin find our own rules, values, beliefs and passions.

Disorientation is a time of confusion and emptiness. "The reality that is left behind in any ending is not just a picture on the wall. It is a sense of which way is up and which way is down…" "… a way of orienting oneself and moving forward into the future" (Transitions, p. 102). The biggest loss of this phase is our sense of the future. These four phases are seldom ever enjoyed; they are to be endured.

Four "endings" tasks

In the *Leader's Guide to Divorce Recovery*, Dr. Frank Williams has identified four tasks that can help individuals navigate through the "ending" and make sense out of the chaos of this time. These tasks get us to the point of being able to say Goodbye.

Venting and clarifying grief—whenever there is a loss, there is grief. Everyone will experience this grief differently. The many faces of grief include sadness, shock denial, despair, anxiety, guilt, anger, depression and confusion. Grief is most intense during an ending; therefore this is where grief work should be done. Give yourself permission to feel the feelings mentioned above and then release them (this takes time). Feelings of grief can be ambiguous as well as overwhelming. The key is to keep doing the work—keep feeling, talking, sharing, moving forward, no matter how slowly or painful.

Developing a support system—this is about community; letting other people in to your life. In our experience, those with an effective support system have a much easier time moving through transitions. Support groups, close friends and family members can be invaluable during this time.

Handling practical matters—this means coming to grips with the tasks that an "ending" may necessitate. This could include going back to school, selling a home, acquiring some job skills, finding a job, changing residences, arranging childcare or reinvesting assets.

Saying goodbye—giving yourself permission to let go. Saying goodbye is the final disengagement and consequently the most difficult. Although former spouses will continue to interact on some basis, particularly if children are involved, this is an emotional disengagement—letting go of the emotional connection between you and your former spouse.

Action Step: Your "endings"

- When did you first become aware that you were in an ending?
- What were your losses?
- How did you know it had "ended"?
- Have you said "Goodbye"?
- Where are you stuck?

The "Neutral Zone" (James 1:2-4)
Letting go is so hard for us. The immense fear surrounding an "ending" is that the future is a giant unknown and the process of "moving on" seems ambiguous and unclear. You have just entered the Neutral Zone. The neutral zone is the struggle in the middle of the journey—a time between what was and what will be. The focus of one's energy now changes from the past and from those outside, to one's self—to the roles, identity and values one has established in their life. This is a time for re-evaluating and re-identifying with life. Interestingly, it is also a time most individuals want to skip because it is a time of so much uncertainty and because we are so impatient—we want to start something new right now! Once the decision has been made to move on and let go of the past, most of us are ready for a new beginning, not more chaos and non-productivity. Endings are traumatic, and we want to move as far away from that trauma as possible. Many see time spent in the neutral zone as boring and unexciting. In our fast paced culture, taking the time to process loss and change seems so foreign. However, this time is so important that much of this workbook focuses on "neutral zone" activities.

The neutral zone is the time when we discover who we were, who we are and who we will be. There is a direct correlation between healthy future choices and time spent in the neutral zone. It is a time of upheaval, emptiness and confusion; a time to mourn and a time to get refocused. For some, it is a time of profound aloneness, a wilderness journey. "For many people the experience of the neutral zone is essentially one of emptiness which the old reality looks transparent and nothing feels solid anymore" (Transitions, p. 117). For this reason, many try to avoid this time—a huge mistake. In many ways the neutral zone is akin to God's work of refining us (James 1:2-4). Bridges sees dealing with emptiness as a key activity during this time. "The first of the neutral-zone activities or functions is surrender—the person must give in to the emptiness and stop struggling to escape it" (Transitions, p. 119). This is true because out of the emptiness of this time we are being transformed and renewed. We have an opportunity to look at life again, from a fresh perspective. The advent of new beginnings occurs when the fear of the past gives way to the hopes of a new future.

During a transition you may find yourself coming back in new ways to old activities. You may resist understanding how to deal with endings. Endings are a time to deal with loss, unpack old baggage and complete unfinished business. The neutral zone is the hallway between endings and a new beginning. There are four critical neutral zone tasks.

Not becoming a victim—many people in transition feel totally out of control. They sense that things are happening "to" them; things they did not choose. To deal with this, set some realistic goals for what you can do. We liken this time to a small ship in a storm. The best thing to do is tie everything down, go below and wait it out. Like a storm, the neutral zone will pass. This is not a time to make life-changing, impulsive decisions, but it is a time to look for new understandings and believe that your circumstances have meaning.

Finding new meaning when the rules are changing and things do not make sense—the neutral zone is a time for re-defining who you are. The old rules do not seem to apply, so it is time to make some new rules—rules that make sense to you. Out of the rubble of a broken past comes the courage to believe in yourself and move forward. God will help you make sense out of the events of your past. You must become open to new ways of looking at things (II Kings 2:8-22).

Partnering with others—it is important that you do not go through this time alone (a common neutral zone experience). Sharing your experiences and feelings with others is growth enhancing. You will discover that others have been there before you and some are there right now. Be open to relating to others in new ways. Join a group or find an accountability partner.

Re-establishing a life purpose based on your relationship with God—the changes going on during this time may render some of your old motivations obsolete. This is a time to establish new values, passions and motivations. Learn to take great care of yourself, and begin planning your future. Ask often, "God, what are you up to in my life?"

Action Step: Spend time in the neutral zone. Bridges gives several practical suggestions for using your neutral zone time wisely. Develop a plan for implementing at least three of these.

- Find times to be alone
- Journal your neutral-zone experiences
- Take this pause in the action of your life to write your story
- Take this opportunity to discover what you really want
- Think of what would be unlived in your life if it ended today
- Take a few days to go on your own version of a passage journey
- Begin developing a list of life lessons

Only at the end of the neutral zone does anyone begin to think positively about the journey. In the midst of pain and confusion, most of us feel that we cannot make it. Only in looking back can we see God's hand at work in our lives. The last book the Apostle Paul wrote was II Timothy. Paul, knowing death was imminent, had learned much about change, suffering and trusting in God. At the end of his life he could tell his young protege to keep the faith because all that he had endured was worth it (II Tim. 4:7-8).

New beginnings (I Corinthians 6:9-11)

Our experiences with abandonment and unwanted change are crisis moments when we must decide whether or not to leave behind the life that is gone forever. We can do that only if we believe in the ongoing creativity of God, who brings light and beauty to the dark chaos of our losses in life M. Craig Barnes *When God Interrupts.*

"New beginnings are accessible to everyone, and everyone has trouble with them. Much as we may wish to make a new beginning, some part of us resists doing so as though we were making the first step toward disaster" (Transitions p. 141). Beginning to work through our fear and apprehension and act on the plans and goals we developed during the neutral zone marks the start of the third phase. The focus shifts again, now toward the future, even though it may at first be a very short-range future. It seems paradoxical that beginnings come at the end of transitions.

When do we know that we have completed the "ending" and have spent enough time in the neutral zone? Bridges suggests it is a form of readiness. "It is when the endings and the time of fallow neutrality are finished that we can launch ourselves anew, changed and renewed by the destruction of the old life-phase and the journey through the nowhere" (Transitions p. 134). New Beginnings are about taking risks, naming our goals and reaching for them, connecting with others in new and meaningful ways and helping others on their journey. So we see that beginnings do come at the end. We have changed from the inside out; we have survived. Genuine beginnings depend on inner change rather than on external shifts, for when we are rooted deep in Christ, we become powerfully motivated and passionate.

You may not experience your transitions like that described above. Perhaps you will leave your endings, enter the neutral zone and return to deal with endings again. Perhaps you have experienced multiple losses and have had very intense reactions. Letting go can be very difficult. Every person's pattern is unique. There are no time limits; this is not a race. We know only one rule, trust God as you keep moving forward.

Dr. P. Rule: Take life one day at a time. Plan and have goals, but be flexible; expect a few twists and turns. No one's path is perfectly straight. Life is a journey full of successes and failures. Learn as many life lessons as possible and stay close to God and a few others.

As the crisis ends I emerge into a new world of possibility and action.
Time is a gift, no longer something to resent or grasp or dread.
I remember the past with gratitude because it brought me to this moment.
I look to the future with excitement because
it allows me an open space in which I am free to become.
I take pleasure in the present moment because
it is the meeting point of all that has been and all that might be.
Healing restores memory, hope, and the capacity for joy.
Sam Keen ***Beginnings Without End***

<u>Action Step:</u> Letting Go (Questions to ponder as you work through this book)

- What is it time for you to let go of?

- Have you identified and sorted out all your losses? What are you going to do with them?

- Have you accepted the necessity of going through a time of mourning?
- Can you use this ending to look at past endings in your life?
- Have you begun to unpack old baggage?
- Is there a pattern to your life choices?
- Are you connected with others who can share your journey?
- Have you begun taking great care of yourself?
- Do have a sense of your purpose? Your passion?
- Have you spent some quality "alone" time?
- Have you challenged any of your habits?
-
- Have you set any goals?

If you wait until the wind and the weather are just right, you will never plant anything and never harvest anything. –Ecclesiastes 11:4

Passages: Emotional Guideposts and Opportunities to Grow

The greatest thing in the world is not so much where we stand as in what direction we're moving.
Oliver Wendell Holmes

Combining the symbols for danger and opportunity forms the Chinese symbol for crisis. Hence a crisis or tragedy, such as a death or divorce contains risk, challenge and opportunity. A tragedy worse than death or divorce however, is to remain in the same place or make the same choices, refusing to change or grow or move on. Being open to change is not the same thing as change. God will always ask us to draw meaning from our circumstances and to deepen our dependence on Him and He will always invite us to grow and change. The change God calls you to, life transformation (Romans 12:1-2), requires persistence and commitment and a willingness to examine who you are. Things have changed, and will never be the same. What is God saying to you? Where is He leading you?

Described below is a passageway to emotional and spiritual recovery and growth. Each of these emotional steps is absolutely essential to your growth as a healthy single and necessary to complete before considering remarriage. These steps function as guideposts, marking a course toward spiritual and emotional health and remarriage readiness (Read Psalm 1, 25:4-5). Woven throughout is the *key task*—developing a healthy single lifestyle that is centered in Christ. Individuals who have not adjusted to a single lifestyle often remarry too soon and with less than positive results. The following steps are developmental in nature, which means that each step is built on the one before. However, going through these steps is personal—take as much time as you need and re-visit any prior steps. Skipping steps or remarrying before you have completed this process is ill advised and will inevitably lead to relationship failure.

Developing a Rock-Solid Relationship with God

The first step in your passage toward wholeness is your relationship with God. He is the source of your identity and fulfillment. God will bring situations into your life to help you grow and individuals into your life to help meet your needs. No matter what your past circumstances, God does not want you to remain broken. He wants to infuse your brokenness with His life-giving Spirit. Wholeness is His legacy to us. The question is, do you want to be whole? Be clear on this, God does not want you to remain a victim. Nor does God want you to live in condemnation for your past. Wholeness is about letting go of the past and embracing a future God has in store for you. Not sure how to do that? Keep reading. Are you spending quality time with God? Are you sharing your life with a few others? What is God doing in your life? Where is He active? Where is He asking you to serve? Where are you being stretched or challenged? Put your trust in Him (Phil. 4:19); keep asking God to reveal Himself. God will always help you draw meaning from your circumstances. Slow down and spend some quality time with God. Your relationship with Him is much more about "being" than it is about "doing." You do not need to know the outcome of this journey, because you know the Guide and He knows you.

How can I grow spiritually? (Psalm 37)
A spiritual life consists in that range of activities in which people cooperatively interact with God—and with spiritual order deriving from God's personality and action (Dallas Willard, *The Spirit of the Disciplines).*

The truth is that the term spiritual life is simply a way of referring to one's life—every moment and facet of it—from God's perspective. Another way of saying it is this: God is not interested in your "spiritual life," God is just interested in your life. He intends to redeem it (John Ortberg, *The Life You've Always Wanted).*

The key to spiritual growth is to acknowledge that God is in control. Life is unmanageable without Christ at the center. The challenges of life, particularly coping with loss or disappointment, can be devastating and overwhelming. An intimate relationship with God helps us make sense of our suffering and leads us to real peace and joy as we allow God's Spirit to fill our lives. There is no spiritual growth without change, no change without loss, and no loss without pain. It is the only path we know that really works.

How does one mature spiritually to the point where Christ is Lord?
Below is a brief outline of the process. For a more in-depth study, see *Mere Christianity* by C.S. Lewis, *Ragamuffin Gospel* by Brennan Manning, *How People Grow* by Cloud and Townsend, *The Life You've Always Wanted*, by John Ortberg, *Lifetime Guarantee*, by Bill Gillham or *The Sprit of the Disciplines* by Dallas Willard.

Repentance (Acts 17:30-31, II Cor. 7:9-10, II Peter 3:9, I John 1:9, Romans 6:15-18)
You can believe in Christ intellectually and admire him. You can say your prayers to him through the keyhole as I did for many years. You can push coins at him under the door. You can be moral, decent, and good. You can be religious and pious. You can have been baptized and confirmed. You can be deeply versed in the philosophy of religion. You can be a theological student or even an ordained minister and still not have opened the door. (John Stott)

Our pain leads us here. More accurately, the failure of our attempts to numb our pain leads us here. Repentance is admitting our brokeness and that our lives are out of control. It is calling upon a holy God to forgive and restore us. Repentance is letting go of our unhealthy and blatantly sinful behaviors and acknowledging our need for God. Alcoholics Anonymous (AA) calls this "hitting bottom." It is when you and I come to the end of ourselves; when we realize that our way isn't working.

Accepting our own personal realities (Ps. 34, 139. Romans 7: 10-11)
Accepting the reality of our situation can be difficult. There comes a time to be honest with ourselves about our spiritual state. No more denial or secrets; no more blaming others. Total honesty means accepting that you are powerless over some aspect of your life and that you are here, now, to settle this.

> *God grant me the courage to change the things I can change, the serenity to accept the things I cannot change, and the wisdom to know the difference.* (Serenity Prayer)

Confession (Psalm 32, 51; James 5:16; II Tim 2:21; I John 1:9; Rom. 10:9-13)
Faith is not so much believing this or that about God, as it is hearing a voice that says, come unto me. We hear the voice and we start to go without really knowing what to believe about the voice or ourselves. And yet we go. Faith is standing in the darkness and a hand is there and we take it. In that moment of surrender, we stand in an open doorway to freedom from our seemingly irreparable past. (Frederich Buechner)

Confession means becoming vulnerable; no more secrets. We are only as sick as our secrets. Confession is the natural progression of a life that is passionate to change and has experienced the touch of a loving God. No more pretense or hiding behind masks because the pain of not being intimate with God is greater than the pain of disclosure. Confession is about sharing our deepest concerns and our most internal battles with fellow strugglers in such a way that spiritual connecting occurs. The masks come off, we tell our story and in doing so we relinquish our proud independence that has isolated us from God and others. Freedom is just around the corner.

Responsibility (I John 1:8, 2: 4-5, James 1:22-25, 4:10)
I repent and respond to God in obedience, taking personal responsibility for my situation and my growth. I begin surrounding myself to those who can help me. I continue to let go of behaviors, environments or relationships that do not move me toward God. I consistently move toward spiritual maturity. Not what I want, but what God wants. No longer a victim, blaming others for my situation or in control, allowing no one access to my choices.

Forgiveness (Psalm 103:10-12, Isaiah 43:25, Matt. 6:14-15; Eph. 4:32)
Forgiveness is an unnatural act. Truly, it is an act of the will. It is a decision you make to cancel the debt owed to you, and that makes it an expensive act. Forgiveness doesn't restore what was broken; it doesn't repair the damage done—it writes it off. And you can do it because on the cross Jesus showed you how. Forgiveness doesn't erase the deed, if simply frees us from its grip on us so we can heal (Ron Deal, *Building a Successful Stepfamily*).

Receiving God's forgiveness can be difficult. A lifetime of pain, guilt and shame can make us feel undeserving of God's grace and forgiveness. Experiencing forgiveness comes at the point of our brokeness, when we know that we desperately need His love and acceptance. The peace that comes from being loved, forgiven and accepted by God allows us to forgive others as well as ourselves.

Transformation (Romans 12:1-2, II Cor. 3:18; Gal. 4:19, 5:22-23)
God's desire is to transform us—change us from the inside out. Spiritual transformation literally means being changed into the likeness and character of Christ. Transformation occurs as you integrate Biblical truths into your life and begin applying those truths to everyday circumstances. As individuals grow in Christ, they assist one another on their journey and thus the body of believers is nurtured, strengthened and matured.

Community (John 15:9-17, 17:15-26; Acts 2:42-47, 4:32-35; Romans 12; I Cor. 12 & 13; Gal. 6:2; Eph. 4:1-13; Hebrews 10:24-25; James 5:16; I John 3:11-19)

Community is God's gift to us—the fellowship of traveling companions. Spiritual growth cannot happen in isolation; it happens in the context of community. The transforming power of community is drawn from the Holy Spirit, who gifts each individual so the body of Christ "may be built up until we all reach unity in the faith and in the knowledge of the Son of God and become mature, attaining to the whole measure of the fullness of Christ" (Eph. 4:12-13).

Celebration (Romans 8:1, 15:7; Eph. 1:4, 2:6; Col. 2:10, 13)
As redeemed believers, we can celebrate the truths of our redemption. We are holy, accepted, blameless, complete, heaven-bound and totally forgiven.

Servanthood (Gal. 6: 1-2, Phil 1:6, James 2:14-17, II Tim. 2:2, 20-21)
Servanthood is giving back—not because we have something special to offer, but out of gratitude for what God has done in our lives. We give out of our fullness in Christ.

Action Step: Where are you in your spiritual journey? If you are near the beginning of if you are stuck, please talk to a pastor about resources for spiritual growth. No matter where you are, connect with a few others. This journey was never designed to travel alone.

Letting Go of Your Marriage

Why is letting go so hard? Perhaps because letting go means finality—the relationship is over. Perhaps it is because it is difficult to cope with all the changes and grieve all the losses. Perhaps because, as we discovered earlier, endings are just plain tough and the "neutral zone" experience is very frightening and ambiguous. It is critical to bring closure to a marriage, whether the marriage ended by death or divorce. Few people realize how totally bound they are to their past relationships. Children, shared experiences, traditions, years spent accommodating one another, mutual friendships, overcoming hardships, possessions, even obligations can keep us emotionally tied to another person. For many, much of their identity is interwoven with the other person and the various roles played out in the relationship. For them, letting go feels like losing a part of themselves.

The way you *end* a marriage is an important determiner of the quality of your life prior to and even after remarriage. Lack of closure means you may still be holding on to many negative and potentially self-destructive thoughts, feelings and attitudes. When we talk about "letting go," we are referring to resolving all the pain and emotions associated with your loss. This can be a slow process, but it is a journey you must make. In the midst of tragedy and loss, God is always there (Romans 8:35-37; II Cor. 1:3, 4; Hebrews 13:5). This is an important time to connect with Godly people. Many who suffer a loss isolate themselves and grieve alone. God's word is clear that life is a community affair.

Many individuals are *legally* divorced but not *psychologically* divorced. The marriage may be over, but they are still consumed with sadness, guilt, anger or bitterness. *The story is told of two monks who meet a young lady at a river crossing. One monk carries her across the river where they part company. Later, the other monk remarks that it may not have been prudent to carry the young lady. "I let her go after the river" the first monk replied, "You are still carrying her."* Letting go is perhaps the most difficult task you will confront.

A client repeatedly interferes with her former -husband's efforts to date or move on with his life. She feels wronged by him (legitimately so) and is still full of bitterness. Unfortunately, she risks negatively impacting her children as well as her own emotional and spiritual well being. Her marriage has clearly not ended emotionally. She is looking for vindication; a way to make sense of her divorce and perhaps a way to punish her former husband. She is angry and bitter. We are encouraging her to forgive her former spouse, move on with her life and seek comfort from God and a few others.

Letting go is not about needlessly taking the blame or denying the pain or pretending everything is okay. It is not about denying good times or developing a permanent dislike for the other person. It is an *intentional process* of not living in the past or allowing the past to define who you are. Paul, in Philippians, reminds us to keep focused on the goal—Christ, and to not look back (Phil. 3:13; 4:6-9). God encourages us to live life in the present. He reminds us that we are precious to Him. In *Ruthless Trust*, Brennan Manning has some strong words for those who have difficulty trusting God with their future. "Uncompromising trust in the love of God inspires us to thank God for the spiritual darkness that envelopes us, for the loss of income, for the nagging arthritis that is so painful, and to pray from the heart, Abba, into your hands I entrust my body, mind and spirit and this entire day—morning, afternoon, evening and night..." (p.12). "Wallowing in shame, remorse, self-hatred and guilt over real or imagined failings in our past lives betrays a distrust in the love of God" (p.15). God understands your pain. He does not judge you or condemn you for it. He wants to heal you through your trust in Him. Part of His plan is that you move forward; grow through your struggles and develop a healthy dependence on Him. How do you do this?

How do I let go of my past?

The past can control us in many ways:

- Harboring fantasies about a return to a past relationship
- Dreaming of revenge
- Closing ourselves off to others and to God
- Seething with bitterness and resentment
- Being consumed with guilt or shame
- Abusing and punishing oursleves with harmful habits or behaviors
- Acting out sexually to attempt to validate our worth

Letting go of the past is amazingly difficult. We hold on to things, even painful things, so tightly. Jesus will always call us to let go of the heavy, but deeply cherished things we are carrying because His dreams for us are bigger than our fears of the future. Ultimately letting go is an act of the will and an act of faith. We really cannot go back, but we can stay stuck. Letting go is placing your trust in a future that you cannot see because you trust a God who has never abandoned you or let you down. Below are some practical letting go strategies. Are you stuck on any of these?

Forgive your former partner and yourself. Forgiveness is a process and it is also a gift. Forgiving someone else frees you from the bonds of anger and resentment. Forgiving yourself frees you from guilt and shame. Letting go starts here.

See the past as life lessons. The past can be our teacher or our harsh critic. It can shame us or leave us with valuable lessons. The choice is yours.

Deal with your emotions. Work through anger, guilt, shame or other emotions with a close friend, support group, pastor or counselor. The key is to face these emotions head-on. Do not let them rule you or define you.

Become accountable to someone. Allow someone you trust to give you feedback, support you with your goals and most importantly, speak the truth to you in love.

Get active. List things you would enjoy doing and do them. Set a few short-term goals. Spend time with people—do not isolate yourself.

Begin identifying unhealthy relationship patterns. What can you learn from past relationships? What patterns are beginning to emerge? What role did you play? If you are not clear about your role in past relationships, you are destined to repeat old patterns and powerless to make changes.

Start taking great care of yourself. Self-care is a critical "letting go" function. You must learn how to identify and meet your own needs. There is a direct correlation between the quality of future relationships and your ability to recognize and meet your needs.

Develop strong boundaries. To know and respect your personal boundaries builds your self-esteem. Learn how to say "no" and "yes." Understand your limits. Work hard to respect the boundaries of others.

Create a healthier perspective on your past. If you get trapped in the past by trying to keep pain out of your future, you will forfeit the present. Do not plan your entire life. Trust God with your present, give your hurt and pain to Him. If you did not like the past, pick a healthier path and start a new one. Use your past as a landmark of where you have come—it is meant to hold great memories and greater lessons. Mountaintops are shaped by the valleys below. The glory of the journey is determined by the climb, not the height. *Twenty years from now you will be more disappointed by the things that you didn't do than by the ones you did do. So throw off the bowlines. Sail away from the safe harbor. Catch the trade winds in your sails. Explore. Dream. Discover.* Mark Twain

<u>**Action Step:**</u> **Where are you in the letting go process?**

- ❑ I am still struggling
- ❑ I still cannot talk to my former spouse
- ❑ I do not want to be around others right now
- ❑ I do not like myself very much right now
- ❑ I am overwhelmed with emotions

- ❑ I cannot forgive myself
- ❑ My former partner and I can at least discuss things civilly
- ❑ I have forgiven myself for my past
- ❑ I am beginning to love, respect and accept myself
- ❑ I am starting to take great care of myself
- ❑ I have forgiven my partner
- ❑ I am learning to set boundaries for myself and to respect those of others
- ❑ My relationship with God is strong and growing
- ❑ I have let go of my former relationship
- ❑ I am open to learning from my past
- ❑ I am connecting with others
- ❑ I am comfortable taking my time in looking for a new relationship

Dealing with Intense Emotions

"So often...feelings make only a brief appearance at highly emotional times such as weddings and funerals. And then, once those events are over, back the feelings go into the deep recesses of the mind. I don't want to let that happen to me. Now that I have let my feelings out into the sunlight, I never want them to slip back into the shadows again" Gene O'Brien, *Learning To Live Again: The Journey Through Grief For The Widowed Or Divorced.*

A divorce or the death of a spouse can generate intense feelings; feelings that can easily consume or even overwhelm us. Even years later, these feelings can be re-kindled. The remarriage of a former spouse, financial struggles, difficulty adapting to changes, or modifications in parenting time or custody can re-ignite these feelings. James tells us to consider it pure joy—a gift, when tests and challenges come our way (1:2-4). Who is he kidding? How could this be true? God wants to stretch your faith during times of trial. It is in those tough moments that you and I come face to face with the Creator and our real faith has a chance to flourish. Until it is tested, none of us know how our faith will hold. "What if I fail?" You might stumble, you might even fall. What God is interested in is perfecting you. Trusting in a God who loves you and will never leave or forsake you is the only cure for our feelings of insecurity, shame, anger, guilt or fear.

Facing Feelings

Most of us avoid dealing with our feelings because we believe they are overwhelming, unfacable, intolerable, or unbearable. We see having feelings as being weak or losing control. Facing feelings can be painful and can force us to deal with our choices and our pain. It is easier to focus on behavior or to intellectualize our feelings than it is to feel them. We would rather deny and avoid than deal with our feelings, especially if they are painful. How do you personally avoid facing your feelings? Do you eat, spend money, run away, stir up excitement or medicate yourself? Have you experienced these thoughts:

If I deal with feelings, I'll hurt and will have to change or be dysfunctional.
I think I shouldn't feel anger or hate, especially toward my former spouse. So I'll pretend I'm bad if I have less than "ideal" feelings.
Someone might feel hurt or angry and leave me, and I'd rather sacrifice becoming whole.

Feeling alone or left is unbearable and can't be dealt with, and my entire life will end." "I can't sit still with my feelings to understand them.
When I hurt someone, I feel better. I want someone to hurt as much as they have hurt me.
If I face my feelings, I am afraid I will hurt someone or myself.

Jesus experienced intense feelings. He expressed his feelings; He thought and prayed about them. He asked His disciples for prayer support and he spent alone time with God to be sure his feelings and mission were in line. He was never ashamed of his feelings. Growing to become whole like Christ is a process we must embrace. Feelings of anger, shame guilt, aloneness or being abandoned can be devastating and overwhelming, but they are faceable, especially if we invite others into our lives for support and encouragement. God will always be with you (Mt. 10:34-36). Revenge is not the way to deal with feelings (Rom. 12:19, Prov. 24:17-18, Eph. 4: 27-32). Revenge does not allow you to deal with or understand your feelings. Avoiding your feelings sentences you to reenact them—over and over. Feelings are God's gift. The goal is to understand them, not to deny them or beat yourself up with them (Jesus in Mt. 26:31-46, Eph. 4:26, Ps. 4:4.).

What feelings are you facing?
Anger—is a form of self-protection, it serves to defend us from future loss and hurt. Anger can mask other emotions such as hurt or fear. Where does all our anger come from? Some anger comes from years of bottled up frustration and resentment due to a lifetime of betrayals, abuse or disappointment. You cannot change the situations that caused this anger. Anger also comes from the definable present, from current hurts and here and now situations. This anger can be dealt with directly if you accept responsibility for your anger. Letting go of anger is a process. There are no magic solutions. Below are some suggestions for releasing anger

- Learn to recognize the many faces of anger in your life: impatience, intolerance, sarcasm, irritability, etc. (Matt 5:22)
- Understand that all angry expressions, good or bad, are the result of choice (Prov.19: 11)
- Take full responsibility for you behavior (Eph. 4:26-27, 31, Col. 3:8)
- Let go of excessive dependencies
- Choose to relinquish your cravings for control in exchange for freedom
- Ground yourself in truth
- Practice radical forgiveness (Eph. 4:32)
- Keep your lifestyle habits consistent with your emotional composure
- Live in humility rather than self-preoccupied pride
- Hold your defenses to a minimum; trust your healthy assertions
- Accept the inevitability of loneliness as you struggle to be understood
- Relate to others as equals, neither elevating yourself above them nor accepting a position of inferiority
- Avoid the temptation to rationalize your anger; assume full responsibility for who you are and what you do
- Be accountable for your ongoing growth

- Work through your emotional wounds
- Find ways to rechannel your negative energy in more positive ways
- Let go of the need for revenge or vindication
- Stop investing emotional energy into making yourself miserable
- Focus on God's love and experience His forgiveness and acceptance
- Laughter

Hurt—develops because we have experienced deep pain and disappointment. We hoped for love and instead received pain. Instead of togetherness and partnership, we received loss and loneliness. Hurts are most often buried and hidden. Most of us suffer in silence or dream of retaliation. Hurts can build up to the point where we experience little joy in our lives. Our emotional cup is filled to the brim with negative experiences that have lead to negative feelings. How do I empty this cup of hurt, pain and sorrow?

- Know that God cares (Psalm 34:18, Romans 8:18-19, II Cor. 1:3-4, I Peter 5:7)
- Abide in Christ (John 15:15)
- Let God lead you through the process of turning despair into joy (Romans 5: 3-5)
- Allow others to share in your sorrow and to provide you comfort (Matt 5:4, Romans 12:15, Eph. 4:32)

Guilt—is a feeling of self-condemnation that we experience after we do something we think is wrong. Guilt can cripple our emotional health by causing depression and eroding our self-esteem. We need to distinguish between true and false guilt. False guilt comes from the experiences of our past. This guilt tells us we are inadequate or inferior. It is based on a lifetime of negative messages and hurtful experiences. True guilt concerns our standing before God and is felt when we are disobedient to Him or unwilling to place our faith in Him. True guilt results in Godly sorrow which leads to repentance and restoration (II Cor. 7:10). To respond to guilt in a healthy fashion:

- Own your feelings; be responsible for them, no matter how or why they occurred.
- Seek repentance—be truly sorry for the behavior that has caused the guilt.
- Surrender your need to act out—let go of any thought of revenge or tendency to be a martyr or victim (James 4:10).
- Determine to make every effort to turn from guilt-producing thoughts and behavior. If it is false guilt, challenge the belief systems and the idealized images you feel you must live up to. If it is true guilt, deal with your issues of pride, self-deception or a need to be in control (Phil 3:13-14).
- Have compassion for yourself. Accepting yourself as someone Christ loves and forgives is critical to reconciliation and restoration (Romans 8:33-34).
- Remember that your worth is determined by God, not by others.
- Allow God to restore you. He does not condemn you so don't live in condemnation (Rom. 6:23, Eph. 1:4, Is. 44:22, Rom. 8:1-3, I Peter 1:16)

Fear—we can become prisoners of fear, especially the fear of change. Yesterday's pain can prompt fear about tomorrow. Fear can keep us trapped in old patterns that can make us feel alone and inadequate, and sabotage our relationships. Relationally, our fears can move us to control intimacy or to avoid it altogether. What kinds of things do you fear?

- The unfamiliar and the unknown.

- Embarrassment, rejection, abandonment, being out of control.
- Negative events from your past that may reoccur at some future time. These result in our dwelling on past failures and possible bad outcomes, instead of focusing upon present reality.
- Change—moving out of your comfort zone. We fear change because it has to do with an unknown future. We are creatures of habit. We like the predictable and the familiar.

To cope with fear we must understand the language of fear in our life. What does fear say about you, your relationships, or your future? Tips for facing your fears include:

- Learn to live life in the present (Joshua 1:5-9, Is. 41:10)
- Acknowledge your fear, do not deny or avoid it (Ps. 23:4)
- Begin recognizing your fear patterns—fear can become self-reinforcing
- Change your response to fear—form new beliefs; replace fear with the behavior your want (John 8:32; Heb. 13:5-6)
- Stop believing the lies that lurk beneath your fears
- Seek feedback from others
- Take in compliments. Feel good about them. Accept what others say.
- Love others from your fullness in Christ (Phil 2:3-4)
- Learn from mistakes and constructive criticism
- Stop punishing yourself
- Learn to forgive and accept yourself
- Celebrate your successes; build on your strengths. Take great care of yourself
- Take a step at a time and celebrate each step
- Trust God's love—His perfect loves casts out fear (I John 4:18)

Depression—sometimes grief and sadness can last for what seems like a lifetime. Soon we are struggling with feelings of worthlessness and hopelessness. Few things are pleasurable and the future seems just as gloomy as the present. Fortunately, our negative forecast seldom lasts as long as we fear it will. However, depression can become overwhelming, to the point of feeling like running away, giving up or even harming ourselves. If any of these are true, please see a pastor or counselor.

There are several things you can do to cope with depression. One of the best natural remedies is exercise. Perhaps some of the following ideas can help lessen the intensity of your depression.

- Do something—take action. Action tends to lessen depression (I Thess. 5:18)
- Connect with others—depression often leads to isolation
- Look at your spiritual life. What is God trying to say to you? God asks us to draw meaning from our circumstances (Romans 8: 28,31, James 4:8)
- Look at some aspect of your life differently. Ask, "how can I see this (issue, problem, etc,) in a different way?" (Phil. 4: 4-13)
- Focus on areas of your life that are going well.
- Do something nice for yourself.
- Resolve to do things better or differently in the future. Thinking about the future tends to uplift our mood.

- Remember a time of joy or success from your past.
- Spend time with someone who is fun or playful.
- Do not feel compelled to make life-changing decisions
- Do not get caught up in the "shoulds" of your life.
- Pray or meditate on God's character and love for you (Psalm 42, Heb. 4:14-16).
- Deal with any self-destructive habits or addictions.

Negative feelings can dominate or even destroy a person who feels wronged. Take the time to work through your emotional issues. Face your feelings; do not run from them. Seek spiritual help from a close friend, pastor or counselor. Do not allow your emotions to consume and control you. Be clear about taking time for healing.

Action Step: What feelings are you avoiding right now?

Mourning Your Losses (Ps. 30:11, Matt. 5:4, Romans 3:3-5, II Cor. 12:9)

"Over the years, I have learned that every life circumstance, even a crisis, can nourish your soul. Recently, the farm and home that I have loved so much for so many years burned down in a horrible fire. Everything that I owned, without exception, was lost. There was even speculation that foul play was involved. At moments like this, we stand at a fork in the road. If we take the fork most commonly traveled, we collapse, we give up, feeling hopeless and defeated. We focus on the negatives, losing ourselves in the "problem." We point to our unhappy circumstances to rationalize our negative feelings. This is the easy way out. It takes, after all, very little effort to feel victimized. We can, however, take the other fork. We can view the unhappy experience as an opportunity for a new beginning. We can keep our perspective, look for the growth opportunities, and find an inner reservoir of strength." Elisabeth Kubler-Ross

Life brings many losses and these losses require grieving. The pain of loss can reverberate throughout our lives and enter every one of our relationships. Most of us have not adequately grieved our losses, partly because grieving is so painful and partly because we do not understand just how important grieving is to our emotional and spiritual well-being. The hurt, pain and disappointment of loss must be acknowledged and ultimately grieved. However, before this can happen, we must understand and accept that loss has taken place. It is natural to avoid this process, loss is indeed painful. If the pain is too great, denial can occur, placing the loss out of our awareness.

Loss and the trauma surrounding it have many faces. Some losses are from the distant past, such, the divorce of our parents, abuse, neglect or abandonment, or the death of a parent. Some are more recent, such as disappointments, physical, mental or sexual abuse, failed relationships, the death of a spouse, or a divorce. Loss is also embedded in change, such as changes in finances, custody, lifestyle, residence, neighborhoods, friends or churches. Every change involves loss and every loss impacts us; we lose something of ourselves with each one. Most of us deny our losses and pretend everything is okay. We rush through the grieving process to avoid the pain. Our pleasure-driven culture teaches us to avoid pain at any cost. The result is that we block our own grief process and do not allow our children or ourselves an opportunity to mourn. However, blocked, frozen or denied grief can slow down or even stop personal growth and limit our ability to bond to others. Inadequate grieving is a major cause of remarriage failure.

What is a loss? A loss is a broken emotional or spiritual bond. Over time, we develop emotional attachments to people, pets, ideas, things, or situations and these things are sometimes taken away from us. The natural response is to grieve these losses. However, we do not grieve, instead we deny, act out, isolate, or pretend—anything but authentic grieving. We nurture the false illusion that life should not bring suffering, pain or loss. Grieving truly is painful, but losses and their impact on us must be acknowledged. God allows us to experience loss because it is the natural way of things and because without loss we would be totally self-reliant, never learning to depend on Him. He allows us to grieve because He grieved. He wants us to embrace grief and not be afraid. What losses do you need to grieve?

Why is grieving so important?

Grieving is the natural way to help us accept and endure our losses. It can take as long as ten years to fully recover from severe loss. Successful grieving frees us to form new bonds. Our culture, our wounds and our past often keep us from acknowledging our losses, experiencing our feelings and growing through our grief—we get stuck. God calls us to embrace our losses and grow through them. How does inadequate grieving impact our family?

- Children experience the least amount of control and the greatest amount of loss. Yet their loss and pain is the most minimized. If a child is not allowed to grieve, he or she will likely reject even the kindest stepparent or stepsiblings. Lack of grieving can result in depression, fears and phobias, anxiety or adjustment problems. Visible signs include: poor grades, withdrawal, changes in eating and/or sleeping patterns and acting out behavior.
- Inadequate grieving on the part of adolescents can lead to depression, isolation, acting out, defiance, unhealthy relationships, sexuality and even substance abuse. Wounded parents can miss this and see the child as simply rebellious.
- If biological parents do not grieve properly, they will experience intense guilt and shame for their children's pain and be unable to provide consistent structure or nurturing. In addition, due to intense loyalty conflicts, they will have difficulty adequately bonding with a new partner. Instead, they may be tentative, angry and report feeling "caught in the middle."
- Stepparents who do not complete the grieving process may experience tremendous resentment over their losses in a remarriage. Many report anger over the loss of privacy, the loss of control, the loss of money and the loss of closeness with their new partner. This anger may be vented at the *inconsiderate* or *ungrateful* stepchildren or the parent who is *too lenient* or *too busy with his or her children.*

Individuals stuck in the grieving process will display some characteristic symptoms. For example, they may be unable to speak of the loss without re-experiencing intense shock and grief. They may engage in intense, self-defeating behaviors in response to minor trigger events. They may talk about their loss but deny that it hurts or impacts them or they may persistently avoid talking about the loss. Other symptoms include, denial, sleep and/or eating problems, thoughts of suicide, depression, addictions, physical symptoms, radical, impulsive changes and ritualizing or 'enshrining' the loss. Individuals operating from a childhood message or current environment that discourages grieving will report that they are fine—they probably are not. Adults and children need clear permission and encouragement to express their deep feelings of grief, hurt, sadness, anger, loneliness and confusion.

"Good Grieving!"

You have turned my mourning into dancing (Psalm 30:11). What does healthy grieving look like? In her landmark book, *On Death and Dying*, Elizabeth Kubler-Ross first introduced the world to the "process" of grieving; she called it the process of separation. Studying and observing hundreds of families grieve their losses, she identified five emotional stages that people pass through when they are experiencing deep grief. These stages are shock or denial, anger, bargaining, depression and acceptance.

- Shock and denial often manifest themselves as numbness, disorientation or hysteria, "This can't be happening to me."
- Anger can be overt and become rage, or covert and develop into bitterness.
- Bargaining can present as fantasizing, magical thinking or irrational pleading.
- Depression presents as profound sadness, despair or even apathy.
- This uneven process finally leads to acceptance and resolution.

Not every one goes through these stages in this order. Grief is very personal; each of us has his or her own style. The *key* is to allow yourself and your children to grieve—fully.

What about the grief of a divorce, is it the same as a death? Researchers Pam and Pearson asked the same question. In *Splitting Up*, they examined the grieving process for divorces based on Kubler-Ross's material. They discovered that two grieving processes or cycles actually exist, one for the initiator or "emotional leaver" and one for the receiver or leavee, the one "emotionally left."

The "leaver" cycle begins with alienation. Grieving begins early for the leaver, as he or she becomes disillusioned and disappointed with the marriage. Most often, the leaver feels he or she has changed and that the marriage no longer "fits" them. Long before anything is said or done, the seed of discontentment is growing. The thought of actually leaving begins when the leavee and the marriage are seen as having unreconcilable faults. Apparently, we cannot leave someone we still like. Ambivalence grows into discontentment and disenchantment; leaving is seen as the only alternative. Leaving happens when the ambivalent, disenchanted leaver becomes the alienated leaver.

Actual physical separation starts the next phase, as the leaver moves from contemplating to actually leaving. This is followed by (or co-exists with) a period of exploring alternatives. This has been termed the Quest phase because for so many leavers this is a time of fantasy fulfillment—being free, having more money, finally living alone, uniting with an existing lover, finding the perfect mate, playing the field, etc. During the cycle there are periods of looking back at the one left and perhaps attempting reconciliation. The cycle ends with letting go for good. Needless to say, this cycle is very difficult for the one left.

The receiver grief cycle closely resembles Kubler-Ross's five phases. *Joan was shocked when Allen said he was leaving. Sure, they had been arguing, but it didn't seem that bad. When she asked him where he was going, he said he already had an apartment. He had been planning this move for several months.* This cycle begins with shock and denial as the leaver informs the receiver of his or her desire to leave the relationship. The more sudden or surprising the departure, the greater the shock The receiver cannot believe this is really happening and implores the partner not to leave. Unknown to the receiver, the leaver had already begun moving through his or her cycle for a good deal of time, perhaps up to a year. The receiver refuses to believe that this is really happening, convinced that the leaver will return.

Most often the leaver does not return. When the realization of being left finally hits home, the intense mourning process begins. All the symptoms of traumatic depression occur: stress, despair, loss of appetite, inability to sleep or function, social withdrawal, loss of esteem and feelings of abandonment.

At some point however, anger over being left crashes through the depression and the cycle moves to rage. This is quickly bridled by a desire to restore the relationship, creating a chaotic period of cycling anger and fear, rage and forgiveness, pleading and attacking. During this period the leaver is actively courted. Attempts are made to woo the leaver back though courting still alternates with fighting. Courting involves a host of behaviors, including begging, threats, manipulation and seduction.

The courting period ends when it becomes obvious that nothing will help. Now the receiver begins pushing away to avoid negative emotions. Suddenly the leavee is cool to advances that they once welcomed. During this distancing phase, the receiver could be cold, rude, or harsh. Strong feelings for the leaver may still exist, but having the leaver around is too painful. Indifference and resolution is the final phase. Acceptance is complete.

Loss can be excruciating. Mourning our loss is critical. What we do not mourn, we carry inside, perhaps forever. Going through the grieving steps is important, but to be successful the process must include a period of synthesizing and embracing the losses you have personally incurred. As you come to understand what you have lost, you must determine to the best of your ability how this loss happened and why. You must determine your role in the loss and assess what this loss means to you. Drawing meaning from our circumstances is a critical part of our spiritual journey. Healthy grieving involves the following elements:

- Acknowledging the loss and its impact on you.

- Understanding your loss. "What did I lose?" "How did it happen?" "What does it mean?"
- Talking about your feelings to another person (Romans 12:15).
- Developing personal faith in your ability to survive the loss.
- Allowing yourself to grieve without guilt, shame or bitterness.
- Involving a support network of pastors, friends, loved ones and professional helpers if necessary.
- Taking personal time (as much as is needed) to sort out your feelings.
- Journaling your feelings and your struggles; keeping track of lessons learned and progress made.
- Understanding that there is no "right" way to grieve, only the way that works best for you.
- Refusing to become a victim.
- Partnering with a holy God who "knows our sorrows" and is "acquainted with our grief." (II Cor. 1:3-4, Rom. 8:35,37)

The process of grieving

Work through the denial that hides the anger
Work through the anger that hides the hurt
Work through the hurt that hides the loss and loneliness
Work through the loss and loneliness that hides the lack of self-esteem
Work through the lack of self-esteem that hides the total confusion
Work through the total confusion that hides our unwillingness to
give up our own control and to surrender our lives to our creator God.

AUTHOR UNKNOWN

God desires to be intimately involved in your grief process. However, many individuals are angry with God, feeling that He has abandoned them or let them down. "How could you let this happen to me" is a familiar question for God. Sometimes we cannot ask God for forgiveness because we have not forgiven ourselves. Sometimes our hurt, anger or shame prevents us from forgiving others and we continue to hold on to the hurt, often resulting in bitterness.

The deep fear lying behind every loss is that we have been abandoned by God who should have saved us. The transforming moment of conversion comes when we realize that even God has left us. We then discover it was not God, but our image of God that abandoned us. This frees us to discover more of the mystery of God than we knew. Only then is change possible (*When God Interrupts*, C. Barnes p.123)

How to support someone in grief

- Be available
- If you are not sure, ask what they need
- If they can't tell you what they need, just be there
- ***Never*** use pious platitudes
- Be present—emotionally and spiritually
- Listen with your heart

- Be okay with prolonged periods of silence
- ***Never*** try to ***fix*** things
- Allow them to grieve their way and at their pace
- Stay within your limits

Action Step: Grieving is a normal part of life. Where are you in the grieving process? Have you adequately grieved your losses? Have your children? If not, please make this a priority. If you need assistance, contact a pastor or counselor familiar with grief work. How do the above factors play a role in your grief process?

Do a loss inventory. Write down your losses, starting from childhood. With each loss, try to identify what was lost and how that loss has impacted you.

Where you are in the grieving process?

- Shock/denial/ numbness
- Grief or rage
- Courting (bargaining; attempting reconciliation)
- Distancing (depression; emotional withdrawal)
- Resolution (acceptance)

My current stage of grieving is ____

Where is God in *your* grief process? (Read Romans 8:35-37; II Corinthians 1:3-4; James 1:2-18) If grieving is a problem, find a counselor that specializes in grief work.

Forgiving Yourself and Others

Mary had been severely abused by her ex-husband. She struggled with self-esteem and wondered if she could ever trust again. Forgiving him and letting go of the pain seemed impossible to her. We agreed that is was a process. It is difficult to forgive someone who has abandoned, abused or neglected us. The hurt and the wounds are very deep. It is equally difficult to forgive ourselves if we were the one who brought the pain. True forgiveness acknowledges the wound or hurt and extends grace through the pain or disappointment. Many individuals tell us they cannot or will not forgive. They go through life hating the one who abused, neglected or abandoned them. As we listen to their stories, we certainly can understand. Others have difficulty forgiving themselves; their lives are full of guilt and shame. God's solution is always the same, He embraces us with His love. Forgiveness is character defining. It makes us free. Forgiveness may not always lead to reconciliation, but it always leads to personal peace. Unforgiveness can breed a lifetime bitterness and resentment (Hebrews 12:15). It may seem easier to use superficial or quick forgiveness to avoid the process of facing feelings about what has happened, but superficial forgiveness seldom leads to peace or joy. God asks us to forgive (Matthew 6:14-15; Eph. 4:32). It is a part of His character (Psalm 103:10-12; Isaiah 43:25; Hebrews 8:12). Jesus clearly taught and role-modeled forgiveness (Matthew 18:21-35).

The path of forgiveness

Forgiving others is critical to our spiritual growth (I Peter 3: 8-9). Healthy forgiveness is an intentional act of the will. It is a long journey that starts with a decision to forgive. Feelings come later. Forgiveness heals us. In *To Forgive is Human*, McCullough, Sandage and Worthington define forgiveness as "an increase in our internal motivation to repair and maintain a relationship after the relationship has been damaged by the hurtful actions of the other person "(pg. 22). Even so, forgiveness is a process one must embrace when the time is right.

Care for the Soul contains a powerful essay by Myrla Seibold called "When the Wounding Runs Deep." Included below are several excerpts from her essay.

> *Forgiveness creates the possibility for justice, mercy and grace to meet. It is the mysterious wedding of hope and love that gives birth to the possibility that something beautiful will arise...* (p. 301).
>
> *Forgiveness is about learning how to live again without being overwhelmed by self-pity or driven by a passion for revenge. It is facing life soberly and realistically without repression, denial or escape/avoidance behaviors (p.306).*
>
> *Forgiveness is about telling my story—not to impress others with my victimization or to smear the reputation of the offender, but simply to affirm that I am my story, that I am a person of dignity and value, worthy of respect(p.306).*
>
> *Forgiveness is letting go of the past, but not in the sense of forgetting what happened or disconnecting myself from the pain. Forgiveness is refusing to allow the past to be the sole determinant of my life's course (pp. 307).*
>
> *When we have been deeply wounded, someone has acted unlovingly toward us. The antidote is to be bathed in love until we are so filled up with love that we can begin to imagine letting some love flow out into forgiveness. Forgiving must flow from love, and forgiving is a form of loving (p. 307).*

Finally, Seibold asks the question, why forgive? Her answer suggests that without forgiveness, we cannot experience the fullness of God in our lives.

> *To move toward freedom from hatred and bitterness that can keep us from living life with joy and enthusiasm. To know more fully what it means to share in Christ's suffering, to unite our spirit with His. To give God more opportunity to work in the world—in the victim's life, in the offender's life, and in the lives of everyone they*

touch. And finally, we forgive because these light and momentary troubles are minimal compared to the glory we shall someday share with Jesus Christ our Lord (p. 308).

The process of forgiveness

The **first step** is to be clear about the wrong or pain you have experienced. You cannot forgive if you do not fully embrace the pain or the wrong done to you. You must feel the hurt and name it. Do not minimize it or excuse it or deny it—face it. Acknowledge the impact the pain or wrong has had on you. Name the damage—clearly and comprehensively.

The **second step** is to acknowledge your right to feel the way you feel. *I feel wronged, betrayed, violated, used, abandoned, etc.* Acceptance of hurt and pain is critical.

The **third step** is to intentionally surrender your right to get even. *I have been wronged. I have suffered because of that wrong. I have a right to feel hurt. I now surrender my rights and humbly release my need to retaliate or get even.* Now you can begin moving from hatred and bitterness to acceptance (Matt. 6: 14-15, 7:1-6, 18:21-35, Romans 12: 9-21).

The **fourth step** is to revise your picture of the one that hurt you by praying that God will allow you to see him or her through His eyes. Pray that God will give you the freedom to wish this person well. Begin praying that God will bless this person. Read Matthew 5:38-48 and the book of Philemon.

The **final step** is to be open to whatever God wants you to do. Forgiveness is about humility and a deep appreciation of God's work in your life. Loving and praying for someone who has truly hurt you is a gift of God's Spirit. Open your heart to God's leading. God asks us to forgive; true reconciliation with another will not occur without repentance (Matt. 7:33). Denial of any of these steps will not lead to real forgiveness, but pseudo-forgiveness.

Forgiveness involves risk

No human interaction occurs without the possibilities of pain, suffering and alienation. The hurts are always there. Relationships at any level involve risk. Without forgiveness, we can only achieve a level of safety via superficiality and self-protection. Forgiveness says more about us than the individual we are forgiving. With forgiveness, we are set free to interact authentically and to risk being fully present with others in integrity. Such forgiveness draws people to one another. Spiritually, we all relate at the point of common pain and truth:

I'm a sinner-you're a sinner; I've been wronged-you've been wronged
I've wronged others-you've wronged others; I've wronged you-you've wronged me

Misconceptions about forgiveness

You have likely behaved in ways that have been hurtful, even damaging to others. When you have been on the receiving end, you go through a whole gamut of emotions, from rage to hurt. Sometimes there is a desire for revenge. All too often, you may react to the offense and simply move on, holding the grudge tightly. Few things are more damaging than the crippling effects of unforgiveness. Below are several key misconceptions about forgiveness.

You are not doing the person who wronged you a favor by forgiving. So often we want to hold on to anger or hurt, often believing that the person who has caused us harm does not deserve to be forgiven. The gift of forgiveness is for our own spiritual and emotional growth, not just for the person who caused us pain.

You are not protecting yourself by not forgiving. In fact you are regaining the power that you handed over to the person that hurt you. It is the forgiving that gives us freedom. Staying under the control of our unforgiving emotions and attitude stunts our spiritual growth.

Forgiving does not necessarily mean forgetting. It simply means that the sting is gone from the memory and we have a willingness to detach. Forgiveness means I will no longer hold you accountable for the wrong. Forgetting comes in time, however, and normally after true reconciliation.

Forgiving is not an instant process. Forgiving starts as an act of obedience to God. "Cheap" forgiveness is not real. To entirely forgive requires acknowledging and venting feelings, regaining God's perspective, being faithful and allowing for healing. We know forgiveness has occurred at the deepest level when we are reminded of the memory, but not held hostage by the old feelings.

You do not have to punish yourself for bad choices. We are responsible for our own actions, but we have to stop holding ourselves hostage. We can repent, forgive ourselves, accept our own humanness and move forward. God tells us He separates our sin as far as the East is from the West.

Forgiving someone does not obligate you to a repeat performance. Some people and some situations are to be avoided because it is wise and prudent. God rightly asks, "What fellowship do darkness and light have? Reestablishing a trusting relationship with someone takes time and a commitment from both to do so.

You are not a "giant" because you are forgiving. By holding a grudge, we become voluntary victims, giving the offender the power to make us miserable. That is not the freedom to which God has called us. Forgiveness is about obedience. It is about the bigness of God who fills us full of Himself, not about how spiritual we are for forgiving someone. Forgiving another is my recognition of the wonderful forgiveness that I have been afforded by God through Christ.

Steps to obtaining forgiveness
Forgiveness is tough—being forgiven may even be tougher. Because forgiveness is beneficial for both parties and God asks us to forgive others, there is often a belief that

anyone who is a spiritual person should offer forgiveness immediately. Certainly, to be able to forgive is beneficial to the forgiver. However, for the perpetrator, repentance must be a precursor to forgiveness. Repentance does not just mean saying you are sorry, especially if the sorrow is more about being caught than about regretting the original act. Repentance also means communicating sincere regret, and taking steps to be sure that you never repeat the action. If you feel you need forgiveness from another person, consider the following steps:

Take responsibility for the choices that led you to cause the pain (or harm). Get real with God; ask His forgiveness. Accept that, regardless of your reasons for doing whatever you did, it was your actions or words that caused pain for someone else.

Search your heart to be sure that it is the pain or harm caused to the other person that you regret, not just your experience of your own consequences. Develop genuine sorrow for the other person (II Cor. 7:10).

Understand that, however much you want to explain, and however much the other person wants to know why, once they know, the hurt will not change. Their feelings towards you may change, but don't count on it. The hurt will still be the hurt. "Why" is rarely a useful question and explanations often sound painfully like self-serving rationalizations.

Decide what you need to do, how you need to change, to ensure that you do not ever again make that kind of choice, and so cause others more pain. Make those changes in yourself. Until you have learned the lesson and sincerely attempted to make the changes it is unreasonable to expect that the human heart will truly be able to forgive you, and it is questionable as to whether it should.

Plan how you will communicate with the person you have hurt. Do you need to prepare them with a letter or a third-party communication? You need to let them know that they no longer need to fear hurt from you. You also need to be absolutely sure that this is true. Be clear in your mind that you will make an apology without excuses and rationalizations. Decide what could or should be done to make amends to the person(s) that you hurt. This will be in addition to an apology.

View your offenses from God's point of view. Only God knows the full impact of our behavior. Confession means to agree with God. Ask God and the other person to forgive you.

Make the apology and offer the amends with no strings attached. Forgiving you is not the same thing as returning to old situations and/or making it possible for you to repeat the behavior. Do not count on a return to a previous relationship as a part of the forgiveness.

If the individual wants no part of your apology or your making amends, be prepared to accept this too. If that hurts, do not turn the pain into anger against them.

They may need time to heal. Know then that you have done the best you can do, and plan on how you can use the process you have gone through for your own spiritual and emotional growth.

Be actively involved in community. In a world of flawed communication, community is possible through understanding others. In a world of painful alienation, accepting others creates community. In a world of hurt and broken trust, community is sustained by forgiveness.

Dr. P. Rule: Forgiveness means taking the initiative to extend grace to someone who has wronged you. Forgiveness takes one, reconciliation and trust takes two.

Action Step: List the people in your life you need to forgive. What did they do to hurt you? How did you feel? What were the consequences? List your reactions? Prepare to forgive and extend grace. List the people from whom you need forgiveness. What's your plan to accomplish this?

Developing a Healthier Identity

Once you have let go of your relationship and allowed yourself to feel deep feelings and grieve the loss, you can begin to develop an identity separate and distinct from your past. This involves establishing a new sense of self, with perhaps a new set of skills and a commitment to healthy self-care. Self, or more accurately, self-concept refers to your emotional well-being; literally your view of yourself. A healthy self-concept suggests that you know yourself well and like who you are. Healthy self-acceptance means that you accept yourself just as you are, warts and all, and that you are committed to taking great care of yourself-emotionally, spiritually and physically. If you struggle with self-acceptance, commit to work on it—take a class, see a counselor, read a book. Healthy relationships require healthy partners.

Developing a healthier identity also involves dealing with self-esteem issues. Losses or failures in our life can damage our esteem, leaving us feeling inadequate or unwanted. To help raise your esteem, try some of the following.

- Use positive self-talk
- Take good care of yourself
- List your skills and strengths
- Learn some new skills (start small)
- Stay close to supportive, positive people
- Learn to be assertive
- List changes you would like to make, pick one and start working
- Be clear on your needs
- Join a small group or support group
- Make new friends
- Get involved in your church

You may be exhausted as a single parent and need "R & R." Emotional overload is a common problem with divorced singles and especially single parents. In *Margin,* Dr. Richard Swenson talks about the steps of restoring margin in our lives. He defines margin as "something held in reserve for contingencies or unanticipated situations. Margin is the gap between rest and exhaustion, the space between breathing and suffocating. It is the leeway we once had between our limits and ourselves. Margin is the opposite of overload" (pp. 91-92). Dr. Swenson makes several suggestions for restoring emotional margin. These include:

Cultivating social support
Getting a pet
Reconciling relationships
Serving others
Resting
Laughing
Crying
Creating appropriate boundaries
Envisioning a better future
Offering thanks
Granting grace
Being rich in faith
Loving others (pp. 111-120).

Based on Swenson's definition, describe your margin (or lack of).

What can you do to improve this area?

Dealing with Loneliness

It can be a bottomless, nameless fear and an overpowering boredom. You would give anything to escape it. You wait for the phone to ring. You pace. Watch TV. You can't sleep well. You can't eat well—but go to the fridge 50 times. You try to read but nothing holds your attention. You can't concentrate. Who do I call? You make a call or two-no lasting help there. You are ashamed of yourself for not being able to handle a little solitude—although it doesn't seem like just a little—it seems like it will last forever. You wonder if this feeling will ever go away. You ask yourself—why is this so upsetting? Somehow you get through the night. You hope you don't have another day (night) like that for a long time. Have you ever felt this way?

Millions of people are lonely. One study reports that over 90% of men do not have a true friend. Perhaps you have never experienced the level of loneliness and despair described above, but loneliness is for real and it is a powerful consequence of broken relationships. Most of us are afraid of loneliness—our fear is that the pain will never end. The good news is that the pain will end, but only if you embrace your deep feelings of loneliness and allow God and a few others to minister to you.

Coping with loneliness has important relationship consequences. Loneliness can drive us to make poor relationship choices. Lonely people often get involved in relationships that are unhealthy. Loneliness can prompt us to get involved too soon or rush us into physical intimacy. One of the deepest needs of the human spirit is to connect with others. Yet our busyness and fear of rejection keep us from reaching out to others. Which of these statements below applies to you?

- ❑ Other people are really important to me, but I haven't taken adequate time for them.
- ❑ Other people, while important to me, aren't everything, and some unwanted time alone is the price I have to pay for devoting myself to other things.
- ❑ I have been a. too proud, b. too lazy, c. too fearful to put myself into situations where I can meet others
- ❑ My relationships with others have been too superficial and leave my need for intimacy unfulfilled
- ❑ Because of painful relationships in the past, I have been avoiding people who could be important to me now
- ❑ I allow my lack of a partner to restrict my contact with married friends or couples
- ❑ I am doing some things that drive people from me, such as a. complaining too much, b. depreciating myself excessively c. being too aggressive, or d. withholding myself
- ❑ I have very few meaningful activities to engage in while alone
- ❑ I prefer being alone
- ❑ Being alone is strange and fear provoking
- ❑ I have just gone through, or I am going through a life transition, and need time to develop friendships.
- ❑ I do not know how to have fun by myself.
- ❑ I feel that I am uninteresting to others
- ❑ I have a hard time admitting that I am lonely or that I need friends
- ❑ I am wounded and have a tough time trusting others right now
- ❑ The thought of being alone is terrifying

If you fear reaching out to others or just don't know how, talk to your pastor or a counselor. Join a small group or support group.

How do you experience loneliness?

- ❑ I never feel in tune with those around me
- ❑ I feel empty inside.
- ❑ I often feel no one really knows me well
- ❑ I can never find companionship when I want it
- ❑ I feel like I have a hole in my stomach.
- ❑ I often feel that people are around me but not with me
- ❑ I'm not sure anyone cares
- ❑ No one knows what's going on inside me
- ❑ I feel abandoned.

How can I deal with my loneliness?

The Christian way of life does not take away our loneliness; it protects and cherishes_it as a precious gift. Henri Nouwen, *The Wounded Healer*

The ultimate solution to our loneliness is intimacy with God. He made us in His image. He announced that it was not good for man to be alone. He designed us for intimacy with Himself and others. Jesus spent time alone, but He also developed many healthy relationships. Jesus also suffered the pain of aloneness in the garden on the night before His death. To deal with loneliness effectively, we must understand the relationship of three terms—aloneness, loneliness and solitude. Our spiritual goal is to turn aloneness into solitude, not into loneliness.

Aloneness may be painful at times, but it is not a character flaw or a sign of insecurity or inferiority. It is a physical state of being separated from other people (Tom Hanks in Cast Away). Loneliness is an emotional state of feeling disconnected from other people. Aloneness is the recognition of being alone, loneliness is the painful feeling of being separated, unwanted or abandoned by others. Aloneness is seen as temporary, loneliness feels like an eternity. Aloneness moves us to connect; loneliness moves us deeper into isolation.

Loneliness is not a physical condition but a state of mind. One can be alone and not feel lonely. One can be surrounded by people and still feel very lonely. Our most common response to loneliness is to try to escape it via distractions. At some point in our life, all of us are alone. Being alone is an inevitable condition of man; and since our society is so afraid of "aloneness" loneliness is an almost universal problem.

Christian thinker Henri Nouwen says that loneliness is a gateway to God. Aloneness is something we must embrace. We must learn to move from loneliness to solitude—intentionally embracing being alone and not feel lonely. Solitude is a time of peace and reflection; a time when we can find ourselves and become intimate with God.

> *It is probably difficult, if not impossible, to move from loneliness to solitude without any form of withdrawal from a distracting world, and therefore it is understandable that those who seriously try to develop their spiritual life are attracted to places and situations where they can be alone, sometimes for a limited period of time, sometimes more or less permanently. But the solitude that really counts is the solitude of the heart; it is an inner quality or attitude that does not depend on physical isolation. On occasion this isolation is necessary to develop the solitude of heart, but it would be sad if we considered this essential aspect of the spiritual life as a privilege of monks and hermits. It seems more important than ever to stress that solitude is one of the human capacities that can exist, be maintained and developed in the center of a big city, in the middle of a large crowd and in the context of a very active and productive life. A man or woman who has developed this solitude of heart is no longer pulled apart by the most divergent stimuli of the surrounding world but is able to perceive and understand this world from a quiet inner center (*Henri Nouwen, *Reaching Out*, p.25.).

In *The Life you've Always Wanted,* John Ortberg writes, "Solitude is the one place where we can gain freedom from the forces of society that will otherwise relentlessly mold us" (p. 90). Solitude is being alone with a purpose. Our culture dos not value aloneness or solitude. In order to counter loneliness and move to solitude, we must rethink some of our assumptions about aloneness. One way is to understand God's solution to our loneliness, namely His abiding presence (John 15 and 16). You and I "belong," we are part of God's family. His promise is that He will never leave or forsake us. Read Isaiah 54:10, Hebrews 13:5-6, Psalms 95:6-7 and Eph 2:19.

What does aloneness mean to you? Does it mean being miserable or free? We attach our own unique meaning. It could mean, "I am alone right now, no one is here" or "I am alone because no one cares. I am unlovable, undesirable, a social failure, a bad person; no one would ever want to be with me. I will never be a whole person unless I have a partner or spouse."

Aloneness gives way to loneliness if we believe these inner negative messages. Loneliness can overwhelm us and take us down a road of despair and disconnection with God and others. Loneliness can turn into solitude when it is motivated by a desire to know and be known by God. Before every major trial, Jesus chose time alone as a way to get clear about His mission and stay connected to His Father. Solitude is finding a time and place for God, and God alone (Matt 6:6). Henri Nouwen calls solitude a place of conversion; where the old self dies and the new self is born. It is not just being alone, but being alone with God. Have you moved from loneliness to solitude in your life? If you have not, you are missing out on valuable quality time with God.

Do not let the "busyness" of our culture control you. Learn to see aloneness as a gift, not a declaration of your inadequacy. Where are you stuck? If loneliness is overwhelming you, seek out a pastor or counselor, connect with others and have the courage to tell them about your feelings. Chances are they may be feeling the same things.

How do I start dealing with my loneliness?

- ❑ Change your mind about "alone" time (Romans 12:1-2)
- ❑ Start spending time alone (a little at first)
- ❑ Start building a few great friendships
- ❑ Get involved with a community of believers
- ❑ Start asking yourself the following questions. If any answer is no, make plans to fill that need.
    - Do I have at least one person I can call in times of distress?
    - Do I have someone who can pray with me who knows what's going on in my life?
    - Do I have several people with whom I can visit with little warning or apology?
    - Do I have several people with whom I can have fun?
    - Do I have people who could help me out in a pinch?
    - Do I have one person to whom I am accountable?
    - Do I have several people who could provide guidance during a decision making time?
- ❑ Build contentment into your life (Phil 4)
- ❑ Start practicing solitude—listen for God, He always nearby
- ❑ Meditate on God and His word (Psalm 1) don't just "check in"
- ❑ Develop healthy self-care skills

<u>Dr. P. Rule:</u> We are never alone because God is always with us. He is ever present. We learned this from Job. Read Job 7:16; Lam. 3:28; Is. 54:10; Heb. 12:1, 13:5-6; I Cor. 1:19; Rev. 3:20; Ps 1, 31: 9-11, 34:18;

Action Step: Write your own definition of solitude

Do you have a social/spiritual support system?

Do you have an accountability relationship with someone?

Are you spending quiet time with God?

Dealing with emotional wounds (James 5:16; II Tim. 1:7)

Relationships have nearly unlimited potential for joy and meaning. When our relationships with God and others reflect a healthy level of intimacy, the oneness we experience can be deeply fulfilling. Sadly, most of us have never experienced that level of intimacy. Abuse, neglect, abandonment, rejection, disappointment or conflict are much more likely to be experienced than deep unconditional love and caring. The impact of failed relationships, abuse or betrayal often results in incredible emotional woundedness. Soon feelings like joy, happiness, peace or contentment are just distant memories. When you think of past relationships, what feelings come to mind?

The most common response I have heard is hurt. This is followed by anger, fear, guilt and shame. These all result from unmet emotional needs. Unfortunately, these negative responses become expectations and patterns (Prov. 23:7). *"No one will meet my needs so I will have to take care of myself and protect myself from being hurt or rejected by others.*" These patterns can become extreme, leading to deep depression, intense panic or anxiety, or debilitating emotional and/or physical symptoms that make it difficult to function. These patterns ultimately take the form of emotional wounds—deep cuts in our soul that cause us spiritual and emotional pain. While there are many ways these wounds manifest themselves, there are five primary traits of severe emotional woundedness.

- Shame—feeling flawed, defective, unlovable, worthless
- Fear—of abandonment, change, the unknown, failure, rejection
- Trust—too much and therefore repeatedly betrayed and hurt; or too little and living in anxiety, suspicion and isolation.
- Denial—fantasies, repression, delusions, lack of awareness, numbness
- Alienation—difficulty bonding, loving or committing yet longing for these; intense loneliness and disconnection from others

What do emotional wounds look like?
Emotional wounds are invisible scars caused by harmful events in our life; most woundedness is out of our awareness. Wounds are adaptive forms of self-protection each

individual develops to cope and survive. The toxic events of our lives cause us to develop these defenses. The younger we are and/or the more obtrusive the event, the greater our need for defense and the more resistant we are to change. At some point, these defenses become defining characteristics of our personality. These wounds become life-guides. We choose partners, careers, friends, etc. based on the needs created by these wounds. Wounded people feel "stuck" in a revolving door of poor decisions, unwanted emotions and situations over which they feel they have no control. The dynamics of divorce and remarriage trigger these wounds—creating a sense of continually being re-wounded. The feelings are very powerful; the behavioral reactions are almost reflexive. Below is a list of emotional wounds. Do you struggle with any of these?

- ❑ Ambivalence—indecision; lack of self-confidence; inferiority
- ❑ Confusion—feeling lost; not knowing what you want or need
- ❑ Rigidity—seeing things and/or people as black or white, good or bad, right or wrong; inflexibility
- ❑ Perfectionism—needing things to be "just so," must be better to be the same as others; needing to be right
- ❑ Control issues—overly aggressive and domineering or subtly manipulative
- ❑ Irrational fears—of losing control, abandonment, criticism or rejection
- ❑ Shame—"I am a bad, worthless person" low esteem, self-abuse
- ❑ Disconnection from others—strong feelings of emptiness, loneliness or isolation
- ❑ Trust issues—trusting too much or too little, ambivalence, under-trusting safe people and over-trusting abusive or hurtful people
- ❑ Difficulty bonding with others—believing you cannot be loved; inability to love oneself; confusing love with lust or pity or codependence, alienation and isolation
- ❑ Spiritual and emotional numbness—not feeling anything; alienation from God
- ❑ Lack of spontaneity—restricted emotions, don't know how to play; stay in adult mode all the time; can never relax or have fun
- ❑ Repressed affect—difficulty expressing emotions, especially strong emotions
- ❑ Conflict avoidance—fear, withdrawal, "freezes" when confronted
- ❑ Limited affect— uncomfortable demonstrating affection; inadequate boundaries; self-conscious; avoidant, awkward when receiving gifts
- ❑ Depression—profound feelings of sadness, hopelessness or helplessness
- ❑ Stress—anxiety, tension, nervousness, restlessness, insecurity
- ❑ Lack of awareness—difficulty getting in touch with inner struggles; denying the existence of debilitating problems
- ❑ Reality distortions—denial, repression, catastrophizing, delusional thinking
- ❑ Addictions—self-defeating habits, self-medicating with sex, food, shopping, substances, gambling, work, etc.

The impact of woundedness

How many did you check? The emotional wounds you identified will play a major role in any future relationships. Emotional woundedness makes it difficult to be a healthy partner, to wait for or be discerning about healthy partners, or to do the things relationships need to thrive. How can these emotional wounds impact your life? The biggest impact is spiritually. Deeply wounded individuals struggle in their relationship with God. They have difficulty trusting God or experiencing joy in their lives. They may even blame God. In addition, they have a hard time trusting themselves and others. Wounded individuals often do not know that they are wounded and they certainly do not know how their woundedness impacts their life. This lack of awareness leads to great personal and relational pain. Underlying our wounds is a lifetime of unmet needs. As adults, we are driven to have these needs met in our relationships. Often this intense "neediness" overwhelms a partner, leading to further rejection. Below are several specific consequences of woundedness.

Wounded individuals have self-sabotaging core beliefs and expectations. These distorted beliefs soon become "our guiding truths" and are out of our awareness and not readily open to scrutiny. The result is that unresolved issues from our past get replayed over and over again in our lives and particularly in our relationships.

Wounded individuals tend to make poor relationship choices. Wounded individuals are not perceptive. They frequently pick emotionally unavailable partners. Red flags are typically ignored. They lack the accurate information needed to make informed relationship choices.

Wounded individuals tend to attract one another. Wounded individuals tend to pick the same kinds of partners over and over. Consequently, patterns of control, abuse, dependency, chaos, neglect or abandonment tend to be repeated—over and over.

Wounded individuals have unhealthy relationships. God designed relationships to meet our needs and to reflect His character. Relationships between two extremely wounded adults are very volatile and chaotic—full of love and hate, confusion, turmoil and distortions of reality. Mistrust is common in relationships between wounded individuals. Neither individual trusts him or herself and usually functions in deep denial.

Wounded individuals are unable to meet each other's needs effectively. Woundedness leads to self-absorption; therefore a wounded partner will not be able to meet your needs. Emotional woundedness also leads to self-centeredness and a tendency to focus on my needs over yours. We develop relationships to have our needs met and to meet those of a partner. Relationships require give and take to be successful. Wounded partners enter relationships to have their own needs met; they seldom see the needs of others and become agitated when asked to meet someone else's needs.

Wounded individuals pass this woundedness on to their children. Wounded individuals tend recreate the dysfunctional systems with which they are comfortable. Guilt, shame, lack of nurturing, unhealthy rules and roles, denial of problems and poor communication characterizes these environments. Since problems are never acknowledged or dealt with, children never learn healthy coping skills. The skills they do learn are generally how to deny problems or pretend everything is fine. Wounded children produce challenges that wounded parents cannot handle effectively.

Wounded individuals tend to isolate themselves. Community is God's solution to life's challenges. God created us as relational beings—we really do need each other. One of our deepest needs is the need to belong. This need is distorted by emotional woundedness. We respond by either isolating ourselves from others or developing one-sided, codependent relationships.

Wounded individuals are very poor problem solvers and decision-makers because they are usually immersed in and distracted by their own inner turmoil and conflict. They have few or no communication or processing skills. *Problems are always treated like catastrophes*, never as opportunities to learn or grow. The result is that conflicts never get resolved—they stack up. Unfortunately, unresolved conflicts do not just "stack up," they lead to emotional blowups and tremendous relational pain and despair.

Wounded individuals are seldom at peace. Every day is a struggle. The needs they experience are intense and the belief that these needs will never be met drives them emotionally. There is little hope or joy in their lives.

"If I am attached to another person because I cannot stand on my own two feet, he or she may be a lifesaver, but the relationship is not one of love." -- Erich Fromm

Understanding the impact of a dysfunctional childhood

You may have grown up with the awareness that something was wrong with your family. Perhaps you are still trying to understand and undo the damage. It is difficult to face the pain of dealing with the past, so sometimes we *stuff* our feelings and choose to avoid meaningful intimacy. We often become victims or perpetrators, perpetually giving or receiving the pain that we once absorbed. The results of growing up in an unhealthy childhood environment are painful to acknowledge—relationships in shambles, incredible woundedness, self-protection that keeps us disconnected from others, and spiritual distancing from God. Healing cannot occur until the truth is out in the open—we must embrace our past and allow God to free us and heal us. Below are some of the characteristics of non-nurturing families.

They shame people. Family members are negatively compared. Name-calling and humiliation are common. Expectations are unrealistic and standards are impossible. No one ever feels "good enough." The basic message is: "You are defective," or "You will never measure up."

They are performance oriented. Value and acceptance are achieved by doing rather than being. Members are told they will never measure up, but to keep trying. Family members keep trying harder because they believe this is the only way to be loved and accepted. Children seldom grow up feeling valuable or worthwhile. Love is always seen as conditional. Failure to perform leads to shaming messages.

Rules are unspoken. Behavior is governed by a set of rules that are only articulated when broken. These rules are shaming and change without notice. Examples include:

Don't talk: "There are no problems here, if you think there are, then you are (have) the problem." Everything is private and unspoken.
Can't win: "Never lie, but tell the person on the phone that I'm not here." "Tell your parents everything, but don't tell this to Mom, it might upset her." These create confusing double binds.
Don't feel: "No one cares how you feel." Feelings are messy; only performance and appearance count. Feelings become irrelevant.

Communication is always coded. Needs or feelings are never expressed directly. You are shamed for being selfish if you talk about your feelings or needs. Talking about issues or concerns breaks the no-talk rule so families learn how to talk in code. Verbal statements are not to be taken at face value. For example, "Do me a favor" really means, "Do it now or else" or "It sure would be nice if someone around here took out the trash" really means, "You do it now (or else)." Non-nurturing families develop a personal "codebook" to help them decipher messages.

A client shared that in his home, messages were never direct. Dad would get angry and Mom would try to soften him up. She acted as the go-between. If Dad got mad and hit him, Mom would say, "Dad has had a hard day." Or "You know your Dad didn't really mean to..."

They encourage emotional idolatry. Idolatry is turning to something other than God as a source of value and identity. In dysfunctional families, value is given for obeying the implicit, unspoken rules. *Don't feel, talk, think, upset anyone, etc.* Value is gained by how you look, how you act or what other people think. Needs are never really met, except in a distorted way of maintaining the family balance. People become numb to their own needs, and, in fact, are discouraged from having needs. True spirituality and intimacy with God comes from personal struggle. To effectively struggle, we must express our inner turmoil, as well as our need for healing and deep relationship with a Holy God. In non-nurturing families people are not encouraged to share (No-talk rule). Relationships are never deep; they are abusive, enmeshed, codependent even incestuous, but never deep, intimate and life changing or life giving.

They are adult-focused. Non-nurturing families have a hard time with kids. Since there is an emphasis on everything looking *perfect*, children represent an extreme challenge. A child discovering life can be messy; kids are hard to control. Also, wounded parents are very self-absorbed, unhappy and unstable. Shaming and oppressive rules are used to control behavior. "Act your age," "Don't embarrass us," "Don't touch," "Don't be a pest," "Don't have too much fun," "Don't laugh too hard," "Don't ask for anything." "Don't get dirty." The message children hear is, "You are not valued or wanted."

They are preoccupied with fault and blame. Mistakes are normal and it is important to be held accountable. Dysfunctional families do not merely hold others accountable, however, they indict them. The message is, "Don't ever make us look bad, embarrass us, bring attention to us, expose us, etc." Since performance is the focus, mistakes are dealt with harshly, with shame and blame. Overreaction is common. One can never be good enough or sorry enough. Finding out "who is responsible" is not about forgiveness and accountability and grace but about blame and condemnation. The safest approach is to deny responsibility or to find someone else to blame.

They are strong on "head skills." Individuals in non-nurturing families are very defensive. Shame and blame hurt. Survival means becoming an expert at self-protection. Skills such as learning how to hide, denying the existence of problems, blaming others, rationalizing things away or becoming a good debater become critical to survival. Questions are asked for which there are no right answers. *"What possessed you to say/do that, is your brain malfunctioning?" "What's wrong with you?"* The only safe answer is, "I don't know." Real issues are never discussed.

They are weak on "heart skills." Feelings are relevant; no one really cares how you feel. Emotions must be thought, not felt. Ask an adult who grew up in a dysfunctional home how he or she feels and you will hear thoughts, not feelings. If you cannot explain the feeling, it must not exist. Experiencing certain feelings, (i.e. loneliness, sadness, hurt, etc.) is viewed as weakness. Denial is common. The result is shame and emotional numbness, as well as an incredibly deep, but unexpressed sadness. Spoken messages deny your humanness, *"Don't act like a baby." Don't get a big head about this." "What's the big deal?" "Why don't you go cry about it?" "Who do you think you are?" "You're not special."*

People appear healthy, but are, in fact, incredibly needy. Since love and acceptance are achieved by performance, family members have no sense of worth apart from their behavior. True joy is seldom experienced. Individuals look great on the outside, but inside they carry some strong, negative inner beliefs. *"I do not know how to be loved or accepted," "I am only okay when I perform," "I am not capable, valuable or worthwhile," "I don't know where I fit in or belong." "I don't know what makes me okay."* Family members exist to perpetuate and support the system, it does not exist to equip, nurture or affirm them. Shame, neediness and woundedness get passed on to future relationships.

There is secrecy and denial. Problems are denied and swept under the carpet. Even major personal violations such as abuse, rape, fondling, beating or neglect, are never talked about or acknowledged. The victim (typically a child) is never quite sure of the validity of his or her experience. The no-talk rule forbids him or her from discussing these things with anyone—making the child a silent partner in the dysfunction. Due to self-protective forgetting, adults growing up in this environment often have large gaps in the memory.

The individual has a distorted sense of self. Children in these systems are taught to subordinate their needs to those of the family. By doing so, they never develop distinct identities. Instead they create adaptive roles to help them cope. These roles are nearly always exaggerated. There is either over-adaptation—going along with everything—or total rebellion. Problem solving skills are non-existent. The grown child is clueless as to his or her needs and does not possess the tools to meet them if he or she did know them. Behavior patterns are rigid, self-defeating and insight-resistant.

Did you grow up in a family like the one described above? Shame is a major consequence of growing up in a dysfunctional family. If you struggle with shame or the impact of abuse, please seek out a pastor or counselor.

<u>Dr. P. Rule:</u> *Every one of us* is emotionally wounded to some degree. Addressing your wounds will be painful, but you must address these wounds and the issues they raise before you can move forward with future relationships. The traits mentioned above will not go away with time and they will adversely affect any future relationships. If you and/or your partner struggle with more than two or three of the above traits, ***please consider putting your relationship on hold and addressing these issues.*** If your partner is wounded and in denial, understand that it will be impossible to build a healthy relationship with him or her. Locate a Christian counselor or pastor familiar with abuse issues.

Healing emotional wounds

Healing your emotional wounds is a process. These wounds and the issues surrounding them must be dealt with to be a healthy individual and to be a healthy member of a relationship. Make recovery a priority. Below are a few suggestions to get you started.

1. Review the following scriptures: II Cor. 1:3-6; Rom. 5:3-5; II Cor. 12:9; Rom. 8:1, 18, 26-28; II Cor. 7:5-6; Ps. 23; Is. 41:10. What application to your wounds can you draw? Stay connected to God's word.
2. Make a *commitment* to yourself to deal with these issues now. Start with one area first. If possible, work on these emotional wounds before getting into a permanent relationship. If you are already in a relationship, take some time for yourself and work on these issues. It is not necessary, however, to leave the relationship.
3. Any work toward wholeness always begins with spirituality—work on your relationship with God.
4. Join a support group.
5. Explore your past. Understand the source of your pain and woundedness. Work through your numbness.
6. Identify your core beliefs and challenge them if necessary.
7. Identify negative self-talk and unhealthy thinking patterns. Below is a list of faulty thinking patterns, which describe you?
    - All or nothing thinking—everything is black and white, perfect or a total failure
    - Overgeneralization—allowing the past to predict the future
    - Personalization—seeing events as personal attacks; seeing yourself as the cause of negative events
    - Emotional reasoning—assuming that the way you feel is the way things are
    - Mind-reading—making assumptions about the motives of others without ever checking things out
    - Fortune-telling—forecasting the future
    - Catastrophizing—exaggerating the importance of events or your response to them
    - Minimizing—denying or discounting your feelings

- Labeling—attaching negative labels to yourself or others. "Loser" "worthless" "lazy" "crazy" etc.

5. Practice positive self-talk. The truth will always set us free (John 8:32). We need to experience God's truth and healing in our lives. Catch your negative thoughts and change them into positive ones. Below are some examples of positive thinking.
   - I can change
   - I can ask for help
   - I can take responsibility for my actions
   - I can learn new ways of thinking
6. Turn your positive thinking into positive behavior (Romans 12:1-2, James 1:25).
7. Develop one or two healthy friendships. Stop *any* unhealthy relationships.
8. Get any addictions or bad habits under control; addictions cloud our mind and numb our pain.
9. Forgive yourself and others; make amends for any wrongs you have done.
10. Get your finances in order—cut spending, take pressure off yourself.
11. Spend some time understanding the role your childhood may have played.
12. Turn off the TV—read and meditate; don't get lost in distractions.
13. Do something different—laugh more, get some exercise.
14. Do something that helps others.
15. Avoid making major, life-changing decisions during your time of healing.
16. Stop and reflect. If you struggle in this area, you will sabotage any future relationships. Please take the time to work on these issues.

Working through spiritual and emotional blind spots

John Chapter 9 tells of Jesus healing a man blind from birth. Read this great chapter because it contains a story of God's compassion and healing power, but also an indictment of spiritual blindness. After the man's healing, religious leaders question and ultimately chastise the man because Jesus healed him on the Sabbath. "*All I know is that I was blind but now I see" (v. 25)* is the man's fabled response. In a later interaction, Jesus reveals himself as the Son of God and proclaims that there are two forms of blindness—physical and spiritual. "I *have come so the blind will see and those who see will become blind* "(v. 39).

The point is that the emotional wounds of our past can leave us with many "blind spots." Good people can have blind spots; they are difficult to identify and change because we do not know we have them. *We don't know what we don't know.* Many remarrying individuals are blind to the effects of the past (Remember our gal marrying five alcoholics). They wrongly assume that time itself will heal them or somehow change their personality. Without making changes, a person addicted, abusive, sullen, passive or cold and insensitive in a prior relationship, will be just the same in the next relationship. Time does not heal; hard work and spiritual transformation heal. Below are some common blind spots? Do you struggle with any of these? Ask someone you trust?

- A critical spirit

- Fear of commitment
- Fear of failure
- Addictions or self-defeating habits
- Anger and rage
- Dependency
- Lack of boundaries
- A deep sense in inadequacy
- Pride or arrogance
- Being a victim or martyr

In *Should I Get Married*, M. Blaine Smith discusses how blind spots have affected him. "When I reflect on my experience as a single Christian, I'm struck by two things. First, I'm certain that some of the difficulties I experienced were unavoidable. There is a mystery—in short, a risk—in human relationships that can never be avoided if we are to experience the adventure of life as God has designed it and move toward the goal of an intimate lifetime relationship. Yet I also realize only too well that some of my problems resulted from certain well-intentioned but misguided perspectives which made me prone to bad judgment and a sitting duck for disappointment" (Pg. 13). Smith goes on to summarize three types of misguided perspectives or blind spots.

Spiritualizing—expecting an unreasonable measure of guidance from God. This can mean taking no initiative in the dating process at all and waiting until God unmistakably brings someone into your life, or upon finding a partner, waiting for some supernatural sign from God before proceeding with the relationship.

Idealizing—having unreasonable ideals about the perfect mate. This can mean looking for someone who will be 20 out of 20 on your list of desired traits and passing on someone who is only 18 out of 20. It can also mean setting yourself up for failure so often that you finally "just pick someone" out of desperation.

Catastrophizing—harboring unreasonable fears of risk by obsessing over potential problem areas. This can mean giving small incidents too much power or dwelling on problems that are not likely to occur. It can mean worrying yourself to the point of relationship avoidance.

How are you—

Spiritualizing?

Idealizing?

Catastrophizing?

Action Step: What are your blind spots? You can work through blind spots with a friend, pastor or counselor. Ask for an honest appraisal. "Do I have traits or behavior patterns that can sabotage a relationship?" "Am I seeing a potential mate clearly?" "Am I over or under-analyzing certain traits?" "Am I avoiding relationships due to fear of failure or rejection?"

Reconnecting with Others

Aside from strengthening your relationship with God, reinvolving yourself with others may be the single most important post death/divorce growth activity. Many individuals lose confidence in their own judgment. Many isolate themselves after a loss and put off reconnecting until they eliminate all their negative feelings. This is a mistake; reconnecting actually helps us grow. Finding the courage to try new relationships, new roles, and new solutions to old problems, helps us restore a sense of competence and self-esteem.

The best advice we can give is to move ahead slowly. Make new friends and strengthen old relationships. Spend time with close friends and loved ones, stay spiritually connected and enjoy the journey rather than focusing on the outcome. Learn as much as you can about your goals and needs. Become comfortable with who you are as a person, understanding that you are complete in the Lord. Past relationships can be a reminder of hurt or even failure, but they are powerful windows through which to see issues, wounds, and expectations that must be addressed if you are to make healthier relationship choices in the future. The key is to not remain isolated. Get connected. Develop friendships and accountability relationships. Join a small group. Listen to others and feel safe before sharing your story. Allow others to get close to you—do not keep them at arms length.

Rebuilding Your Life

I have learned one important thing in my life—how to begin again.
Sam Keen, *Beginnings Without End*

What life do you want to build? The path you choose will lead you to certain social, spiritual, emotional and relational outcomes. In *For Better or For Worse*, Mavis Hetherington, based on 40 years of research, has observed six pathways a person can take after a death or divorce. Each of these leads to very different outcomes.

- **The enhancers.** This group took responsibility for their growth. They became more socially and emotionally healthier and more confident, well-adjusted and self-fulfilled over time. Future relationships were generally more successful and fulfilling.
- **The good enoughs.** This was Hetherington's largest group. These individuals were in the middle on most of her measures. They experienced successes and failures. Many remarried into relationships very similar to past relationships.
- **The seekers.** This was the second largest group, characterized by an eagerness to find a new mate as soon as possible. They did little to grow or change.
- **The libertines.** This group, predominately men, were interested in the singles life. Hetherington notes that within a year or two, most libertines became disillusioned and began looking for stable relationships.
- **The competent loners.** This group is comprised of well-adjusted, self-sufficient and socially skilled individuals. However, unlike enhancers, members of this group seldom remarried.

- **The defeated.** This group had the poorest level of adjustment. Many of these individuals were experiencing problems long before the break-up. Most saw themselves as victims, with no control and few options. Future relationships were extremely unhealthy and unsuccessful.

What path will you take? You do not have to be a victim. You can create a spiritually and emotionally healthy, balanced life for you and your children. Before you can be a healthy relationship partner you *must* be a successful single person and/or single parent. The big question is, "Are you willing to take the time to accomplish the steps we have outlined *before* you remarry?" It takes time to develop a close, intimate relationship with God and to understand and heal your brokenness and hurt. It takes time to understand your role in past relationships and to learn new patterns of relating to others. It takes time to define what being a "healthy single" looks like for you and then to live that life consistently. Be patient; give yourself the gift of time (Read Psalm 37 and Isaiah 40 about waiting on the Lord). Consider the "gifts" you brought from your past relationship. These gifts refer to lessons learned, changes you have made, issues you have resolved, even accomplishments that your relationship made possible. Even if you feel you did all the giving and changing, look back and compare the person you are now with the person you were before. Every relationship offers an opportunity for growth.

Summary: Signposts of emotional and spiritual health

The following ten signposts are designed to help you gauge your progress so far. Rate yourself on each using a 1-10 scale, with 10 meaning you are more complete in this area. A score of 70 or above suggests that you are progressing well. If you score below 50, please consider re-examining the growth steps we just covered.

Signpost one: Getting serious about your relationship with God. Is God truly Lord of your life? Have you made a commitment to live your life for Christ? Do you have an accountability partner? Do you attend a small group where you share your issues and receive support, love and encouragement? Do you spend time reflecting on God's word and attempt to apply it to your everyday life? Do you try to discover what God is up to in your life?

Signpost two: **Accepting that you cannot change what happens to you.** You cannot control others or your circumstances. What you experience in any given moment immediately becomes frozen in history, and you cannot change that. When something "terrible" happens, it is immediately over, gone, irreversible. Change happens—you cannot stop it or control it.

Signpost Three: Realizing that you have almost absolute power over how you respond to your circumstances. You can choose how you will respond to life. Your past does not have to dictate your present or your future. Choose not to be a victim.

Signpost Four: Letting go of old patterns and learning new ones. When your patterns of behaving, thinking, believing and living are no longer working positively, you can let go and learn new ways of responding. No matter how difficult, you can choose new, healthier ways of relating.

Signpost Five: Becoming patient with change. Change seldom happens overnight. Old ways of thinking and behaving die slowly. New ways of relating seem awkward at first. Being clear about allowing yourself to be "in" the change process is critical to growth. This is a "crockpot" versus "microwave" process.

Signpost Six: Taking responsibility and making choices.
As you grow, you learn that life is not just "black or white," but rather a full spectrum of colorful options from which you are free to choose. Few choices you make are permanent or cannot be modified by yet further choice. You can always choose how to respond to others.

Signpost Seven: Learning to love
God calls you to love yourself and others unconditionally. You can do this when you love from your fullness in Christ, rather than from your tendency to allow circumstances or others define who you are. If you allow God to transform you with His love, you can go beyond your childhood habits, beyond your self-defeating behavior, beyond your narrow view of life, beyond your fear or anger-ridden responses to being alive. When you love, you expand your awareness to realize the freedom of having abundant life, and the peace, joy and hope that sharing life with others has to offer. By loving, we become healthy.

Signpost Eight: Learning to forgive. Forgiveness is a gift we give others and well as oursleves. Forgiveness frees us from the bonds of bitterness and resentment and allows us to live life fully in the present.

Signpost Nine: Leading from strengths. There are several indicators of healthy adjustment. Individuals who display these traits fare much better after a death or divorce and have healthier relationships in the future. These indicators include a strong support network, spirituality, adaptability, the ability to plan, the ability to control one's emotions, independence, the ability to solve problems and a strong work ethic. Risk factors include emotional instability, impulsivity, lack of social support and an unhealthy attachment to a former spouse.

Signpost Ten: Developing healthier relationship patterns
Growth frees us to live life differently, to learn new habits, to genuinely connect with others and to develop a healthy lifestyle that reflects God's character. Below are examples of a healthier mindset toward others.

- Appreciating people for who they are.
- Allowing friendships to naturally emerge into relationships.
- Feeling free to enjoy others versus needing others.
- Always addressing others from your real self.
- Knowing and articulating your needs
- Knowing and respecting your boundaries and those of others.
- Being clear about your definition of an ideal relationship.

- Taking care of your companionship needs. Making friends; not becoming dependent on a relationship to validate your worth.

How did you score? Which signpost still needs some work?

Dr. P. Rule: The time you invest in yourself—grieving, healing, identifying your needs, understanding the role you played in past relationships—is invaluable. If you are going to make better partner choices in the future, you must give yourself this vital gift. Too many singles have married the wrong person, at the wrong time, for the wrong reasons.

Growth Activities

The following activities will help you grow after a divorce or death of a spouse.

- Keep writing your story. Be clear about your circumstances and the role you played. What life lessons have you discovered to this point? There are several reasons to do this: to get closure, to prepare for future relationships, to see God at work in your life, to grieve the losses and to aid in confession, repentance and forgiveness. Begin the process of learning from your experience. If you do not understand why you are divorced, you are destined to repeat unhealthy patterns.
- Take great care of your kids. Get them into a support group, counseling or whatever it takes to help them process the divorce. Encourage them to spend time with their friends. Don't become dependent on your children. Children must grieve and adjust in their own way, so be observant and sensitive to their needs, but not overindulgent or inconsistent with discipline. Help them rebuild their trust. Children need stability after a divorce. Do not rush into new relationships too soon.
- Take great care of yourself, emotionally, spiritually and physically. Attend a divorce recovery group or get some counseling. *Work* on yourself. Take the time to improve your health and fitness. The greatest gift you can give your children is a healthy you. Denial is a huge problem after a divorce. Many individuals do not see how the divorce has affected them. Be clear about this, divorce wounds everyone. Develop healthy boundaries.
- Find a church singles group that focuses on building friendships and helping you become a healthy single, not one that serves as a dating service. Be discerning. Get involved in serving in your local church.
- Set some new goals and priorities.
- Try some new things. Take a class, find a hobby or learn a new skill.
- Build a new social network—new friends and support network (Proverbs 27:17).
- Consider new educational or vocational opportunities.
- Get clear on your career. Find something you really enjoy.
- Get your financial house in order.
- Join a community organization, volunteer your time.

- Read books on divorce recovery and how divorce affects children. Learn all you can about how to build a better life for you and your children.
- Get into God's Word and find an accountability partner. An accountability partner is someone who can laugh and cry with you and is willing to ask you hard questions about your life.

Action Step: The tasks and activities outlined above are critical to your development as a healthy single. Becoming a healthy single-adult is necessary for remarriage readiness. Please give yourself the gift of time. Review these tasks and activities; be clear about which still need attention. Check all that apply:

- ❑ dealing with loneliness
- ❑ resolving emotional wounds
- ❑ working on my relationship with my children
- ❑ taking care of myself
- ❑ finding a home church and a small group
- ❑ getting an accountability partner
- ❑ developing healthy friendships
- ❑ career exploration
- ❑ personal boundaries
- ❑ grieving losses
- ❑ forgiveness
- ❑ making amends

Dr. P. Rule: You can never know enough about your own pain, struggles, emotional wounds, feelings, values, beliefs and expectations.

Taking Great Care of Yourself: Building a Healthy Lifestyle

The world breaks everyone and afterward many are strong at the broken places—
Earnest Hemingway *A Farewell to Arms*

God wants our lifestyle to reflect the "great commandment" Jesus described in Mark 12:31-32—deep love for God, others and ourselves. Having a healthy, vital single life is a key to building Godly, enriching relationships. Below are several components of a healthy single life.

"Doing" life with others (Eccel. 4:9-12)
Loneliness and a sense of disconnection can overwhelm us after a divorce or the death of a spouse. We can begin believing that the only way to get our emotional needs met is through a new partner. Community is God's way of meeting our needs. Community means having people care about you who will hold you accountable and who will be there to celebrate or mourn with you. In Acts 4 we see the church, the community of believers, sharing their lives and resources with one another. Needs met in the context of community help us grow spiritually and emotionally. Consequently, we are less "needy" and therefore less dependent on a partner to meet our needs. It is far healthier to "choose" a partner rather than "need" one. Build community by getting connected. Join a small group, share your life, and get involved in helping others. The Christian life was meant to be played—out on the field, not observed—up in the bleachers.

Healthy self-care
Self-care means doing things for yourself that are nourishing and nurturing. Examples include, taking extra time to relax, pray or meditate, getting to know God a little better, or changing negative self-talk into positive affirmations. Write a list of the things for which you are grateful. Do something special for someone else. Forgive someone; being angry drains your energy. Forgive yourself; being angry hurts your soul. Ask yourself often "How important is this?" Caring for others does not mean that you have to constantly please them. Learn how to say "no." Ask friends and family members for support. Set goals and priorities for your life. Spend time with good friends. Exercise. Eat well. Get enough sleep. Read a book or listen to music.

Choosing joy
In *The Hidden Adventure*, Tim Hansel says that joy is the key principle of life. Joy is a choice and it defies our circumstances. "When we spend time regretting the past or worrying about what the future will bring, we rush past God, who is the ultimate source of joy" (p.135). Paul, in Philippians, says that joy comes from the contentment of knowing that God will supply all our needs. Even in prison, Paul could say, "Rejoice in the Lord always" (Phil 4: 4). Celebrate your life; do not get bogged down in the details. You are a wonderful work in progress in the hands of the great life-giver.

Living life in the present
Life after a tragedy such as a death or divorce is still your life; it is not a waiting room or dress rehearsal for when you have a partner. When you stop participating in life, you stifle your growth and your joy. Resentments accumulate and you lose touch with

yourself and others. You risk becoming co-dependent. Being present is life giving and keeps us open to God. Unfortunately, many individuals wait until they are in a relationship to live the kind of life they want and do the things they love to do.

Putting the past in the past

There is no surer way to sabotage future relationships than continuing to carry hurt, resentments or anger about what happened in the past. We hold on to the past for several reasons: fear, too punish others or ourselves, to prevent hurtful or harmful things from re-occurring, or because we do not know how to let go. Holding on to the past drains our joy and peace, leaving us bitter, depressed and discouraged. God does not want your past to define or control you. Learn how to let go of your past. Forgive yourself and others. Read books, go to workshops, or see a counselor. Keep learning new ways to let go of the past. Read Phil 3:8; Col. 3:12-13; Rom. 12:9-21.

Finding passion and purpose in your life

Passion is what "gets us up" and makes our eyes sparkle. A life without passion and meaning is like a hot fudge sundae without the hot fudge. What motivates you? Perhaps the items you pinpoint will help you create a list of activities. Focusing on your passions pulls you through life rather than pushing and prodding you to live a life you do not really want. Don't settle—live life as fully as you can. Purpose is what you do after you wake up in the morning—it guides your activity. What career path do you wish to take? What do you want to contribute to others? Where is God at work? Take action. Your life's purpose is your own, and will energize you when pursued. You will be happiest when following your passion and purpose. Do not make the mistake of waiting for a relationship to infuse your life with passion and purpose; a loving partner is not a substitute for a meaningful life.

Knowing who you are

Self-acceptance is powerful. Identify your values, your core identity. What are the traits that make you who you are? Identifying what defines ***you*** is so important because you are at your healthiest when you are being who you are—the person God created you to be. What are your likes and dislikes? What do you do really well? God endowed you with skills, abilities and gifts. How are you using yours? If you do not know who you are and if you are not comfortable being you, you risk relating to others through a false self.

Surrounding yourself with healthy people

Surrounding yourself with Godly, healthy people can help you grow emotionally and spiritually. Some individuals are "takers" and some are "givers." Too many takers and you will be drained and bitter. Too many givers and you will be not be challenged nor will you develop a servant mindset. How do your current relationships stack up? Examine your relationships. Be clear about the kind of people you want in your life, remembering that they will challenge, influence, counsel and comfort you.

Developing healthy boundaries
Are there things or people in your life that you tolerate? Tolerations are people or situations in your life that you endure but wish you could change. These drain our energy and steal our joy. It is so important to set personal limits and identify and articulate your boundaries. Make changes in your life to eliminate distractions or annoyances. Learn how to say "no." Define you limits, needs or level of involvement. Respect others and ask for respect in return. Love from fullness, not selfishness or co-dependency.

Giving yourself the gift of "alone" time
Each of us needs time when we focus on ourselves. Jesus spent time alone before every major event. If you do not take time for yourself, you will not be renewed. Poor self-care leads to burn out. When you leave yourself off your own list it is nearly impossible to enjoy or appreciate the life God has given to you. Find ways to have time alone to nurture yourself. Neglecting yourself ensures that you will not be at your best. Experiment and discover how much time and space you truly need. Then, make sure this time for self-care is part of each day. Schedule time for yourself. Take a personal "mental health" day at work every so often. Learn to say "no" and "later." Jesus renewed His strength during alone times; this sharpened His focus and reminded Him of His purpose.

Knowing how you would live if you were to die in one year
By considering the remainder of your life compressed into a year's time, the truly important things will bubble to the surface. Rather than waiting for the "right time" to do something, do it now. If you continually put off what really matters, you end up living a life of urgency and unimportance, instead of creating a life you can thoroughly savor. Focus your real passions. Stop tolerating things that are distracting or draining. Clean up any issues from your past. Bitterness, anger, guilt and shame drain your energy and steal your joy. Get very clear with God.

When you honestly address the components above, you will identify the life you really want and begin to create it right now. God calls us to live life to the fullest. Jesus said that He came to give us an abundant life. The gifts and fruit of the Spirit are meant for you— now. God has gifted you for life and for service and does not expect you to wait until you are married to use these gifts. Get in the game. Give yourself the gift of acknowledging your own mortality so that you will begin to live as if each moment you have matters—because it really does.

Action Step: Write your own personal definition of a healthy single lifestyle. Here are a few suggestions:

- ❑ Differentiating between aloneness and loneliness
- ❑ Finding solitude
- ❑ Determining your passions
- ❑ Finding fullness an contentment in Christ
- ❑ Identifying goals that you want to achieve

- Discovering your areas of passion
- Identifying areas that need some work
- Enjoying the journey
- Developing a group of solid Christian friends
- Involvement in serving in my local church
- Getting your finances in order
- Finding a career that works
- Having strong values about sexuality and dating
- Giving yourself adequate time to heal
- Developing boundaries
- Writing your story
- Finding out what "fun" is in your life

Are you rebuilding your life or are you stuck? If you're stuck, what will you do?

What is keeping you from accomplishing this task?

What does a healthy single lifestyle look like?

Do you know anyone living a "healthy single" lifestyle? Spend time with them.

Here are some important tasks for single parents?

- Helping your children work through their grief issues.
- Staying connected to others for support and encouragement.
- Staying a parent, not just a friend to your children.
- Encouraging parenting time, no matter how you feel about the other parent.
- Learning to let go; you cannot control everything.
- Telling your children the truth; be sure they hear things from you first.
- Modeling forgiveness.
- Seeing yourself as whole in Christ, not just when you have a partner.
- Not becoming codependent on your children or using them as a confidante
- Being consistent with boundaries, expectations and discipline
- Having a social life, but not dating too soon.
- When dating, not feeling guilty.
- Deciding when to introduce your children to a potential partner.
- Taking care of your needs and getting yourself as healthy as possible.

Dr. P. Rule: Be clear about the fact that God not only loves you, He likes you. Not convinced? Read Brennan Manning's wonderful book, *The Ragamuffin Gospel.*

Taking Care of Your Children: Understanding Their Losses

*For adults, divorce brings **a** world to an end; for young children, whose lives are focused in the family, it seems to bring **the** world to an end* Mavis Hetherington *For Better or For Worse*

Second chances are a big theme in divorce and remarriage. Many adults hope to get another chance at love and happiness. Those who were left, abandoned or abused, for example, hope to find someone who will love and respect them. Those that left a marriage are perhaps looking for vindication or absolution, a "second chance" to do it right and a partner they can bond with for life. What about the children, what do they see, want and need? To your children, second chances do not mean the same thing. For them, loss is the big theme. Many children we talk to never quite get over the loss of their biological family. Despite all the explanations, "This had to be done." "We will be better off." "Your father was hurting us." et cetera, most children still only see a loss.

Johnny is seven. His mother just left. He cries most nights. He wants to see her, but she has moved to another town and hasn't yet made contact. Divorce is traumatizing for children. They experience an abrupt transition from a predictable, orderly secure life to one filled with change, uncertainly, disorder and unpredictability. Their world does not feel safe anymore and their parents become less trustworthy, competent and involved. Normal routines are totally disrupted and life presents little stability. The break-up of a family does not "compute" for children, so many assume it must be their fault. To make matters worse, most children are given very little information about a divorce and very little warning that their family was in danger of collapsing. Separation, divorce and remarriage come as a shock to most children. Their whole world is turned upside-down. People they thought would be there forever are gone.

Myths concerning the way divorce affects children

Many parents do not appreciate the traumatic effects divorce can have on their children. Below are several common myths about how divorce affects children.

Myth: Children are resilient and bounce back in a few months without any negative consequences.

Fact: There is a high degree of drug abuse, school-related problems, poor grades and lower economic well-being in single parent families. The trauma children experience when their parents divorce is substantial. Many children have been firsthand witnesses to violence between their parents. When their dreams of a happy and loving home are broken, their security is shattered and their faith in adults is diminished.

Myth: If the parents are happier, the children will also be happier.

Fact: Parents cannot fathom how their children think. Most children want their parents to stay together. Children are not happier, in fact, they feel anxious, lonely, isolated, angry and afraid. Further, "happier" parents do not necessarily become better parents. New relationships take time and energy. Parents weary of working through past issues or the challenges of parenting alone find new relationships a welcome distraction.

Myth: Children do well in new families after divorce.
Fact: After five years, fifty percent of children do not consider their new family an improvement. If they were given a choice, they would return to the family that failed. Children are not nearly as troubled by marital problems as adults. They assume adults will work out their differences, leaving the home intact.

Myth: Children will relate to each parent in the same way after a divorce.
Fact: Relationships with both parents will never be the same. Some parents become more attentive and indulgent, some more possessive and overprotective, while most become more distant and uninvolved. Custodial parents are often so wearied with the tasks of single parenting that they do not have time to be attentive to their children's needs. Soon both parents are involved with other adults, further limiting their time with their children. Established rules and routines change, discipline becomes inconsistent, parents are less emotionally available, anxiety and stress increase and the future seems less predictable. Only one thing is certain, relationships will be changed and children will be impacted.

Myth: Divorce is a temporary crisis; kids get over it quickly..
Fact: True, divorce's impact is most pronounced in the first two years. However, particularly in situations where parents remain adversarial, children can experience the effects of divorce long into adulthood. In fact, much of the impact of divorce will be experienced not in childhood but in adulthood. Divorce can be a life-changing experience for some children.

Myth: Divorce rescues children from an unhappy marriage.
Fact: This is mostly wishful thinking and denial on the part of parents. Most children are "blind-sided" by divorce; having no idea their parents were even thinking of divorce. Children assume parents will have disagreements and arguments and that these will be successfully resolved. These children feel rejected, abandoned or betrayed by their parents. Most feel a deep sense of sadness and loss; some blame themselves. Many adult children of divorce talk about the divorce of their parents as a defining moment in their lives.

> "A central finding of my research is that children identify not only with their mother and father as separate individuals but with the relationship between them. They carry the template of this relationship into adulthood and use it to seek the image of the new family. The absence of a good image negatively influences their search for love, intimacy, and commitment. Anxiety leads many into making bad choices in relationships, giving up hastily when problems arise, or avoiding relationships altogether" (Judith Wallerstein, *The Unexpected Legacy of Divorce*, p. xxix.).

Wallerstein goes on to say that the divorced family is different from the intact family. The children feel less protected and more uncertain about their future. Relationships are never the same and the cast of characters often changes without notice. Have you treated any of these myths as facts? If so, understand that divorce is tough on children; even through they may not show it. This is not about guilt; this is about being aware of what is going on inside your children. Start developing a plan to help your children adjust to life after divorce.

Questions children have asked

- What will happen to me?
- Will you and Dad (Mom) ever get back together?
- Who will take care of me?
- If my parents stopped loving each other, will they stop loving me?
- Where will we live?
- Where will I go to school?
- What about my friends?
- When will I see my Dad/Mom?
- What about my cat/dog/ fish?
- Will you leave too?
- Will we have enough money?
- Can I still take piano lessons?

Children tend to fill in the blanks. In the absence of information, they will create their own stories and explanations. Children's questions are endless and their anxiety and worry over things you may see as trivial is real and intense. Answer your children's questions with confidence and candidness. Children are looking for honesty, structure, support and consistency.

Characteristics of children of divorce

The thought and behavior patterns of children of divorce, even into adulthood, can be summed up by the following general characteristics:

- Trust issues
- Unresolved anger
- Lack of accountability
- Low self-esteem
- Difficulties with social learning
- Difficulty with cause and effect reasoning
- Fear of abandonment
- A value system focused on self

The dysfunctional thought and behavior patterns of children of divorce are not "learned" in the ordinary sense of the term. Rather they come from the traumatic experiences of the child and the resultant view of the world. The most fundamental thought is, "I'm all alone in the world. Because I'm not certain who will always be there to take care of me, I'll take care of myself." *Jeff asked a five-year-old boy whose parents had divorced to draw a picture of his family. After a moment's thought he said, "I have a small family. In fact, I'm the only one in it. So, I'll draw a picture of myself."*

What are some of the long-term effects of divorce on children?

Researchers vary on the lasting impact of divorce on children. Two factors however, seem to play a vital role in how well children will adjust. The first is pre-divorce adjustment. Children who were well adjusted before a divorce seemed to handle the trauma of divorce far better. The second factor is parental conflict. The more adversarial the relationship between the child's two parents, the worse his or her adjustment. Below are some common ways divorce impacts children.

Children often accept responsibility for the divorce. "If I had only cleaned up my room . . ." "If I had only been born a boy . . ." "If I would have made better grades in school . . ." Children often carry the burden of guilt. Many parents do not even tell their children they are getting a divorce, let alone give them plausible reasons. They mistakenly think children are too young to understand. This often has the effect of confusing a child or perpetuating false ideas and unnecessary guilt or trauma.

Children often feel unloved. "If my parents had really loved me, they would have worked their problems out." It does not matter how many times a parent verbally affirms love or brings gifts on visitation days, the child bears a sense of resentment. A child may ask, "Why did my parents have children if they were going to divorce?"

Divided loyalty. Many divorced parents compete for the loyalty of their children. Children are hurt and confused when they hear demeaning and derogatory things about a parent they love. Children often feel disloyal to one parent when they are with the other.

Loss. Children of divorce feel a powerful sense of loss. Even in those families where life was difficult for the children, there were good times and those times are firmly etched in the memories of the children. It can be compared to the death of a loved one. You remember the good things and block out the bad things. We can eventually adjust to a death because we know the deceased person will not return from the grave. In the case of divorce, the other parent is still alive and it is harder to give up hope that somehow mom and dad will re-unite.

Insecurity. Many young children experience separation anxiety. They will cling to their mothers when left at a day care facility. They cannot bear the sight of having their mother leave. Some try to deny their insecurity by claiming to be happy all the time. Many children have terrible dreams of their parent dying. Some develop fantasies. One little girl claimed that her daddy (who had left) slept in her bed every night. A little boy told stories in class of trips never taken with an absent father. These behaviors are symptoms of the fear that parents will go away and never return.

Anger. The two people who were supposed to love the children more than anyone else deserted them. Life is more complex than it used to be. Grownups are acting like children. A stranger who moves into the house to take the place of their birth parent may further complicate a child's life. Anger may be expressed in numerous ways—uncooperativeness, withdrawal, rage, tantrums or rebellious behavior. Some children may show physical symptoms. Rarely will a child tell you he/she is angry.

Future relationships. Many adult children of divorce struggle with relationships. They are not confident that they can make a marriage work. The images of their parents divorce may linger, even into their 30's and 40's. Some still secretly hope their estranged parents will remarry someday.

The unavailable parent

A child's most important buffer to the stresses of change is a competent, available parent. Yet, one of the key consequences of death or divorce for children is the lack of parental availability. At a time when children are very concerned about the future (and present), parents are often absorbed in their own issues. Due to their own worry, fear, anger, grief, etc. many parents become emotionally unavailable to their children. Divorce or the death of a parent is a hard reality for children as well as adults.

Parents also become less available when they start dating. The emotional and time demands of a new relationship limit time and emotional availability with children, many of whom are still grieving the loss of their family. Children of deeply wounded parents often become caretakers, and are forced to assume many of the parental duties. These children are robbed of their childhood as they attempt to meet the needs of their parents. Children need healthy parents who are committed to their welfare. They need encouragement and permission to grieve their losses. They also need structure and boundaries. Most importantly, they need spiritual and emotional support from their parents. Fortunately, most parents revive their skills within two years of a death or divorce, and much of the stability in the child's life returns as well. However, parents that continue to neglect their children leave a powerful legacy. Without nurturing or guidance, children develop few healthy skills and have significant problems with life and relationships long into adulthood.

Action Step: What is your plan to avoid the "unavailable parent" syndrome?

Emotional tasks for children

Divorce or the death of a parent can leave a child in deep pain. Due to a parent's own pain, the pain of children can go unnoticed. Children of divorce learn firsthand that relationships can be broken, and they are afraid of being abandoned. Having seen their parents say and do cruel things to one another, they are afraid of being caught in the middle. Having seen their parents fail, they fear future failures in their parents' and their own lives. The following is a list of emotional tasks you must help your child address.

Understanding the divorce—explaining what the divorce means in their family and what the consequences are. Children need to be given concrete reasons why the divorce ended and why reconciliation will not occur. This is not to suggest "open season" on defaming an ex-spouse. Children deserve a reasonable explanation for why the marriage ended. They need to understand that they did not cause nor could they prevent the divorce from occurring. Children need closure.

Coping with change—helping children get on with their lives. Children need to experience as little change and as much consistency as possible. They need to know where they will live and with whom, when they will see each parent and any other important facts that may affect them. They need to resolve any ambivalent feelings they have towards their biological parents.

Dealing with loss—helping children deal with many losses, including the loss of the intact family and the loss of one parent. They need to work through their anger and anguish, which usually comes in the form of acting out, but less often as depression. Coping with all the losses a child experiences may take years.

Dealing with anger—children are caught between anger and love for their parents. This makes it difficult for many children to even acknowledge their anger. They need to recognize their parents as human beings capable of making mistakes and still respect them for their efforts. It is important for children to stabilize their view of their parents. Part of this task is forgiveness—of their parents, themselves, perhaps even God.

Working out guilt—young children often feel responsible for divorce, thinking that their misbehavior may have caused one parent to leave. Children must be reassured that both parents love them and that they are in no way responsible for the divorce. Many children exit a divorce with large amounts of guilt and shame.

Accepting reality—denial is often the beginning point of the coping process. Many children will struggle with the permanence of divorce, maintaining a fantasy that someday Mom and Dad will re-unite and once again create "one big happy family." For some children, this hope carries with it their own hope for happiness in the future.

Adjusting to new situations—new routines and responsibilities. There are numerous changes a child will face: visitation schedules, a new home and school, new friends as well as the loss of old friends, a familiar room or teacher. Children may also have to cope with ongoing legal battles between parents and the possibility of being used as a weapon in the divorce.

Developing a new identity—as a child of divorce. They will need assistance drawing clear boundaries separating themselves from their parents and re-building a sense of identity and security.

Coping with new parent figures—as parents begin dating and eventually remarry. New relationships for the parents often result in the loss of parental attention. Children need help dealing with new parental figures and stepsibling relationships, new living conditions, new rules and new roles. "Family" will come to have a new meaning.

Restoring hope—this may be the most important task of all. Despite all the hurt, fear and disappointment, children must grow and become open to the possibility that they can find love and meaning in a marital relationship. This task involves re-building trust with both biological parents. Children's faith in marriage must be restored.

Reducing parental conflict

Conflict between parents is the single biggest cause of adjustment problems in children. Children exposed to prolonged, ugly battles over custody, parenting time, child support or child-rearing are damaged because they internalize these issues, blaming themselves. No matter how you feel about a former spouse, your child will likely never see that person the way you do. In fact, the more you demean the other parent or attempt to limit contact, the more drawn to that parent and the more resentment your child will ultimately have toward you.

Generally speaking, children receive the worst parenting during the first year of a separation or divorce. Please stop any behaviors that keep you in conflict with your former spouse, no matter how much you believe he or she deserves it. Respect your former spouse and the role he or she plays in the life of your child. Keep the welfare of your child at the forefront. Follow the model Jesus presented in Matthew five and six—love your enemies, turn the other cheek, go the extra mile, seek first the Kingdom of God. *There are not many one-on-one correlations in human psychology, but one is that a child who hears a parent attacked thinks, in some way, he is also being attacked; another reliable correlation is that the hurt and anger such attacks cause eventually will be acted out in destructive behavior* (James Bray, *Stepfamilies* p. 83).

Parenting time

Regular visits, when there is low parental conflict, are important to a child's self-esteem. Children seem to do best when they have access to both parents and when the parents commit to "co-parent" their children. Parenting time seems to work best when the following measures are taken:

- The child is allowed to move freely between parents.
- Visitation logistics are simple, stress-free and consistent.
- The child is not forced to declare allegiance to one parent or family.
- Children are encouraged to enjoy each household.
- The focus is on the needs of the child, not of the parents.
- Parents avoid fighting in front of the child.
- Visitation details are not discussed with the child (okay if teens).
- Parents inform one another of any changes in the child (e.g. diet, hairstyle, music, friends, health, physical, spiritual or emotional development).
- Both parents stay involved in the child's life and activities.
- Both support the spiritual development of the child.
- Children are never used as messengers or spies.
- Parenting time is never used as a weapon or as punishment.
- Respect for the others rules, values, friends, activities or dating choices.

How can I effectively parent my child?

- Be open and honest. If there was a divorce, children should be told the details. Obviously, the explanation given to a four-year-old will be much different from the explanation given to a teenager.

- Remember that you are the adult. Let your child be a child. Do not use him or her as someone to lean on or as a sounding board. Solve your own problems. Talk to a friend, counselor or a pastor. Keep adult things adult. Children should not be exposed to all the details of your separation, court proceedings, spousal maintenance or child support. Let them be children and help them to feel safe, well loved and protected.
- Model healthy self-care. It is very important to take great care of yourself, but make sure you do not leave your kids out. Too often children are left on their own while parents are off finding themselves. They did not ask for this change in their family, it is imperative to make their needs a priority.
- Be an example. Your children will observe you and learn from you. Model responsibility, forgiveness and persistence. Children need to see real adults handling real struggles.
- Do not just focus on the negatives. So often when we get divorced we only remember the pain and hurt. It's important for kids to hear about and remember the fun you all had as a family. It is important for them to know that they came from parents who did love one another at one time.
- Be consistent. Maintain routines as much as possible. With so many aspects of their lives changing it is important to know that some things stay the same. As much as possible have dinners together, keep bedtime routines and any other things that you did before.
- Be responsible. Do not bring a parade of dates through your home. It is ***never*** appropriate to have dates sleep over. You are teaching your children by your actions—how do you want them to behave when they start dating? Children should not be introduced to every person you date, because of the likelihood of attachment. We recommend introductions only after a few months and only if the relationship has become serious. Before any introduction, talk to your child one-on-one. Be open, expect questions.
- Be aware. Keep a watchful eye for changes in behavior with your children. Children communicate through their behavior. If they seem to be having a hard time, seek professional help. Often it is very helpful to have someone neutral to talk with. They do not want to hurt you so they might not always tell you how they are feeling. Sometimes just a couple of visits to a counselor can make a huge difference
- Remember that you are still a family. It is easy to feel that you are in this "never-never land" surrounded by intact families. You are certainly not alone, and you are still very much a family. It may look different from before, but it is not less special and vital.
- Be careful how you talk about a former spouse. Children identify with a missing parent. If you portray your former spouse negatively, they may believe you at first, but the time may well come when they realize that your view is biased and they will resent you for interfering with their ability to bond with the other parent. Offer comfort when a child needs it.
- Do not overindulge a child. Parents who feel sorry for their children, or who want to win their affection do this. Children need quality time, love and structure, not more stuff. This kind of behavior keeps children from growing and encourages manipulation and dependency.

- Maintain discipline. One of the hardest things to do is to maintain consistent discipline. Firm, consistent loving discipline teaches children about boundaries, self-control and responsibility.
- Do not overprotect your children. Help your children learn how to solve problems and deal with negative situations. Teach them how to express themselves. Role-model how to deal with situations over which you have no control.
- Allow children to talk. Children need to process through their issues—in their own way and time. However, do not allow them to perseverate on negatives—it can become self-reinforcing. In these situations, re-direct their focus.
- Stay informed. Read books, attend classes, or join a support group. Talk to their teachers, coaches or scout leaders.
- Allow your children stay connected. Be sure your children have access to friends, teachers, counselors and family members, even those of a former spouse.
- Develop a support network. Parents with good social support systems have better morale and make better parenting choices. Networking with other parents can provide help in areas such as emotional support, finances, babysitting, repairs and transportation.
- Build their esteem. Children can feel lonely, rejected and powerless. Show them encouragement and respect. Limit put-downs and critical language. Focus on your children's positives. Involve them in positive activities.
- Develop and maintain a co-parenting relationship. Parents working together for the welfare of their child are the best positive adjustment factor.
- Model a clear and consistent faith. Everything you say and do is a reflection of your life in Christ and a model for your children. In *The Smart Stepfamily*, Ron Deal provides some excellent advice for nurturing your children spiritually (pp. 202-212). Specifically he suggests three activities to share with your children. Share the biblical story of God's work in the world and the sacrifice of Jesus Christ. Share your own personal faith stories. Live your faith. God admonished the Israelites to live out their faith so as to preserve it from generation to generation (Deuteronomy 6: 4-9).

Adults adjust to radical changes much sooner than children. For children, life (school, friendships, holidays, vacations, etc.) may never be the same. Adult children of divorce often carry regrets to their grave. Ten to twenty years after a divorce, some children still hope their parents will re-unite. Adults who undergo the stress and transition from divorce and single parenting to remarriage may have less time and emotional stamina to deal with the emotional turmoil of their children. Yet, they may find themselves caring for biological children, stepchildren, aging parents, and a new spouse. Many parents have difficulty dividing time between their children and their new spouse. Difficulties in the disruption of time, attention, and financial burdens complicate remarriage and stepfamily life even further. You need to do everything you can to help your children feel loved and needed. What are some possible areas of concern for your children?

Getting Spiritually Connected

Every part of scripture is God-breathed and useful one way or another—showing us truth, exposing our rebellion, correcting our mistakes, training us to live God's way. Through the Word we are put together and shaped for the tasks God has for us (II Tim. 3:16-17, The Message).

You and I were created to connect with others. At the very core of who we are—we have a deep longing to know and be known, love and be loved. Part of this connection is spiritual. Just as God is connected to the universe and to us, we are to be connected to Him and to one another. The dynamic of fellowship, *Koinonia* in the Greek, however, is more than just potlucks or volleyball. It is part of God's provision, sharing life together as the Body of Christ. Spiritual growth happens inside this fellowship. It is clear that God wants us to live out our lives in our culture, to be salt and light to our world. It is also clear that the energy to do this comes from a spiritual connection to other believers through His Spirit. If you want to grow in your walk with Christ—get connected.

<u>Action Step:</u> What are your spiritual needs? Check all that apply

- ☐ To practice spiritual discipline
- ☐ To see myself as a whole person in Christ
- ☐ To be affirmed as valuable to God
- ☐ To live life in the present and not put things on hold until I remarry.
- ☐ To invest in my life now—relationships, church, serving others, etc
- ☐ To build margin into my schedule—time alone to heal, to set goals and to commune with God
- ☐ To become more intentional in serving others
- ☐ To commit myself to accountability relationships as a hedge against temptation and an antidote for isolation and loneliness
- ☐ To choose joy and celebrate the life God has given me
- ☐ To forgive myself and/or others and experience God's forgiveness
- ☐ To love others out of my own fullness in Christ

Why do I need to connect with others?

Community is the place where the person you least want to live with always lives. Henri Nouwen.

One of God's greatest gifts to us was the Church—the community of fellow strugglers and believers (Acts 2:42-47, Romans 12, I Cor. 12, Eph. 4). It is in this community that we share life with others and grow as believers. Transformation (Rom. 12:1-2) into Christ-like servants happens in community.

What is community? Community is...

- A place to learn the truth about yourself.
- God's plan for the church.
- Where you and others are being formed into the likeness of Christ.
- Where the real you meets the real me.
- Where everyone matters and no one stands alone.
- About unity in Christ, sharing experiences, trusting others and being vulnerable.

- Being committed to others and choosing to be accountable to them.
- A safe place where you can be yourself—flaws and all, and feel accepted.
- Where you are loved and encouraged.
- Where you discover how to apply God's word to your daily life.
- Where Biblical transformation happens.
- Where you are spurred to repentance.
- Where others speak truth and love to you.

Jesus believed in community. He did not write a book, he started a community. He gave His life to establish that community. Dietrich Bonhoeffer believed in community and he too died for his beliefs. The day before he was executed in a Nazi prison camp, this incredible man of faith was busy ministering to others. He speaks about community in his book *Life Together*, a book that celebrates community, the shared life. Bonhoeffer believed that the gathering of God's people was a gift of God, a celebration symbolizing the life that Christ gave to us through the cross. As we share life together, we live in expectancy of Christ's return. Bonhoeffer maintained that it was a privilege to live in community with others. "It is by the grace of God that the *ecclesia* (Grk. gathered ones) is permitted to gather visibly in this world and share God's Word and Sacrament" (p. 22).

What about small groups, why are they important?
There are practices that are critical for our spiritual growth and development that can only happen in small groups. Below are five such practices.

Confession (II Cor 3:18; II Tim 2:21; James 5:16; I John 1:9; Psalm 32, 51)
Confession is the free and appropriate disclosure of my brokenness, temptation, sin and victories given for the purpose of healing and forgiveness and spiritual growth. It is about taking off our masks in an atmosphere of safety and trust. Most of us keep our masks on because we fear rejection. Community, such as we find in small groups, is where we learn the truth about ourselves. It is where we can make our brokeness public and be accepted and supported. Self-disclosure is tough, but there is little personal growth without healthy disclosure.

Application (Psalm 25:9, James 1:22-25, II Tim. 3:14-17)
James 1:22-25 speaks of looking into the revealing mirror of God's Word. Small groups are a place where we can look in that mirror. Once we see our need for change, the people in our group can help us apply the scripture to our lives and circumstances. Small groups are like "schools of life" where God's word is applied to every aspect of who we are. We all need someone who will *walk with us through* an issue.

Accountability (Eccles. 4:9-12; Hebrews 10:24-25; Gal. 6:1-6)
Accountability means opening our lives up to others and taking responsibility for each other. The Poet John Donne penned these famous words, "no man is an island, unto himself." God did not design us for the kind of "rugged individualism" that we find in our society. He designed us for relationship, for community. Accountability has been defined as the process of having someone take us "kicking and screaming to a place that

we really want to go." Small groups can be a place for valuable feedback when we are making life decisions. We will not simply "drift" into a mature relationship with Christ—we must decide to grow. Therefore, we must allow others to get close enough to help us grow. Our part is to be clear about our decision to grow and then to share this decision with others.

It is interesting to note that the word for person (*persona* in Latin) comes from the Greek word *prosopon*, which is translated "face to face." In contrast, the word *individual* comes to us much later, from the Latin word *individuus*, meaning "not divisible." It reminds us that we are persons, standing face to face, turned toward one another, engaged in dialogue, involved in relationship. Not separate individuals, but people in community who need others to bring us to spiritual maturity.

Guidance (Acts 13, II Tim. 2:22, I Peter 5:2-5)

The whole purpose of spiritual direction is to penetrate the surface of a person's life, to get behind the facade of conventional gestures and attitudes which he or she presents to the world, and to bring out his or her inner spiritual freedom, the inmost truth, which is what we call the likeness of Christ in his soul. (Thomas Merton, *The Ascent of Truth*)

Community is where I intentionally involve others in my important decisions. Any decision is a time to enter into prayer and listen to God. Do you involve others in your decision making process? Guidance is about helping someone find his or her direction and learning how to listen to God together. God is always active in your life; do you know what He is doing or where He wants to take you? Below are some ways your small group can help.

- Providing a safe setting where you can be honest about your struggles, reflect on your pain and face up to the questions with which you struggle
- Sharing life with others who have struggled and gaining from their strength and experience.
- Drawing power and encouragement through other's stories of struggle and victory
- Empowering others to ask you tough questions
- Allowing others to speak truth into your life
- Getting clear about your limitations and priorities
- Helping you make choices that reflect God's character
- Never allowing you to struggle alone

Love and encouragement (Romans 12:9-21, Eph. 4:1-18)

We need to know that there is someone committed to us who loves and accepts us as we are. We need to see love in action. We need to be part of a close-knit group that helps us put our faith into practice. Love is where faith is given hands and feet. God becomes real through our caring for one another. We need to know that we matter to someone. This need for love and encouragement is a hunger that will never go away. Experience teaches that people will find this, good or bad. This kind of love is transforming. We don't venture out of our shells very often. When we share our problems and concerns and feel genuine love, the boundaries that separate us drop away and we feel a part of something larger than ourselves.

These five spiritual practices are so important to your spiritual development. Are they present in your life? If not, what can you do to get connected?

What does God's word have to say about divorce and remarriage?

The only way to answer this is to do a thorough investigation for yourself. Below are some scriptures and thoughts to assist you. God has some powerful things to say about divorce and remarriage as well as about who you are in Christ. There are consequences to our selfish choices and there is forgiveness when we come before God in humility—just ask the Prodigal Son.

God loves you. The truth is that God hates divorce but He loves divorced people. If you are to place your hope and trust in Him, you must understand who God says that you are and the incredible forgiveness that He offers. In Christ you are a new creation, made righteous by the redemptive act of Jesus on the cross. Many believers live in shame because of their divorce. Jesus makes it clear that from the beginning, God intended for marriages to last until death. Long before the Law was given, God shared this one-flesh vision of marriage (Genesis 2). However, after the Law, God instructed Moses to allow divorce, "because of the hardness of man's hearts" (Matthew 19:1-11). Only God can judge a heart. Where is your heart concerning your divorce?

- Are you bitter and unforgiving?
- Are you hard and unrepentant?
- Are you angry with God?
- Have you rejected God?
- Are you denying any responsibility?
- Are you continuing to play the victim role?
- Do you live in shame?
- Are you prideful and self-righteous?
- Have you sought forgiveness from God and those you hurt?
- Have you asked God for a forgiving spirit?
- Are you truly repentant?

God calls us to painstakingly apply His truths to our lives. James reminds us that obedience is God's will for us. *Don't fool yourself into thinking that you are a listener when you are anything but, letting the Word go in one ear and out the other. Act on what you hear. Those who hear and don't act are like those who glance in the mirror, walk away, and two minutes later have no idea who they are, what they look like* (James 1:22-25, The Message).

God's Word is truth and life for all of us, whether you left your family for another life or you were left to pick up the pieces with three small children. God's incredible love draws us all, just ask the thief on the cross, the woman at the well, or the woman caught in adultery. Each of us needs the power and strength that only God can provide. The catch is that we must come empty-handed, no excuses or rationalizations. We must claim Jesus as our Lord and Savior. We must turn from our old self-centered lives and receive the new life He offers. Make no mistake, God's love, forgiveness and acceptance are waiting for you.

Examine these Old Testament scriptures**:** Genesis 2:24-25; Exodus 20:14-17, 21:10-11; Leviticus 18:6-18; Deuteronomy 24:1-4; Psalm 23, 71:20-21, 94:18-19, 127:1; Jeremiah 3; Malachi: 2:14-16

God made us relational beings

Relationships in general and marriage in particular have always been God's idea (Genesis 1 and 2). God is a relational being. He asserted that notion when He said, "let us make man in our own image" (Gen. 1:26). After creating Adam God said, "It is not good for man to be alone" (Gen. 2:18). Adam needed human companionship. Eve was created to meet his needs and he hers. Later, God instituted marriage by calling man and woman to become one flesh (Gen. 2:24). Mankind, however, has always found a way to pervert and distort God's creations. Like everything else, marriage went through the fall, left the garden and became part of mankind's struggles (Genesis 3). A beautiful thing became cursed.

Relationships changed after the fall. Before the fall, relationships were complete and needs were met. After, relationships were broken and needs became distorted and unfulfilled. Perfect companionship turned into competition. God's intentions for man and relationships would not be complete until the advent of Christ. Ephesians 5:21 is a powerful statement about relationships in the spirit—mutual submission; it lies in sharp contrast to life after the curse—competition for headship (Genesis 3:16). The concept of "one-flesh" was now distorted and relationships between men and women became more adversarial. Control, power, selfishness and hard-heartedness replaced oneness and mutuality.

Implications of the certificate of divorce (Deut. 24:1-4)

In Old Testament times, divorce was not a court procedure as it is today, but rather an action taken by a husband against his wife. The passage in Deuteronomy does not necessarily provide grounds for divorce as much as it seeks to protect the rights of women. A husband could "put away" a wife for any reason. All he need do was give her a written certificate in the presence of two witnesses and return her dowry. This was humiliating and terrifying for women, who often had few resources and perhaps no place to go. Divorced women carried a stigma in that culture. This written certificate was very specific, and allowed a properly divorced woman to marry again, and thus be cared for. The practice of divorce was not questioned, but simply taken for granted as an accepted part of life (Isaiah 50:1). Only Hebrew men could initiate a divorce and only they were permitted more than one spouse. Without a written divorce document, a wife who had been "put away" would be committing adultery if she remarried, which was punishable by death. It is clear the divorce certificate was for the woman. A man needed no such certificate. No respectable Hebrew male would marry another Hebrew male's wife.

Family dynamics changed when the Law of Moses allowed for the certificate of divorce. When Hebrew men married, they did not vow exclusive faithfulness, since they were allowed more than one wife. From the beginning, God did not intend for divorce or polygamy to occur. His ideal was one man-one woman for a lifetime. When the ideal was upheld and maintained, family life was relatively uncomplicated. However, God recognized that it is our nature to be self-willed. He accepted divorce as a social reality. Deuteronomy 24:1-4 describes the procedure for issuing a certificate of divorcement, literally a "cutting away."

Examine these New Testament scriptures: Matthew: 5:31-37, 19:3-12; Mark 10:2-12; Luke 16:18; Romans 5:1, 7:2-3, 8:1-11, 12:1-2; I Corinthians 7; II Corinthians 6:14-18; Galatians 5, 6:1-5; Ephesians 5:21-33; Philippians 3 and 4; Hebrews 13:5; I John 2:1.

The Gospels tell us that Jesus arrived on a scene where appearance was more important than integrity. He spent His time here challenging this view. He called people to honesty and disclosure; to live a life without pretense. Those who acknowledged a deep sense of their own sin and woundedness were not shamed but embraced, affirmed and refreshed. Those who denied any sin or need continued living in emptiness. That same call exists today. The heartbeat of God is still about healthy relationships and the abundant life. God's call is to repentance and obedience, no matter what our circumstances. Healthy relationships in a broken world are only possible through His Spirit. Because of His deep love, He provided His son to free us from the bonds of our sinful tendencies and empower us to have healthy relationships. Few places however, can reveal the worst of mankind than divorce, for herein lies deceit, lust, betrayal, selfishness, insensitivity, revenge, shame and abandonment.

When the Pharisees questioned Jesus concerning His position on divorce law, He quickly moved the discussion from the law to God's intent. He made it clear that from the beginning, God intended for marriages to be monogamous and last until death. Long before the Law was given, God shared this one-flesh vision of marriage. However, after the Law, God instructed Moses to allow (not command) divorce due to man's stubbornness (Ps. 95:8, Jer. 4:4), "because of the hardness of man's heart" (Matthew 19:8).

There are hard teachings in the New Testament concerning divorce and remarriage. These scriptures have been debated for years, much as the early rabbis debated the meaning of Deuteronomy 24. In Matthew 19, Jesus makes it clear that marriage was to be seen as a lifetime commitment and a relationship that reflected God's relationship to us. Marriage is not man-made; therefore God takes it very seriously. In vs. 3 of Chapter 19, the Pharisees seek to trap Jesus by asking a no-win, politically-charged question, *What about divorce; is it lawful for a man to divorce his wife for any reason?* The catch phrase "for any reason" was an attempt to get Him to choose sides between debating factions of the Pharisees. Jesus quickly moved to the real issue, the "heart" issue, not what the law permits, but what God intended.

God's desire is that marriages last a lifetime. Some do not. When we sin, when marriages fail, the law requires a penalty. Jesus came prepared to pay that penalty, but He also calls us to live life at a higher level. Meaningless and capricious divorces and lifeless and spiritless marriages are not about the abundant life to which He has called us. Jesus stood for honesty and integrity. Jesus knew that many of the divorces the rabbis had permitted were not based on substance. He taught that even for adultery, a spouse was not required to divorce his or *her* unfaithful partner. That was big news in 1st century Israel.

The Pharisees focused on the question of law, Jesus quickly moved to the higher issue. Jesus stood against the practice of the Pharisees sitting in court and deciding who could or couldn't get divorced. "*What God has joined let not man separate.*" Life in the new kingdom would be of the spirit, not the sterile law. It would always be matters of the heart that would destroy relationships—not some "unlawful" behavior. God will always look on the inside and man on the outside. Long before divorces happen, men and women become selfish, hard-hearted and uncaring. Someone referred to divorce as a funeral for a marriage murdered by abuse or starved to death by neglect.

Action Step:

What does God say about divorce and remarriage?

What does God say about forgiveness and restoration?

What does God say about transformation?

What does God have to say about who you are in Christ?

What about my situation?

Marriage has always been God's idea (Read Genesis 1 and 2). He called man and woman to become one flesh. However, as with most of God's ideas, man has always found a way to pervert and distort His creations. Marriage went through the garden and became part of mankind's struggles (Genesis 3). A beautiful thing became cursed.

Divorce, however, is not the unpardonable sin (Romans 8:1). Yes, there are consequences to our self-directed, disobedient or prideful behavior. However, God's remedy for sin is always the same—grace. His grace leads us to acknowledge our wrongdoing, to repent and to experience His restoration. Do not let your guilt, shame, hurt or bitterness keep you from experiencing the joy God offers you. Scripture, such as I Corinthians 7:27-28, seems to suggest that if you are "loosed" from the bonds of marriage, you are free to remarry. Read Chapter seven carefully. Paul offers strong teaching on staying single (unmarried or divorced). The New English Bible rendering of v. 27 sheds some light on this admonition. *Are you bound in marriage? Do not seek dissolution. Has your marriage been dissolved? Do not seek a wife.* It seems clear that Paul suggests one stay single, whether divorced or never married. However, he also suggests that marriage is a means of grace for those who struggle with lust (vs. 8-9). Here Paul is heralding God's grace for those who may struggle.

Paul does not command us to marry or remarry, indeed, he encourages those divorced or widowed to remain single. Marriage (remarriage) is allowed, as God's graceful provision, if one struggles with lust. Paul also indicates that remarriage is allowed if the bond of marriage has been broken (v. 27). The most common ways to break the marriage bond are death, adultery or desertion. If your divorce and/or remarriage happened prior to your conversion, II Corinthians 5:17 and Galatians 2:20 tell us that you are covered by the reality of the Cross.

For the Law was given by Moses, but grace and truth came by Jesus Christ (John 1:17). Grace is such a powerful concept. We suggest you read Phillip Yancy's book, *What's so Amazing about Grace.* We also suggest that you submit yourself to the pastors and elders of your local church. God has given them authority in these matters. Tell your story; share with them the details of your divorce. Take responsibility for your role. Demonstrate a repentant heart and a Godly lifestyle since your divorce. If they believe your marriage bonds are broken and there is no possibility of reconciliation, then scripturally you are free to remarry. God wants our behavior to line up with His Word.

Get into the habit fellowshipping with other believers and of regularly reading and meditating on the Word of God. God offers forgiveness and restoration to all who ask. To those wounded by divorce, He offers healing and power. *Are you tired? Worn out? Burned out on religion? Come to me. Get away with me and you'll recover your life. I'll show you how to take a real rest. Walk with me and work with me—watch how I do it. Learn the unforced rhythms of grace. I won't lay anything heavy or ill-fitting on you. Keep company with me and you'll learn to live freely and lightly (Matt. 11:28-29, The Message*

Action Step:

- Have you connected with others?
- Do you have an accountability partner
- Are you applying God's word to your life and circumstances?
- Are you clear on your story?
- Have you shared your story with your pastor?
- Have you taken responsibility for your part in past relationships?

Relationship 101

Ready to start dating? Think you know all there is to know? Here is a refresher course just in case. For a more comprehensive look at relationships, see our book, *Developing Healthy Relationships.*

God made you with a need for intimacy

We are God's image bearers. Created in God's image as relational beings, we have a deep need for relational intimacy. We yearn to experience real, Godly relationships that are motivated by caring involvement, and characterized by deeply knowing and being known by one another. Yet we fear such relationships, since they can only develop through the vulnerability of self-disclosure. We fear rejection, ridicule or disappointment and many of us have stories to reinforce our fears. "Needing" others seems risky or even non-spiritual. Neediness is seen as a flaw in our society; so most of us avoid appearing needy at all costs. Yet, experiencing relational intimacy can only occur through the sharing of our relational needs and these needs cannot be known by others, let alone met, if we never disclose them.

Ten key intimacy needs

In *Discovering Intimacy*, David Ferguson and his co-authors have identified ten key intimacy needs you and I experience. He believes these needs must be met in the context of relationship. The ultimate cure for loneliness is relationship and community—we cannot meet our needs alone. Ferguson says, "We cannot manufacture by ourselves the intangible value that is realized when another person imparts his or her life to us by unselfishly giving to meet a need that we have" (p. 21). Neediness is not a flaw, but a part of our humanness. We really do need each other. Let's examine these needs. Which are primary for you?

Acceptance—receiving another person willingly and unconditionally, especially when the other's behavior has been imperfect; being willing to continue loving another in spite of offenses (Romans 15:7).

Affection—expressing care and closeness through non-sexual physical touch, carefully respecting the boundaries of the other person; saying, "I love you" (Romans 16:16; Mark 10:16).

Appreciation—expressing thanks, praise or commendation; recognizing accomplishment or effort (Col. 3:15; I Cor. 11:2).

Approval (Blessing)—building up or affirming another; affirming both the fact of and the importance of the relationship (Eph. 4:29; Mark 1:11)

Attention—conveying appropriate interest, concern, and care; taking thought of another; entering another's "world"(I Cor. 12:25).

Comfort—responding to a hurting person with words, feelings and touch; to hurt with and for another's grief or pain (Romans 12:15; Matt. 5:4; II Cor. 1:3-4; John 11:35).

Encouragement—urging another to persist and persevere toward a goal; stimulating toward love and good deeds (I Thess. 5:11; Heb. 10:24).

Respect—valuing and regarding another highly; treating another as important; honoring another (Romans 12:10).

Security (Peace)—harmony in relationships; freedom from fear or threat of harm (Romans 12:16, 18).

Support—coming alongside and gently helping with a problem or struggle; providing appropriate assistance (Gal. 2:2).

Let's say it again—needs are not wrong, selfish or unspiritual. God made you with needs. His plan was to meet these needs through relationships and community. It is not wrong to express your needs to others. It is not wrong to develop relationships with those that can and will meet your needs. It is unhealthy to "jump" into relationships, due to loneliness or a weak personal foundation, that have virtually no chance of meeting your needs. It is unhealthy to "use" other people; that is, take from them and give little or nothing in return.

Obstacles to having our intimacy needs met

God clearly calls us to community—to sharing life together in love and acceptance, which includes moving toward others to meet their needs and allowing them to meet ours. However, there are several reasons why this does not happen.

Self-reliance—"I don't have any needs" proclaims the self-reliant individual. "If I had needs, I would take care of them myself." "God said He would supply all my needs." The problem with self-reliance is that it not only blinds us to our own natural neediness, but also to the needs of others. The Church, the living Body of Christ, is the mechanism God has ordained to meet our neediness. Paul reminds us of this in II Corinthians 1:3-6. As you and I face our own neediness we are more aware of the neediness of others.

Self-effacing—"There must be something wrong with me" is the cry of the self-condemner. "I shouldn't need others; I must be selfish or inadequate." "I don't want to burden or obligate anyone." In truth, needs are normal; to have them is not a sign or sin or shortcoming. God encourages us to share our burdens. I need to move toward you and meet your needs as much as you need to share your needs with me. In his classic book *The Wounded Healer,* Henri Nouwen, writes, *Every Christian is a minister. Ministry means the ongoing attempt to put one's own search for God, with all its moments of pain and joy, despair and hope, at the disposal of those who want to join the search but don't know how.*

Selfishness—"You must (should) meet my needs" or "If you love me you will want to meet my needs." Perhaps this is an exaggeration, but it typifies the thinking of selfish individuals. Selfishness is not defined by the expression of one's needs but by the relative unconcern or insensitivity for the needs of others. In Philippians, Paul reminds us not to do anything out of selfish ambition or vain conceit (2:3-4).

Denial—"I don't know what my needs are" is the catch phrase of true denial. These are individuals out of touch with their feelings. They cannot articulate their needs. Their feelings have been pushed down by some pain or trauma in their lives. They need the light, easy yoke of Christ. They need support, encouragement and a safe place to begin exploring their suppressed feelings and needs. John 4 tells the incredible story of the woman at the well. Here was a lonely person whose needs were deeply suppressed. Jesus was tender with her and she responded. If you cannot identify any personal needs, please see a pastor or counselor.

Fear—"I'm afraid to move toward you; I will meet your needs but you won't care about mine." The fearful person does not trust the process. He or she has likely been hurt in the past and is therefore extremely self-protective. He or she probably does not have many "five-criteria" friendships. This person may actually believe no one would want to meet his or her needs. Unfortunately, our inability to move toward others in intimacy results in forms of false intimacy, like sexuality. At its core, this is a spiritual issue. Ultimately our trust must be in God. He wants to meet our needs—His main tool is community.

Acknowledging our needs
We all have needs—physical, emotional and spiritual. Having your needs met is life giving. Unmet needs leave you hungry and wanting. Your ability to recognize and take care of your needs has a direct connection to the quality of your relationships. The extent to which you recognize and take care of your needs influences your ability to develop healthy relationships. When you do not recognize and meet your needs, potential partners see these needs as your defining characteristics. Those who are not needy will see your needs and scatter. Only those who do not meet and recognize their own needs will be attracted to you.

At the same time, the haze of unmet and unrecognized needs can cloud your judgment. When a potential partner strongly meets one of your main needs, you may discount his or her lack of other important qualities. This will lead to unsuccessful relationships, filled more with anger and hurt than love. If you are not taking care of your needs or you are not directly asking for what you need, your partner may feel manipulated and become resentful or they may move into a care-taking role. Such patterns can only produce unhealthy and short-lived relationships.

In order to have healthy relationships, you must be able to clearly recognize your needs and find ways to get them met outside of the relationship. This is the role of Christian community and a radical concept in our culture. Most people think that being in a relationship will get all their needs met, consequently they see no need for community. That is why so many individuals abandon their support network the moment they get into a relationship. It is true that some of your needs can and will be met in a relationship, but ultimately you will always be responsible for your own needs. Even when you are sure you have an established relationship, you must be able to meet your needs when necessary. Your partner will not always be able to do so.

Communicating your needs

In *Who's Really Running Your Life*, Peter Gerlach says that we communicate to get our needs met. Whether your needs are met depends on your ability to clearly articulate your needs to another. However, this process can become complex because we communicate at more than one level. The first level is the one of which we are most aware and the one through which we communicate, "I am hungry," "I am hot," "I am sad," etc. We are much less aware of the next level, but our core needs—the critical relational needs—come from and are expressed through this deeper level. If you are not aware of your deep core needs, you cannot express them to another. Besides the intimacy needs mentioned above, Gerlach includes several other needs we attempt to fill by communicating with one another. They include:

- The need to feel valued.
- The need to give or get information
- The need to cause or block action.
- The need to have someone change a belief, feeling or behavior.
- The need to change or preserve a relationship; to increase intimacy, trust, love or closeness.
- The need to vent or to express deep or intense feelings.
- The need to have our thoughts, feelings, wants and desires understood and accepted without judgment.
- The need to feel stimulated, excited or passionate.
- The need to end uncomfortable silences.

Practice becoming alert to your own core intimacy and relational needs. Think of interactions that were not so successful. What can you learn from your experiences? Ask others if you are clearly articulating your needs or listening well for theirs.

How do I develop emotional intimacy with others?

The keys to intimacy are disclosure (revealing myself to another) and servanthood (reaching out to another in need). Disclosure increases vulnerability. Without intentional disclosure, however, relationships stay superficial and benign and needs are left unfulfilled. Servanthood demands that I am present with someone and willing to move beyond myself. For many of us, this involves some "emotional" stretching. Below are some suggestions for increasing intimacy in relationships.

- Share personally. A pastor's sermon will be more meaningful if he uses an illustration from his own life and admits how he is feeling about things.
- Share honestly. "Speak the truth in love." In the short run, you may make people angry, but in the long run others will see you as a person of courage who can be trusted. Honesty builds trust.

- Account for broken promises no matter how small. Acknowledging your failure to have your actions line up with your words will make others feel that you are treating them with respect and honor.
- Apologize often. The words, "Will you forgive me?" go a long way in creating strong relationships.
- Work on self-disclosure. Intimacy develops when people share deeply with one another. Move past superficial conversations and superficial interactions.
- Adopt a servant mind-set. Reach out to others in need. Sit with someone who is grieving. Pray specifically for your friends.
- Do community. Be accountable. Get involved, be a participant. Share yourself with others. If you sit in the bleachers and watch the game, you won't remember it as well as if you play the game on the field (Romans 12:9-16).

What does a "healthy" relationship look like?

In *Bonding,* Donald Joy gives five criteria for healthy, meaningful relationships. These relationships can be close family, relatives, friends or associates. To determine how many of these relationships you have, he suggests that you list those who would need to be called or contacted if you were admitted to an emergency room in an unconscious state. Here are Joy's five criteria.

- You both have a high investment in the relationship.
- There is frequent face-to-face contact and mail (e-mail) or phone connection when you miss seeing each other for a few weeks.
- Your relationship has a strong emotional dimension. You welcome even a chance meeting in spite of your intense schedules.
- Your relationship has an "instrumental" base. That is, each of you knows that any serious emergency or need would cost you time or money to "be there."
- Your relationship is mutually reciprocal and symmetrical. Healthy friendships are so evenly paired that both persons can give and both persons can receive without "keeping score" (p. 12).

Dr. Joy suggests that we need 20 to 30 "five criteria" people in our lives to be healthy and that at least half of these individuals should know each other. He states that if our connections drop below 10, we will begin showing symptoms—depression, distortions in our perceptions, acute loneliness, etc. If our connections drop below 5 we will almost certainly be the center of attention for our group, who will likely be functioning in some form of "care-taking" role. If you do not have twenty or thirty people that meet these criteria, take heart, few of us do. However, if your number of healthy relationships is very low, please take some time to examine why.

How can I identify an unhealthy relationship pattern?

The experiences of childhood and past relationships provide us with a "blueprint" for how to get our needs met in a relationship. This blueprint forms our relationship patterns—characteristic ways we behave in relationships. These patterns, even if unsuccessful, are repeated over and over again. What are some of these unhealthy patterns?

- Complainer—Procrastinator: nagging begets avoiding; avoiding begets nagging. Which came first the chicken or the egg?
- Pursuer—Distancer: one fears abandonment, the other fears being controlled or smothered.
- Rescuer—Victim: parenting someone perceived as helpless. Soon the rescuer tires of rescuing and becomes the persecutor.
- Interrogator—Denier: passive-aggressive person acts out but denies feelings, frustrating the other, who wants to know what is wrong.
- Attacker—Defender: no one accepts responsibility for their own behavior; attacking leads to defensiveness, which leads to more attack.
- Parent-child—control versus independence; power struggles.

In each of these patterns, individuals become "locked" in a position, yet they justify their behavior by citing the other person's behavior. Neither party will "let go" since they feel they are right. Not one of these patterns is healthy or reflects God's view of relationships. God always call us to be servants and mutually submissive (Eph. 5:21). If one of these patterns describes you, acknowledge that you are stuck, determine the unmet needs that are driving the pattern and replace your unhealthy, unproductive ways of responding with behavior that is more Godly (Eph. 4:22-25).

What characterizes an unhealthy relationship?

Unhealthy relationships do not reflect the character of God. They are not life-enhancing or freedom-producing. The behaviors in these relationships reflect unresolved issues and learned responses to getting our needs met that are totally self-gratifying. As you examine these characteristics, pay attention to the ones you may have done to others or those you have allowed others to do to you. Relationships that contain these characteristics are not healthy and will not meet your needs.

Control and coercion. Coerciveness and possessiveness are signs of control. Forcing your desire for a relationship onto another person is unhealthy. Individuals in healthy relationships choose each other freely. Healthy relationships are mutual and life sharing. Using guilt, care-taking or any other form of manipulation to keep someone in a relationship is abusive and unbiblical.

The relationship is based on impulse. "Red flags" are ignored. Hard questions are never asked. Emotions, not reason, control decisions. There is no accountability. Healthy relationships come from friendships that have been allowed to develop over time. In healthy relationships, needs are addressed and met.

The self is not honored. Relationships thrive in an atmosphere of acceptance and tolerance. Agape love accepts the other just as they are. Relationships that make you feel you must change to be accepted are not real and they will never meet your deep intimacy needs. The goal for all of us is to be loved and accepted by someone for who we are—which is a model of God's love for us.

There is emotional control and manipulation. You do not express your feelings and needs to your partner for fear you will hurt their feelings or make them angry. Your deep fear is that they will leave. Or, you withhold your feelings as a form of punishment or control. Healthy relationships allow for free expression of emotions. Problems are discussed openly. There are no hidden agendas.

Jealousy and insecurity are present. Fear and insecurity control this response. This can lead to several patterns, including smothering, clinging and ultimately abuse. Possessiveness is about insecurity and control. We cannot and should not be forced to give our love or affection to someone. In healthy relationships, we give our love and support willingly.

Truth is not the standard. Even though you know that an individual has been unhealthy in past relationships, you choose to believe that he or she will not do the same to you. Or, you know your partner is deceiving you but you refuse to believe it, even though you know the truth. Healthy relationships are about honesty and truth telling (Eph. 4:15, 25, 29).

The relationship becomes exclusive. Unhealthy dependency can develop when a person looks to only one or two people to meet all of his or her needs. Healthy relationships are built on a solid foundation of other important relationships—family, friends, church, work, etc.

Dependency replaces interdependency. Staying with someone because you don't know how to say "no" is unhealthy. You fear being alone, so you latch onto the first person that comes by and is available. One-sided relationships are unhealthy, often parental. Healthy relationships are characterized by inter-dependency, where two people are autonomous but depend on one another and mutually submit to one another (Eph 5:21).

Personal growth is not encouraged. AA defines insanity as doing the same thing over and over and expecting a different outcome. In unhealthy relationships, individuals keep doing the same ineffective things, over and over. Rather than learn, grow and change, they stay stuck. Change is hard, even painful. Healthy individuals and relationships embrace change because they know staying stuck is even more painful. God calls us to change, "Be transformed" is what God says in Romans 12:1-2.

There is limited freedom of expression. Relationships blossom in an atmosphere of freedom and acceptance. Control limits vulnerability and disclosure, ultimately removing any chance for intimacy.

The relationship is built on externals. Looks and appearance are given more credibility than character. A person shows interest and you respond quickly and passionately, without really finding out if this person represents a good relationship "fit." Healthy relationships are patient and move from the inside out.

None of the patterns or characteristics discussed above will result in a healthy relationship that will meet your needs or reflect God's character. These patterns reflect deep emotional wounds and are primarily motivated by fear. Fear is crippling to intimacy and drives us in one of two directions: a fear of closeness—that our freedom or independence might be restricted or a fear of abandonment—that we might be left alone and insecure. To counter these fears, we move toward one of two defensive postures: control—attempting to control our relationships (via threat, manipulation, dependency, etc.) or avoidance—running from intimacy and closeness (emotional distancing, anger, aloofness, etc.). The longer these fears are left unaddressed and unresolved, the more emotional pain they cause and the more distorted our relationships will become. Which have you experienced?

How do I develop healthy relationships?

Healthy relationships are characterized by truth, trust and transparency and they are built over time. Start by creating community—getting plugged into a local church, a small group and establishing accountability relationships. Next, begin building a healthy personal lifestyle. Healthy relationships have at their core a love for God, others and self (Mark 12:30-31). They share a commitment and connection to the Creator of life. The love of God then allows us to love others as we love ourselves (I Cor. 13). This type of relationship is free and servant-minded, not fearful or controlling. Next, make healthy relationship choices by being clear on the following distinctions:

- Taking charge of your life vs. being a passive victim
- Practicing agape love vs. just seeking personal or physical fulfillment
- Developing genuine friendships vs. looking for lovers
- Building a structure for one's time and relationships vs. just passively waiting around
- Developing one's uniqueness vs. seeking to be entertained
- Accountability vs. secrecy and isolation

We have identified five patterns of unhealthy choices; do any fit you? :

1. Expecting others to make your life interesting, enjoyable and rewarding rather than developing your own gifts and finding interest, fulfillment and reward in oneself.
2. Entering into relationships more to have your needs met than to contribute to others.
3. Placing blame on others when problems occur and avoiding accountability or responsibility for your situation and circumstances.
4. Looking for the "perfect" partner and thus discarding those who do not qualify.
5. Never involving your friends or support group in your relationship choices.

Below are some specific strategies for helping you to develop healthy, authentic relationships. The keys to developing healthy relationships are threefold: absolute dependence on God, healthy self-care and unshakable respect for other human beings.

Place your trust in the "right" person—God (Phil 4:19). God wants to partner with you in everything, including your relationships. Your growing relationship with God will actually enhance your relationships, because you will be relating out of fullness, not weakness and neediness. When we draw our value and worth from God, we do not have to depend on others to fill a role that they ultimately cannot fill. Godly relationships are full of love, acceptance, forgiveness and grace.

Create "grace" filled relationships. Grace is such a powerful word; it instills thoughts of mercy, compassion, forgiveness, tenderness and kindness. Grace is a character trait of God. Colossians 1:6 says that we should extend grace to others. Grace is to be shared. It should infiltrate every one of our relationships.

Discover and celebrate your needs (Eph 4:15). Most of us are uncomfortable asking others to meet our needs. The paradox is that we all enter relationships to get our needs met. There is a direct correlation between the quality of your relationships and your ability to recognize and meet your needs. Everyone has needs—that's a part of human nature. In fact, our needs facilitate relationships. The giver and the receiver both feel better and more connected when each other's needs are voiced and met.

Focus on giving rather than taking (Matt 10:8). Become a great listener. Speak truth to your friends in love. Learn to welcome constructive feedback. Be sensitive to the needs of others. Do not allow your relationships to stay superficial. Lead the way by healthy disclosure and personal sharing.

Develop strong boundaries. To know and honor your limits builds your self-esteem, while earning the respect of others. Boundaries are there to protect you, and to help you honor your needs and wants, not your "shoulds." You have boundaries when you can choose to say yes or no to something, someone or a situation. You have boundaries when you can stop a situation that is hurting you. You have boundaries when you know your needs and ask others to respect them. Having boundaries makes you discerning, gives you self-respect, and inspires other people to both respect you and treat you well. Incidentally, having healthy boundaries makes it much easier to identify and respect the boundaries of others.

Redefine socializing. Many of us socialize for one express purpose—to find a partner. This approach inevitably leads to superficial, short-tem relationships. If you want to find a life partner, stop looking. Socialize as a way to make friends, to build community and to create a healthy, godly lifestyle. Allow your friendships to evolve into relationships.

Develop a life vision. Focus on creating the kind of life that expresses who you are in Christ. God has gifted you. What is the life you feel called to live? What do you want to contribute to the world? The key to creating a healthy lifestyle is to base it on who you are and not wait until you are in a relationship. Being single or divorced is not a bus stop to real life (having a partner)—it is life. Live it now.

Get/stay connected (Romans 12). Build a community. Be a participant. Get people into your life to meet your needs, to support you, to nourish you. Community not only helps meet our needs but it provides vital emotional and relational feedback and accountability. Some of the valuable roles a support network can provide are guidance, application and prayer. Our close friends can help us apply God's word to our lives and to our relationships and provide caring guidance as we make life decisions. They can also pray with us and for us that we remain obedient to God and consistent with our values.

Accept people for who they are—do not try to change them. Demanding or manipulating someone into changing to make you more comfortable is unhealthy and unbiblical. If you are unhappy or your needs are not being met, say so, then allow the other person the freedom to respond to you. Forcing someone to change does not yield true change. Instead of putting your energy into changing others, work on yourself. When you change your own behavior, the dynamics of the relationship will change. You may not get what you wanted initially, but you will be happier with yourself and will stop resenting the other person for not changing to suit your needs.

Understand that the way you see others is a reflection of how you see yourself. Annoyances and irritations can be self-reflections. Irritating character traits we see in others may reveal something we see in ourselves that we do not like. If, for example, you consistently choose partners who do not treat you well, you may want to examine your view of self. You may not like what you see in your "relationship mirror," but your willingness to get real and look will be critical to your ability to have healthy relationships (James 1:19-27).

Allow others to be responsible for their own needs. Never do someone else's work. Do not "care take" a partner, fearing they may leave. With the obvious exception of caring for your children or others who literally need your help to survive, you are not responsible for the needs of others. If you are becoming drained and burned out, you are doing someone else's work and being responsible for his or her welfare. You do not need to "buy love" from others by making yourself an indispensable doormat.

Take responsibility for your own feelings. Just as you cannot change another person's behavior, you also cannot control the way another person feels. We all have choices about our reactions to things. Get clear about this or you will forever be suppressing and withholding your real feelings. Your sole responsibility, when communicating with another person, is to speak the truth from your heart, with love and compassion, and to do it authentically and directly. As long as you are speaking your truth, and doing it in a non-reactive way, you are not responsible for how the recipient chooses to feel about it. Accepting this frees you from a great deal of guilt and allows you to speak the truth in love.

Be authentic in your relationships. Some people compromise their values and beliefs in order to make a relationship work. They say what they think the other person wants to hear, or do what the other person wants them to do, even when that is not a true expression of who they really are. This happens most often in romantic relationships. We fear showing our "real" self early in the relationship, so we pretend to be something else (false self). This always backfires. If you are not being your real self in your relationships, you are doing yourself and the other people in your life a huge disservice. God made you and loves you just the way you are—so be yourself!

Practice healthy self-care. Great relationships start with you. This demonstrates that you are not merely in the relationship to be cared for. Since you're already caring for yourself, you can enter a relationship free of demands and needs. Create a healthy lifestyle for yourself. Make sure that you are living the standard that you would want to invite into your life.

Know what you want. What is it that you really want when you envision your day-to-day life in a relationship? Once you have developed a sense of what you want, write it down and talk about it with friends. Make sure that you say it out loud and repeat it in your mind. Know your non-negotiables. Be clear on your values.

Develop your ability to respond to others emotionally. Intimacy and closeness develop in an atmosphere of trust and safety. One way to achieve this is through being sensitive to the emotional needs of others. Emotional responding means relating directly to the feelings that are present in another, acknowledging and validating their importance. Elements of emotional responding are active listening, gentleness, empathy, concern, reassurance, confession and forgiveness.

Do not try to move directly from loneliness to relationship. Healthy relationships are allowed to grow. Skipping steps (self-care, solitude, community, friendships, etc.) inevitably leads to disaster. The American fantasy is the lonely person who suddenly and mysteriously finds the partner of his or her dreams, gets married and lives happily ever after. This never happens in real life.

Learn to trust others based on your fullness in Christ. Trust is a huge relationship issue. Past hurts and disappointments can make you vigilant and reluctant to lower your guard. Trusting others is not a form of denial if it comes from your faith in Christ and your awareness that God loves and accepts you for who you are. Trust does not mean being a doormat or ignoring reality. It means looking for the good and knowing your limits and boundaries.

Believe in the process. Follow the guidelines outlined above Be a great listener. People will tell you want they want and need. Tell your truth. Share your expectations, dreams and goals. Accept what you hear. Embrace the moment. Be fully present. Allow relationships to grow naturally. Have fun. Become friends. Hold confidences. Never compromise your values. Pray together. Seek wise counsel from your support network. Enjoy the journey.

Action Step: Summarize the relationship strategies given above. How many are you currently implementing? Where do you need improvement?

What Should I look for in a Potential Partner?

Identifying the qualities that characterize the "perfect partner" is truly a daunting task. Actually, we do not encourage you to develop a finely tuned "laundry list." We do encourage you to know yourself and your needs, values and passions. Out of this true sense of who you are comes your definition of the "right" relationship. You have spent time in this workbook working through a process of healing, growth and discovery. We have encouraged you to connect with others, develop a healthy single lifestyle and make friends and allow relationships to evolve, slowly and naturally. The time has come to consider what you want in a life-partner—someone who will be the other part of the "right" relationship.

Fantasies and Realities

In *Building Relationships: Developing Skills for Life*, David H. Olson illustrates the folly of choices. He suggests that compatibility can even become the source of incompatibility.

> She married him because he was such an assertive male;
> She divorced him because he was such a domineering husband.
>
> He married her because she was so gentle and petite;
> He divorced her because she was so weak and helpless.
>
> She married him because he could provide a good income;
> She divorced him because all he did was work.
>
> He married her because she was so attractive all the time;
> He divorced her because she spent too much time in front of the mirror.
>
> She married him because he was so romantic and sociable;
> She divorced him because he was such a fun-loving playboy.
>
> He married her because she was so quiet and dependent;
> He divorced her because she was so boring and clinging.
>
> She married him because he was the life of the party;
> She divorced him because he was such a dud at home.
>
> He married her because she was so sociable and talkative;
> He divorced her because she could only discuss trivia.
>
> She married him because he was such a good athlete;
> She divorced him because he was either playing or watching sports.
>
> He married her because she was so neat and organized;
> He divorced her because she was too compulsive and controlling.

The above comparisons may seem humorous, but they reveal an important principle: for many remarrying individuals, areas of attraction can become areas of conflict. This is true because most relationships begin out of balance, with a person looking for a certain trait, such as submissiveness, while ignoring other important characteristics. Remarrying individuals often seek to compensate for perceived flaws in prior partners. "She was unfaithful, so I will look for someone I can trust." "He did not take good care of us, so I will look for someone who is successful." This process often occurs out of our awareness, but it always leads to disappointment because it focuses on finding the right person, not the right relationship. A healthy partner is someone who is willing to take the time to invest in the courtship process. A healthy relationship is one that will meet your needs and that reflects who you are. Take the time to share your needs, passions, goals and values with a potential partner. Listen as he or she shares these things with you. Look for a "good fit." Meet each other's family, friends, support group, etc.

Positive traits

The old adage, "opposites attract" is not really true. In fact, the healthiest relationships feature two individuals with many traits, values and goals in common. Begin identifying the traits you consider important in yourself. These will guide you as you consider a potential partner. When we ask remarried couples to share the qualities that are the most enhancing to continued growth in their relationship, the most typical responses are:

- communication
- affection
- compassion
- forgiveness
- honesty
- acceptance
- dependability
- sense of humor
- romance (including sex)
- patience and freedom

When we ask couples to identify those qualities or traits that are the most destructive to a growing, loving relationship, their list is a mirror image of the first list:

- selfishness/unforgiveness
- dishonesty
- jealousy
- lack of trust
- lack of flexibility (not open to change)
- lack of understanding
- lack of respect
- apathy
- perfectionism
- lack of communication

How do you rate yourself in these areas?

In *Married People: Staying Together in the Age of Divorce,* Francine Klagsburn lists several characteristics of successful long-term marriages. These characteristics are important to note because they do not reflect the traits normally highlighted by the media or our culture. How would you rank these traits in importance to you? What would you add to the list?

- An ability to change and to tolerate change
- A willingness to live with the things one cannot change
- An assumption of permanence in the relationship
- Trust between the partners
- A balance of depending on one another
- A balance of power
- Enjoyment of each other
- A shared history that is cherished

Qualities of a potential partner
You probably have a "laundry list" of qualities that you are looking for in a partner. We have seen lists with as many as twenty items. Which qualities are really important? Based on our research and experience, five traits stand out.

- Possessing good insight into themselves and how others see them
- Maintaining good emotional controls
- Having effective relationship skills
- Possessing an accurate picture of the challenges of remarriage and stepfamily life
- Maintaining a vibrant, growing relationship with God

How can I know if a potential partner has these traits? Observation and good listening skills are perhaps the best way to determine if these traits are present in an individual. Observe a potential partner in different situations; ask questions and listen to his or her friends and family. Time is a great ally.

How do I determine if a person has good insight? One way is to look for any signs of denial.

- Are certain subjects avoided or discounted as unimportant?
- Are there times when compensation is used to cover-up low self-esteem?
- Is there a discrepancy between words and actions?
- Are there any body language "red flags?"
- Is there a noticeable emotional shift when certain subjects are discussed?
- Are there topics that seem to create uncomfortableness?
- Does this person demonstrate an adequate level of self-respect?
- Does this person have a clear sense of personal identity?
- Are his or her perceptions of others accurate?
- Does this person's honest disclosures encourage you to be more honest and disclosing?

There are also certain cues for determining an individual's level of emotional control.

- Is this person's emotional response to various events what you would expect it to be?
- Can this person experience peace and joy in the company of others and when alone?
- Are there significant differences in mood when this person is around family members?

- Does this person manage his or her emotions well?
- Is this person comfortable expressing emotions?
- Is honesty or denial used when angry?
- Is there frequent use of criticism, withdrawal, depressed mood, or blame?
- What do others say about his or her emotional reactions?
- Do you feel controlled, discounted or patronized?
- Are disagreements or differences handled well?
- Did the words "love" or "marriage" occur too soon in the relationship?
- Is this person a good listener?
- Are there any addictions or self-sabotaging habits?

Relationship skills are critical in a remarriage. Questions to consider about relationship skills include:

- How has this person behaved in other relationships?
- How are past relationships described?
- How does this person relate to parents or other family members?
- Are there patterns of behavior that seem to interrupt relationships for this person?
- How does this person relate to friends and associates?
- Does this person present a Godly spirit when dealing with others?
- Does this individual possess good problem solving skills?
- How does this person handle conflict?
- Can the two of you talk through issues together?
- Are you free to share your point of view?
- Does this person bond well with others?
- Does this person demonstrate empathy and compassion for others?

An individual contemplating remarriage and stepfamily life must have a reasonable sense of the challenges involved and they must have resolved their past issues.

- Does this person bring up his or her past relationships with anger or disdain?
- Has this person forgiven others or sought their forgiveness?
- Does this person acknowledge his or her role in past relationship failures?
- Does this person speak realistically about the challengers of remarriage and creating a stepfamily?
- Is this person clear that remarriages are different from first-time marriages?
- Does this person have a healthy relationship with his or her children and former spouse?
- Does this person relate well to your children?
- Does this person understand and accept that a stepfamily is a "multi" home and person family, consisting of children, stepchildren, former spouses and a host of relatives?
- Does this person have realistic expectations about your future together?
- Does this person understand the key characteristics of stepfamilies?
- Can this person articulate a reasonable plan for stepparenting?

The last factor is the spiritual component. Not only should a potential partner possess a vibrant, growing relationship with God, but there should be compatibility in such areas as maturity levels, theological beliefs and worship styles. Differences in giving, worship styles or belief systems need to be identified and addressed. Issues include:

- Bible study and quiet time
- Stewardship
- Church attendance and involvement
- Maturity level
- Small/support group participation
- Worship styles
- Accountability
- Evangelism
- Spiritual gifts

Use these five characteristics as a guideline. Please be cautious if a potential partner did not score high in even one of these areas. Have the courage to be honest with yourself and to stick to your convictions. Please do not put your head in the sand. Ask God for discernment. Involve your support group. Be a careful observer of the time you spend together. The quality of your dating relationship is an excellent predictor of subsequent remarital success.

Recognizing "emotionally" available partners

When individuals tell us why their past relationships have been unsuccessful, many report that it was because their partners had been "emotionally unavailable." The following traits were listed when we asked them to describe an "emotionally unavailable" partner: *Doesn't talk about feelings; doesn't talk about his/her life; doesn't have time for the relationship; wants a relationship on his/her time frame; noncommunicative; keeps secrets; geographically distant and doesn't want to change the situation; doesn't want a commitment; doesn't want to move to the next level in the relationship; vague and evasive.*

Do any of these behaviors remind you of your past relationship partners, or even of yourself? Each of the behaviors above can be categorized as a gap in communication, a gap in the amount of time each partner wants to spend together, or a gap in the level of commitment. These gaps are what make one partner feel the other is unavailable.

We each have a different level of need for intimacy or availability of a partner. If you connect with a person whose need for intimacy is drastically different than your own, you will struggle and suffer in the relationship. By understanding your own need for intimacy you can accurately assess how much intimacy you need in a relationship. Take time to discover your own need and capacity for intimacy—*before you get involved.*

<u>Action Step:</u> Assess your need for intimacy

- Do you sabotage intimate relationship?
- Describe the behaviors of a partner who is emotionally available?

- On a scale of 1 to 10, how much of each of the following do you need from a partner?

communication
depth in the communication
in-person communication

together time
space/apart time
depth of connection

- What needs to happen in a relationship for you to feel you have enough intimacy?
- Do you want to be in a committed relationship?
- In your past relationships, was there a gap between what you wanted and what your partners were willing to give?
- Did you get the right amount of closeness, distance, communication and commitment?

How to recognize an emotionally available partner.
Remember our adage, "It's not the right person but the right relationship." Listen and observe a person's behavior. People will communicate clearly who they are, what they are looking for and what they have to give. For example, if a person says he is not interested in a committed relationship, and you know you are, then he or she is not "available enough." If he likes working 80 hour weeks and you want a partner with whom to enjoy weekends and evenings, than that person is not emotionally available.

Begin by developing healthy friendships. Allow those friendships to develop into relationships. Be clear about your needs for intimacy and closeness. Work on discovering a partner who wants similar things and has a similar value system. "Equally yoked" is an important concept. Once you begin viewing relationships in this way, you will be free to identify a partner who is "available enough."

Warning Signs?
We have just addressed some positive traits to look for in yourself and ultimately in a potential partner. You may be asking, "Are there some *red flags* (personal traits in me or a potential partner) that suggest caution?" "Are there relationship situations I should avoid?" The answer is yes. There are negative traits, expectations and situations that, when present, nearly always lead to disaster. These include:

- Wanting someone to make your life interesting or meaningful
- Thinking, "I can't live without you," or feeling desperate to remarry right away
- Dating someone who has no friends or close relationships
- Feeling a need to lie or keep secrets or avoid certain topics
- A partner who needs permission from someone else before he or she is free to marry
- A persistent inner sense that something is wrong with the relationship
- Looking for someone who will focus on your needs exclusively
- Wanting someone who will be responsible for the relationship
- Looking for someone who will control the relationship
- Addictions—your own or someone you are dating

- Children (theirs or yours) acting out—ditching, stealing, drugs, depression, lying, academic problems, etc.
- Dating someone who is not living a successful single life
- Dating someone with children if you have no interest in being a parent
- Dating someone who is not interested in your children
- Dating someone who believes that co-parenting in a stepfamily is the same as in a biological family.
- You or a potential partner suggesting that the children will always come first.
- Dating someone who pushes sexual involvement
- Discussing marriage too soon (less than one year after meeting or being separated from prior spouse)
- Dating someone who is not spiritually mature
- Dating someone who wants to co-habitate or who pushes you to commit too soon
- A person who is separated (not yet divorced) or just recently divorced or who is involved in ongoing legal action with a former spouse
- A person who has clearly not let go of the past
- A person who continually puts down or blames a former spouse
- A person who, by choice, has no relationship with his or her children
- Assuming or fantasizing that your potential partner or his or her children will change after the marriage
- Dating a person with obvious emotional wounds
- Dating a person with a history of relationship break-ups
- Dating someone who avoids talking about tough subjects
- Ongoing legal (custody, parenting time, child support) hassles with a former spouse.
- A recent history (past year) of traumatic life events.
- Dating someone who has never had any significant adult relationships
- Dating someone who refuses to acknowledge or discuss the challenges of remarriage and stepfamily life
- Dating someone who is vocationally or financially unsettled.

Are any of these present in your current relationship? If so, what will you do?

Dr. P Rule: Learn to recognize relationship "red flags." The presence of a "red flag" does not necessarily always mean "no," but it certainly means, "wait." We suggest you consult your pastor or a counselor to examine these areas before proceeding with the relationship. If several of these factors exist, please put the relationship on hold and seek professional assistance.

Handling the physical (Romans 6:12, Gal. 5:16-24, Phil. 1:10, I John 2:15-16)

You may be struggling with your sexuality. Some of you may be thinking about becoming involved in a sexual relationship with your partner—some of you already are. Perhaps you are already living together. Some of you may be dealing with the consequences of childhood events such as abuse or incest or more recent trauma such as spouse abuse or rape. You may feel you hate the opposite sex or you may even hate yourself. You may have difficulty seeing yourself as a sexual being or you may be having difficulty with your sexual boundaries. Some of you may be struggling with the unfaithfulness of a partner. You may have even contracted an STD through his or her behavior. Sexuality and understanding your own sexual boundaries are clearly important topics in dating and remarriage. In reality, sexuality is about you. Our goal in writing this section is absolutely not to shame you but to inform you. God has a great deal to say about sexuality. Just as important, however, He has a lot to say about you. He loves you and wants the very best for you. We believe His ideals lead to our best possible destiny. Please review the following material and make informed choices. This is a critical area of discussion with a potential partner. Please take the time to get clear about your sexuality.

First and foremost, sexuality is very personal. God made you a sexual being. You have choices about how you will involve yourself sexually with others. This is true no matter what your past; even if you have traumatized by abuse, incest or rape. These horrible intrusions may have left you feeling ashamed and guilty. You may even hate your own sexuality, the opposite sex or even yourself. If this is the case, please find a caring pastor or counselor to talk to.

The decision to be sexual with a partner is a choice you should make without feeling coerced or obligated. It is a choice that should be consistent with your values. Sexual boundaries can appear vague and blurred to those who have already been married. The stigma surrounding abstaining seems less urgent or less relevant. A strong desire for intimacy, including sexuality, often hastens a couple toward sex or even cohabitating before remarriage. For many, sex is a way of finding acceptance or dispelling loneliness. However, sexual contact tends to make a new relationship "feel" more intimate than it really is. Sex creates a bond, but it does not necessarily create love. Sexuality can create a false sense of oneness, which is a distortion of God's call for a couple to become "one flesh." Sexual contact can result in relationships that do not "fit" and partners that we would normally not choose. God made sex and He meant it to be pleasurable. He also meant it as a gift to be enjoyed in marriage. Resolve to keep your relationships non-sexual until marriage. Be clear about your values before the first date.

Our advice is to not have sex until you are married. Become friends first. Agree to wait. Be firm and intentional here. Sex should be discussed up front. Limits and boundaries should be crystal clear. If a person will not respect your boundaries here, he or she has impulse control or integrity issues and will likely not respect your boundaries in other areas. If a person consistently violates your boundaries or continually pushes your limits, terminate the relationship. If you do not, not only will you lose their respect, but your own as well.

If you are currently having sex with your partner, please stop. You are harming yourself and the relationship. Sex tends to "rush" relationships, not allowing time for two people to really get to know one another. If you are currently co-habitating, one of you should move out. If that is not possible, immediately move into separate bedrooms and stop having sex. Co-habituation clearly *decreases* remarriage success because it emphasizes relationship without commitment. Also, be clear on this, God has forgiven your past. No matter how sexually active you have been in the past, or how many broken relationships you have had, God can heal, forgive and restore you. Please do not continue to have sex out of guilt, shame or fear. Sex will never lead to the intimacy you desire.

Sexuality can drive us into relationships in a sinful context. Many individuals tell us they have become sexual or contemplated moving in with a partner as a way of determining sexual compatibility. Their reasoning is that knowing if they are compatible before marriage will lessen the chance of divorce in the future. In our experience, sexual compatibility is an overblown concept. In over twenty-five years of counseling couples, Jeff has seen very few cases of true sexual incompatibility. Two human beings that deeply love each other can be sexually compatible. Sex is a powerful way to deepen love between two people and enhance their relationship. It is also a powerful way to hurt when it is experienced in the wrong context. While sex creates a powerful bonding, it does not necessarily create love. In fact, it often does the opposite. Many men, for example, begin to have a lower view of their partners once they are having sex with then. Again, the facts refute this anti-abstinence argument. Women who live with their boyfriends are many times more likely to be physically abused than married women. The statistics on cohabitation are overwhelming and compelling—it actually increases the chances of divorce. A strong commitment to God and to one another is still the best hedge we know against divorce.

Find an individual or group who can encourage you and to whom you will be accountable. If you are struggling in this area, talk to a pastor or counselor. If you feel you have a sexual disorder contact a physician. If you struggle with sexuality issues due to past abuse, please contact a professional trained in abuse counseling.

Dr. P. Rule: Intimacy is the gradual development of understanding and appreciation for another person by listening, discussing, sharing, and being mutually involved. It can exist in several realms, not just physical. Onc can be intimate with a person and not physical. Dating someone who is not actively living his or her faith will result in great disappointment. Take the time to find someone spiritually compatible (II Cor. 6:14).

Action Step: Personal sexuality

- How comfortable am I with my sexuality?
- Am I operating with faulty beliefs about sex from childhood?
- Do I feel good about my body?
- Do I struggle with self-acceptance?
- Is sex without love okay for me?
- What role do I want sex and relationships to play in my life at this time?
- What are my values regarding sexual relationships and where do they come from (family, church, friends, media)?
- How well do my values and behavior match up?

- Will a decision to engage in a sexual relationship with my partner at this time enhance/detract from my positive feelings about myself and my partner?
- Can I talk about sex with my partner, my support group, my friends?
- Can I acknowledge my feelings and consider them an authentic part of me?
- Can I recognize my vulnerabilities?
- Am I open to learning about sexuality?
- Can I be authentic in my relationships with other?
- Can I articulate my sexual boundaries and expectations?
- Do I understand the distinction between sex and love?
- Do I fear that my partner might leave if I am not physical?
- Are there unresolved issues from my past that I have not addressed?
- Am I able to trust those close to me?
- Am I taking great care of myself?
- Do I feel vulnerable or defensive around members of the opposite gender?
- Am I clear on God's view of sexuality?
- Can I view celibacy as a gift and an opportunity?
- Do I sabotage relationships because of a fear of intimacy?

Talk about these questions with a friend, counselor, pastor, accountability partner, sponsor or your support group.

Dr. P. Rule: God made sex and He made us sexual beings. He made sex to be a source of pleasure and unity. God did not design sex such that by its avoidance we would grow closer to Him. Sex has meaning beyond itself—it is a gift that reflects the very essence of God. Sexual relationships between a man and a woman should be based on mutuality. Love is more about giving and serving than taking or being served.

Action Step: What are your negotiables/non-negotiables in terms of a potential partner?

Dating

Marriage relationships in our culture all begin with a time of falling in love. During this time, the other person is not really perceived as a different person who is apart from oneself, but as a mere extension of one's own being. It is a time full of illusions and fantasies that have little to do with reality. Dating couples actually contribute to the fantasy by not being totally honest with each other and by being what each believes the other desires. Richard Dunn, *Preparing To Marry Again*

How is first time dating different from remarital dating?

There are several major differences. First, remarriage dating features individuals who are generally older and who have a wider age disparity. This will impact areas such as values and priorities. Second, remarriage dating nearly always involves the presence of children. The needs of children will always compete with the needs of a new relationship. Most children are not ready for their parent to date, especially if dating occurs less than two years after a death or divorce. Third, remarriage dating involves individuals who have been married before, impacting such diverse issues as grief, trust, finances, sexuality or marriage expectations. Remarriage dating leads to marriage much faster than first-time dating. Remarriage daters have far more unrealistic expectations. Remarital daters are painfully aware that the odds of a successful remarriage are lower than those of a first-time marriage. Finally, remarriage dating features two individuals who have been very wounded by past relationships. The result of this wounding is that individuals are extremely self-protective, have difficulty discerning emotionally available partners and operate largely in the false self.

The false self and real self

We tend to cover our weaknesses and insecurities with a self-protective emotional mask called the "ideal self." This is the self we want others to see. This self is created from our observations and beliefs of what we think others expect from us. This false self is driven by our prior relationships failures and losses and is the product of our belief that we are not okay. "If people knew the real me, they would not like/date/marry me." So, we show others the self we think they would want to see. For example, we create the ideal self of the "good" partner. We imagine what we think a potential partner "expects" from us and then try to emulate that in our behavior. This is a great definition of "unhealthy" dating. Suppose both people do the same thing? Let's examine this pattern a little closer. We call it the "false-self to false-self" dating pattern.

This pattern starts with two people, both lonely and looking for companionship. Inside, both are wounded from the past—tentative, weak, insecure, afraid, etc. but they present a healthy looking "ideal" self to one another. They want to appear attractive to one another. Consequently, each of them only sees the external image of the other. If they fall in love, they will fall in love with an illusion.

Why does this happen? Loneliness, our natural God-given desire to connect with others, and "poisonous needs" that we addressed earlier to name just two. The need to find a "good partner" blinds us to the need to be real. The fear of being unacceptable not only drives us to show our ideal self but to also accept another's ideal self without question. We look for other ways to connect to others without having to reveal our private selves. Consequently, we often become entangled sexually, usually after the first or second date, believing sex is a quicker way to intimacy than conversation. Perhaps we can have someone fall in love with them without having to reveal too many flaws.

Thus, most dating is really false self to false self. The relationship is even promoted in ideal circumstances—restaurants, theaters, hotels, etc. Never in real-life situations- friends, work, family, etc. and always when we look the best. Fear of rejection and aloneness and need for approval, acceptance and companionship drive this irrational process. Marrying during this time of "joint delusion" (within the first year) will likely end in disaster.

How can I limit my own false-self dating or recognize it in a potential partner? The goal of "healthy" dating or courting is to develop friendships (allowing a person to discover and embrace your real self) over time and in diverse settings that are allowed to evolve into a close, intimate relationship. False-self dating discourages self-disclosure. False-self dating is intense, exclusive and hurried. It seldom incorporates friends or support groups.

Confront your fears about dating and relationships

Dating can be scary and relationships can fail. God designed you for relationships and intended these relationships to meet your needs and reflect His character. Past experiences, however, can make us extremely cautious and fearful. The fears outlined below are distortions and misbeliefs that are derived from past experiences and from our culture. Confront these misbeliefs and face your fears. God's words of encouragement to you are the same that He had for Joshua and the people as they crossed the Jordan into the Promised Land—*Be strong and courageous, for I will be with you* (Joshua 1:6-9). Which of these are true for you?

This relationship will probably fail, just like the last one. There are no guarantees when it comes to relationships. All relationships involve risks. However, relationships do not end because of some "unknown force in the universe" and you are not "cursed" and therefore doomed to a lifetime of failure. Relationships work because of some very basic principles. Healthy relationships are made up of healthy people who have taken the time to build a great friendship before entering into a deeper relationship.

I will have to give up too much of myself. You have the power to set your own boundaries and to articulate your needs. By exercising healthy self-care, you will be able to bring more of your real self into the relationship; the result will be a healthier relationship. Healthy relationships allow each person to be who they are.

He or she will eventually see the "real" me and reject me. Human beings tend to wear masks. We want people to see a certain "us." We put on an "ideal self" mask for others to see. However, if you spend enough time with someone, glimpses of their real self will appear. Everyone has strengths and weaknesses. Embrace all aspects of yourself. Learn to celebrate who you are in Christ. Work on those aspects of your self that need changing. Until you are willing to accept yourself for who you are, you will have a hard time believing that anyone else can. Healthy relationships involve people who accept themselves and each other just as they are.

He or she will make sexual demands and leave if I don't comply. Many singles dread this area. They are convinced that their partner will eventually demand sex and will leave if they do not give in. God created human sexuality and intended it to be exclusive to marriage. God made sex pleasurable. No one should deny or avoid addressing this issue. Ignoring this issue or "hoping" for the best is a recipe for disaster. It is important to have your boundaries in place about sex. Get the discussion out in the open. Find out where the other person stands. Decide what the two of you will do. The sooner this is resolved, the sooner you can focus on building a great relationship. Our Pastor, Tim Coop, says that lust cannot wait to get but love can wait to give. That is good advice.

Years of research tells us that sex is not the main reason relationships work. If you are being pressured in a relationship to violate your values or boundaries, change the relationship or get out. Sex is not intimacy. As a matter of fact, sex before marriage is false intimacy. Sex makes it seem that the relationship is much deeper than it really is. Do not cave in on this. Honor God and yourself. This is a great area to get support from others. If your partner will not honor your values now, what makes you think he or she will honor them after you are married?

My partner will find my "flaws" and leave me. Relationships involve vulnerability and trust as well as disclosure. We all have flaws; there are no perfect people or relationships. We cannot control the responses of others. It is best to disclose our real self and find real love and acceptance from others. Fearing the rejection of others keeps us in our false self and leads to insecurity. Take risks and trust others. If they do not accept you, forgive and move on.

I really do not trust anyone. Some people are neither honest, nor worthy of our trust. This is a good reason to stay present and in touch with your thoughts and feelings. Assuming that you cannot trust anybody indicates the issue is more related to your own wounds and earlier life issues. In order to have a healthy relationship, it is necessary to allow yourself to be open and vulnerable. Trust and disclosure are a joint process.

Do you struggle with any of these fears? God tells us that His perfect love casts out our fear. I believe fear is real and must be addressed. Perhaps you have experienced many of the fears above. Perhaps you have been hurt or disappointed in a past relationship. Take heart, so have many others. The solution is to face our fears deliberately, with the help of God and a few spiritual traveling companions. Relationships still work best when we allow them to grow slowly over time. Talk about your fears and apprehensions with your friends and support network. Work on them in counseling if necessary.

Strategies for Successful Courting (Dating)

As you may have guessed, we are not big fans of dating, which we define as random interactions that utilize "false-self" tactics and are about superficial, casual and oftentimes physical contacts that do not have marriage as a goal. Courting, on the other hand, is about building long-term friendships that are allowed to develop into lifetime commitments. Courting is "real-self" no matter how painful. Courting puts as many things up front and on the table as possible. Dating "springs" things on people after we think they like us. Dating usually ends poorly, with people being hurt. Courting normally ends with two people remaining friends. "False-self" dating is harmful to you spiritually. It places too much emphasis on externals and performance and not enough on character and what is inside a person. Please remember our most important maxim, **the goal is not to find the right person but to be the right person and find the right relationship.** Okay, here are some rules for the road.

Here are some basic friendship rules

- Listen without judgment—you never learn anything from hearing yourself talk
- Celebrate and enjoy your relationships—laughter is the cement in a relationship
- Do not demand loyalty—it must be voluntary
- Friendships are not just give and take—they are about growing as a person
- Never manipulate anyone into doing something in the name of friendship
- Never hold on to anger, hurt or pain—they will steal your energy
- Live as though your friend is a gift from God—he or she is
- Express your feelings through your actions—"walk the walk and talk the talk"
- Friendship is not a sporting event—do not compete for control
- Enjoy the journey

Follow some basic courting rules

- Do not have a sexual relationship until you are married. Relationships are partnerships. Sexuality is a part of a committed relationship; it is not a good foundation on which to build a relationship.

- Limit your time together in the beginning. See one another or talk on the phone in moderation. You develop friendships over time; does an intimate relationship deserve any less?

- Spend more time courting in person rather than by email or phone. Electronic communication has an aspect of anonymity and safety. It allows for a false sense of closeness. If this is your primary mode of communication, you may feel awkward with each other in person.

- Be yourself at all times in the courting process. Be clear about who you are and what you want. Doing so allows both of you to clearly see if the relationship will work. If you are compatible, you will discover more things to like about each other.

- Be clear from the start about how you want to be treated. It is better to know how your new partner responds to your boundaries and standards.

- Be aware of who your new partner is. At the same time, do not automatically assume he or she will disappoint you in the same ways you have been disappointed before. Give him or her a chance to treat you well rather than testing to see if he or she will cause you pain.

- Know your needs, because you are responsible for them. Articulate your needs and determine which ones can be met by a partner and which can be met by others. Be certain to choose a partner who will satisfy your long term, not just your short term needs. Choosing a partner out of short term needs guarantees that the relationship will not last. Read Philippians 4.

- Accept your new partner as he or she is or do not engage in the relationship. If a certain behavior bothers you but does not bother him or her, you can be sure that this behavior will continue. Accept how your new partner is now, rather than hoping for change.

Love others well, just as God does. In the Message, Philippians 1: 9-11 reads, *So this is my prayer: that your love will flourish and that you will not only love much but well. Learn to love appropriately. You need to use your head and test your feelings so that your love is sincere and intelligent, not sentimental gush. Live a lovers life, circumspect and exemplary, a life Jesus will be proud of.* Here's the key question you must address in courtship. "How can I love this person well who has become so close and dear to me and to whom I am attracted? God's word provides some answers. Love doesn't cause another to sin (Luke 17:1-2; I Cor. 8:9-13). Love considers the interests of others (Phil. 2:4). Love rejoices in truth (I Cor. 13: 6). Love encourages spiritual growth (Heb. 12:25). *Agape* love is unconditional, affirming love. Read Paul's incredible definition of *agape* in I Cor. 13.

Stay connected to your support network. Many people want to simply find "the one" and then proceed to isolate themselves. What a stress on a relationship! Can you put all of your needs, wants, desires, and interests on one person? Do you think one Prince or Princess Charming will somehow meet all of your needs? You need community. You have too many needs for one person to meet them all. Get connected, and stay connected.

Relax and allow relationships to develop naturally. Timctablcs and laundry lists can make us obsessed and very unhappy. The only way to attract a fulfilling relationship is to have a healthy single lifestyle and take great care of yourself. You can have a fulfilling life with or without a partner. When you are living out of your own fullness, you will no longer need to look for a relationship. You can be patient and allow the right relationship to develop. Loneliness and unrealistic expectations drive us into unhealthy relationships much too soon. It is never wrong to have healthy boundaries and limits or to look for certain non-negotiables in a potential partner. What needs to drive our behavior is the patient peace that comes from being content in our situation (see Philippians 4) not loneliness, fear or desperation.

Never expect another person to fulfill all your needs. You, and you alone, are responsible for your needs. Many of our frustrations in relationships stem from our expectations of others. We often expect another person to "make" us happy, to "bring" us love, or to "give" us respect. We expect them to show they care by placing conditions on the relationship: "If he really loved me..." "If she was really a good friend..." Other people cannot "make" us happy, "bring" us love, or "give" us respect. Those things have to come from within us. If you are expecting a partner to provide you with those things, chances are you are feeling rather disappointed on a regular basis, because no one will ever be able to live up to those high expectations.

Be sensitive to the needs of your children. Some children feel replaced, abandoned or deserted when their parents begin dating. Affirm them as children. Never use them as confidants or surrogate adults. Help them understand the value of child and adult relationships in your life. Do not introduce your child to everyone you date. Before you introduce someone, let your child know the nature of the relationship. Reassure your child of your love for them.

Be willing to be vulnerable in your relationships. You cannot have a truly healthy relationship until you are willing to be vulnerable and disclosing. Playing it safe and hiding your true feelings and thoughts is self-protective, and can prevent you from experiencing the true joy of being in healthy relationships. The benefits of personal openness and honesty far outweigh the risks. Vulnerability occurs when we feel fully accepted by Christ.

Discover old relationship patterns. If your past relationships have not worked out, you are at least 50% responsible. If you are unwilling to examine your relational patterns, you will make the same choices and pick the same types of partners, over and over. Explore all aspects of your relationship behavior. Make a list of what you believe about relationships.

- ❑ Do your relationships end painfully?
- ❑ Do you internalize (stuff) painful/negative emotions?
- ❑ Do you run from one relationship to the next to avoid loneliness or pain?
- ❑ Do you feel any remorse when you leave?
- ❑ Do you hesitate to commit "all of yourself" to someone?
- ❑ Do you feel a need to "break up with them before they break up with you?"
- ❑ Have you become good at "playing the game?"
- ❑ Do you hurt others through short-term intensity and sexuality, only to get bored and leave?
- ❑ Do you maintain emotional walls to keep from getting hurt?
- ❑ Are you insensitive to the feelings and needs of others?
- ❑ Do you have a need to hurt others physically or emotionally as a way of diminishing your own pain?
- ❑ Do you experience guilt when you hurt or disappoint someone?
- ❑ Do your carry on multiple intimate relationships?
- ❑ Do you leave relationships suddenly, with no warning?
- ❑ Do you end relationships but maintain the friendship?
- ❑ Do you consistently see yourself as a victim?
- ❑ Are you always wondering if there is something better?

Have the courage to examine your relationship patterns and make needed changes. Unless you identify and change these patterns, you will repeat them, over and over.

Develop new relationship patterns. Most dating is false-self dating and we have already demonstrated that it will never meet your intimacy needs. Changing your old patterns sounds harder than it really is. Deal with your resistance to change first. Then remember that relationships are God's way of meeting your intimacy needs. "False-self dating" will never accomplish that. Relating out your fullness will allow you to be vulnerable and self-disclosing. New patterns of relating should include the following:

- Seeing people for who they are and not for whom you want them to be or who you are afraid they are.
- Developing friendships and allowing those friendships to naturally emerge into relationships.
- Feeling free to enjoy others versus needing others.
- Always addressing others from your real self.
- Being clear about your definition of an ideal relationship and being able to articulate this to a potential partner.
- Taking care of your companionship needs. Making friends; not becoming dependent on a relationship to validate your worth.
- Recognizing your attraction to people, understanding what you are attracted to in them and realizing that you have a choice in what you will do about it.
- Knowing what you need and being able to assess if a potential partner is able and willing to meet your needs.
- Knowing and respecting your boundaries and communicating when they are crossed and being able to respect the boundaries of another.
- Having a strong community and support network and a satisfying social life, one where your needs for companionship are well met.
- Committing to honor God in all your relationships.
- Being willing to be held accountable for your relationship behavior.
- Placing value in finding the relationship that fits who you are.
- Being sensitive to the needs and feelings of others.
- Maintaining friendships that have a basis in Christ.

Share your needs, values and boundaries right from the start. Healthy relationships involve people who share similar goals, values and expectations. Staying in relationships where these values and goals are not shared almost always ends in disaster. It is critical to have an open discussion about the future of the relationship. How many of your values, goals and desires are you willing to give up? How many of your partner's desires are you willing to ask him or her to give up? How long do you think a relationship can survive under those conditions? Relationships are always a choice.

Be yourself. Trying to be someone you are *not* is rarely successful. If you know who you are, what you want and what you can give in a relationship, you will connect with a partner who is a natural fit for you. Look deeply inside yourself and find out what you want in a relationship and what you can give. Do not compromise on who you are. Making huge changes or denying parts of yourself just to be in a relationship will never bring peace or ultimately meet your needs. Relationships of this sort are an illusion. Assess your relationships regularly.

- Is this relationship healthy?
- Can my partner and I talk honestly and openly about our feelings, needs and wants as well as listen to and respond positively to one another?
- Can we make relationship course corrections when necessary?
- Do we have more effective communication and problem solving than drama?
- Is this relationship meeting my needs or his or her needs?
- Can I be "me" in this relationship?
- Does the relationship honor God and reflect His character?
- Do I want to meet this person's needs?

If the answers to these are "yes," there is good chance you are in a healthy relationship.

Learn to identify "red flags." "Instant" love, quick marriage proposal, pressure to have sex, feelings of coercion or manipulation—these are all "red flags." These behaviors are more about needing to connect to someone than they are about a healthy relationship with you. The solution is to take things slowly; a relationship such as this will cool off within a short period of time.

Maintain your limits. Even the best of partners or friends will inevitably do some things that will not be "OK" with you. If you say nothing, they will not know that their behavior is affecting you negatively. This will inevitably lead to unhealthy relationship patterns. Limits keep us healthy because they re-iterate our values. Boundaries also greatly enhance your ability to select the right partner. Healthy partners will respect your limits. Unhealthy partners will cross your boundaries fairly early into the relationship.

Monitor you choices. Relationship choices are often influenced by our parents' relationship. If our parents' relationship did not work well, we may be "stuck" with painful, unhealthy relationship patterns. The solution is to understand your parents' relationship to see how it has influenced your choices. How does your parents' relationship parallel your own relationship history? Next, make a conscious choice to create new relationship patterns. Do the hard work; you are not your parents nor do you have to live out their relationship.

Learn to ask for what you want in a relationship. To stay healthy in a relationship, you need to be able to ask for what you want. It is a myth that people should know what you want or that it "doesn't count" if you have to tell them. The real self is clear about wants and needs and sensitive to the wants and needs of others.

- Discover what kind of interactions you want.
- Ask yourself what kind of a person would be suited to naturally engage in that kind of interaction. You will arrive at a clear description of your ideal relationship.

Define the relationship you want. Ask yourself not what you want but what you need. What can you not live without in a relationship? What do you need to thrive? What do you need from a partner day to day? To purge fantasy from your definition, ask yourself what you want from another that you are not willing to do or be yourself. Look at the relationships you value most and model your love relationship after those.

Practice sexual stewardship. It is normal for all adults to experience sexual desire and even arousal. These sensations are not sinful. These are physiological responses created by God. However, part of God's design was that sexuality would not achieve full expression until marriage. Know your sexual boundaries before you begin a relationship. Respect and honor the boundaries of a partner. Address the issue up front in your relationship. Have your support network hold you accountable (Prov. 27:17). Keep affection appropriate. Paul reminds us in Eph. 5 to not let our love turn to lust. Lust often leads to manipulation and pressure to compromise our values. Healthy individuals will not ask you to compromise your boundaries.

Are you ready for a relationship?

Negative beliefs and lack of skills can prevent us from being able to identify healthy partners. The following checklist can help you identify which beliefs you need to change and which skills you need to acquire. Check every statement that is true for you. Total each section and the inventory as a whole

Letting Go of the Past

- ❑ I have forgiven my mother; she did her best.
- ❑ I have forgiven my father; he did his best.
- ❑ I have forgiven each of my past relationship partners
- ❑ Each of my past partners did the best he or she could.
- ❑ I am working to forgive anyone who abused me in the past.
- ❑ I harbor no hope of reconnecting with past relationship partners.
- ❑ I am complete with and have forgiven the opposite gender.
- ❑ I have forgiven and no longer compete with the same gender.
- ❑ I have forgiven myself for my past relationship mistakes.
- ❑ I no longer harbor deep bitterness and resentment for past wrongs

Total number of statements checked___

Acknowledging My Needs

- ❑ It is okay to have needs. Everyone has needs.
- ❑ I have needs and I have the right to express them.
- ❑ It is okay to have my needs met.
- ❑ It is okay to ask to have my needs met.
- ❑ I know that someone I just met cannot meet my needs.
- ❑ I know what my needs are.
- ❑ I recognize and know what makes me needy.
- ❑ I practice great self care when I feel needy.
- ❑ I consistently take great care of myself.
- ❑ I have a system that meets my top needs.
- ❑ I have a spiritual solution for my needs.
- ❑ I no longer need a relationship to meet my needs.

Total number of statements checked___

Understanding my Relationship Patterns

- ❑ I understand what did/did not work in each of my past relationships.
- ❑ I understand what did/did not work in my parents' relationship.
- ❑ I have compared the two situations above and have discovered my relationship patterns.
- ❑ I have identified the types of partners I tend to attract.
- ❑ I understand how I have developed my relationship patterns.
- ❑ I have identified how my relationship patterns benefit me.
- ❑ I have identified what my relationship patterns cost me.
- ❑ I have discovered what I believe about relationships.
- ❑ I understand my expectations.

Total number of statements checked____

Defining my Boundaries

- ❑ I can say "no" and do so regularly.
- ❑ It is important for me to have boundaries to protect me.
- ❑ I know clearly what my boundaries are.
- ❑ I do not ignore people crossing my boundaries.
- ❑ I have an empowering boundary setting process.
- ❑ I am always heard when setting boundaries.
- ❑ I am being supportive of other people when I set boundaries.
- ❑ I gently but effectively educate people about my boundaries.
- ❑ I respect and honor another's boundaries.

Total number of statements checked___

Discerning the Right Relationship

- ❑ I have defined what I need to thrive in a relationship.
- ❑ I have defined what is important to me living day to day with a partner.
- ❑ I have identified the relationship needs to absolutely be met by a partner.
- ❑ I have defined what I value above all else in another.
- ❑ I have defined what I cannot live without in a relationship.
- ❑ I have defined the worst thing(s) a partner could do to me.
- ❑ I have defined what I absolutely won't tolerate.
- ❑ I have dropped all demands on another that I don't demand of myself.
- ❑ I am willing to be in the process of growth with a partner.
- ❑ I am not willing to negotiate on the qualities most important to me.

Total number of statements checked___

Connecting with Others

- ❑ I engage only in activities that bring me joy.
- ❑ I no longer engage in activities hoping to meet a partner.
- ❑ I no longer put my best foot forward, I am being me at all times.
- ❑ I never use sexuality, power or money as a way to attract partners.
- ❑ I don't expect everyone to be attracted to me.

- ❑ I no longer require attention from everyone.
- ❑ I don't compare myself to others.
- ❑ I readily participate in activities rather than sitting at home.
- ❑ I surround myself with loving supportive friends.
- ❑ I am building a healthy, vibrant, loving community.

Total number of statements checked__

Developing New Relationship Patterns

- ❑ I recognize quickly the types of partners I attracted in the past.
- ❑ I acknowledge this attraction as a reaction to my past pattern.
- ❑ I recognize available people.
- ❑ I recognize those who have a genuine spiritual commitment.
- ❑ I recognize people in the process of growth.
- ❑ I recognize kind, generous people.
- ❑ I see people for who they are rather than for whom I want them to be.
- ❑ I am attracted to partners who will be good for me.
- ❑ I surround myself with people who will be good for me.
- ❑ I have numerous role models of good relationships around me.
- ❑ I recognize people with active addictions.

Total number of statements checked___

Defining My Goals

- ❑ I am clear about my life goals.
- ❑ I have identified the steps that will allow me to achieve my goals.
- ❑ I am living my life to the fullest.
- ❑ I know what type of work I am passionate about and I am doing it or working on creating it.
- ❑ I know what my life purpose is.
- ❑ I know what I contribute to others.
- ❑ I know how I want to spend my time.
- ❑ I know where and how I want to live.
- ❑ I know the legacy I want to leave behind.
- ❑ I have a life mission statement.

Total number of statements checked___

Addressing Personal Faith Issues

- ❑ I have a personal relationship with God.
- ❑ I am connected with other believers.
- ❑ I have my own spiritual practice—prayer, study, quiet time..
- ❑ I take time for silence and meditation
- ❑ I am detached from my own sense of timing, in favor of God's.
- ❑ I am truly happy and living a full life in the present.
- ❑ I can allow God's timing in terms of finding a partner.

Total number of statements checked__

Identifying New Dating Patterns

- ❑ I am a woman and I allow men to pursue me or I am a man and comfortable taking first steps in a relationship.
- ❑ I stay away from verbal foreplay in a relationship.
- ❑ I have clear boundaries around my sexuality.
- ❑ I limit my together time in the beginning of a relationship; I get to know the person slowly.
- ❑ I spend much more time courting in person that I do by phone or email.
- ❑ I am clear about how I want and don't want to be treated and I communicate those desires to my partner.
- ❑ I do not test my partner.
- ❑ I appreciate my partner for whom he or she is and not for his or her potential or to meet my expectations.
- ❑ I have fun in the dating/relationship process.
- ❑ I can be myself when dating.

Total number of statements checked___

Your total score___

What does my score mean?

75 points or more—you have excellent relationship skills. You are clearly ready to pursue a relationship.

50-74 points—you have some areas of strength, but also a few areas that need some attention. We suggest you address those areas before pursing a relationship.

0-49 points—you likely feel frustrated with dating and have had several bad experiences, or you may not be dating at all. Do not become discouraged. We suggest you do some relationship work with a counselor.

> **Dr. P. Rule:** Dating/courting is a wonderful opportunity to make friends and explore the world of relationships. Please have fun. Enjoy the rich diversity to people God has created—each one unique and able to contribute something of value to you. Add value to the lives of others.

What Do I Want From a Relationship?

Personal pictures

Every relationship you will enter involves expectations. Expectations are like a personal map; they are formed by your life experiences and are very often unconscious and out of your awareness. These expectations create a "picture" of how your relationships, and life in general, should be—a picture that is not easily altered. Unfortunately, your picture of remarriage probably does not take into account the complexities and challenges of remarriage or stepfamily life. This is true because you, like most, have a "nuclear family" model of marriage that does not accurately represent the realities and challenges of remarriage. Consequently, these two pictures of remarriage, the one you want and the one that actually occurs, are very different. The solution would be to change your "picture" to match reality, that is, if you ***knew*** the two pictures did not match. However, you don't know, so you hold on to your picture, hoping someday to find the right match (partner). Why do we hold on to our picture so tightly? There are several reasons—fear of failure, little exposure to accurate information, unexamined misbeliefs about remarriage, emotional wounds, etc.

The solution is to acknowledge the fact that you likely have unrealistic expectations about remarriage and stepfamily life; unrealistic expectations that could reduce your chances of remarriage success. Once acknowledged, these expectations must be examined in the light of remarriage realities.

What are your expectations?

The examples listed below will allow you to more easily identify your own expectations. Some of these are very specific to remarriage, others are about stepfamilies. Many of these examples are extremely subtle. Some are verbalized and well articulated—for example, "I will handle the discipline of my children;" others are totally unverbalized and possibly even unknown to the person, "I will never again let anyone close enough to hurt me." Verbalized or not, known or unknown, expectations can apply immense pressure to a new marriage and create an invisible barrier, making stepfamily development very difficult. These expectations will be examined at three levels: those known and articulated, those known but unspoken and those seemingly unknown. It is important to note that every level contains unrealistic or blatantly unhealthy expectations.

Spoken expectations

Many of our expectations are fully known and readily articulated. "I want a man who will love my kids." These expectations cause few problems in relationships, unless they are totally unrealistic or inconsistent with Biblical truth. The goal is to differentiate between healthy and unhealthy beliefs and expectations and work toward healthy, Biblically consistent, workable guidelines. Some spoken expectations are in the form of contracts or family rules:

- My partner and I will present a united front to the children.
- I will discipline my own children.
- Your children will come to stay every two weeks.

- We will pray with the children before bedtime.
- We will share in paying household expenses.
- If we get upset, we will make time to talk.
- My ex-husband paid the bills; I prefer it that way.
- You will stay home and take care of the children.
- We will make time to get away as couple.

Some spoken expectations suggest underlying, unrealistic beliefs about relationships in general and stepfamilies in particular:
- We will be a "normal" family again.
- We will really love each other this time.
- We will not have the problems other stepfamilies have.
- This family will be easier because we are older and wiser.
- Our love for one another will enable us to overcome any problems with the children.
- Their biological father/mother is out of the picture, so we won't have to deal with that issue.
- My son/daughter will be so much better off when he/she has a father.
- Since we don't have custody of the children and they will only be visiting every other weekend, they won't cause any problems.

List some your well-known, easily articulated expectations.

Unspoken expectations

Unspoken expectations involve hidden agendas and frequently contain assumptions about the way that certain things should happen. Most unrealistic beliefs are in this category. Unspoken expectations are typically kept secret during the initial stages of courtship and marriage. Typically, these expectations emerge after marriage and create a good deal of confusion and conflict. Often these expectations are exact opposites of those verbalized earlier. Why does this happen? Most of us are reluctant to verbalize these beliefs, for fear of rejection from a potential partner. However, the more unrealistic the belief, the more important it is for you to confront. Unrealistic expectations can destroy a new relationship. Examples of unspoken beliefs and expectations include:
- I will teach her child how to behave.
- You will learn to do things the way I like them done.
- I am not going to put myself out for his kids.
- I will be the best stepparent a child could ever have.
- You won't drink as much after we are married.
- If things don't work out right away, I will leave.
- You will lose weight after we are married.
- Your kids will call me Mom/Dad.
- I will be a better husband/wife than your first one was.
- My kids will always come first.
- Marriage will solve all my problems.
- Everyone in the new family will get along instantly.

- My new spouse will always take my side.
- The stepchildren will appreciate what I bring to the marriage and family.
- My spouse will intuitively know what I need.
- My new wife will step in and take care of my children.
- Never ask for help.
- Never talk about your feelings.

<u>Action Step:</u> How can I know if I have unspoken, unrealistic expectations?
Are there expectations you are unwilling/afraid to share? Do you avoid certain topics? Are you waiting for the "right" time to discuss something? Are you continuing to operate in your false self? If so, write them down now and commit to share them with your partner. If you are reluctant, share them with a friend and identify the source of the reluctance.

Unspoken and unknown expectations
Unknown expectations are the most difficult to deal with because we are unaware of their existence and likely in denial. These expectations are generally deduced from behavior, most often during counseling. When you encounter struggles in relationships that prove difficult to resolve or define, they likely fall into this latter category. Many of the deep, unresolved wounds from childhood or from prior relationships will manifest themselves here. If you find yourselves getting stuck, contact a pastor or counselor to help. Remember that we all bring disappointment, pain, hurts and fears from prior relationships. Examples of unknown beliefs and expectations include:

- If you give your child more attention than me, I will leave
- This house belongs to me; don't ever think it is yours.
- I want you to be just like/the opposite of my Dad/Mom.
- I don't really trust men/women, so I will be cautious with you.
- You must prove that you love me, although it will be hard to do.

Examples of unspoken and unknown roles include:

- The pleaser
- The controller
- The planner
- The comic
- The cleaner
- The worrier
- The worker
- The martyr
- The caretaker
- The hero
- The scapegoat

Double bind expectations are emotional "set-ups." These misbeliefs come from past relational wounds that can sabotage relationships very quickly.

- If you really loved me, you would know what I want and do it. Since you don't do what I want, you must not love me.
- If you really loved me, you would always agree with me. Since you don't always agree with me, you must not love me.
- If I let you get to close to me, you will see my inadequacies and not love me. But if I don't let you close, our relationship will struggle/end.

- If we don't agree, one of us must be wrong (probably you). If it is me, I will feel bad, so I have to prove it is you.
- If I have to tell you what I want, even if you do it, it doesn't count.
- I do what you want instead of what I want and resent you for it. I don't tell you what I want because I fear you might reject me or leave me.

<u>Action Step</u>: Worksheet on Expectations

- Identify your remarriage expectations?

- How are these expectations influenced by your childhood? Past relationships?

- List any unresolved issues from your past. (Hints: places where you are still hurt, angry, or extremely sensitive; issues you can't talk about, etc.)

- Using the above lists, identify your own unrealistic expectations. Everyone remarries with these. (Hints: are there hopes, dreams or fantasies that you cannot talk about? Are there areas of your relationship that are not okay with you, but you are accepting them or not saying anything because they are "not that big a deal" or you feel you "don't have the right to" or you think, "things will be okay after we get married"?)

Part 2

Relationship Skills

If you plan to have healthy relationships, you must possess some effective relationship tools. The most important tool is communication, because the communication process is how we share who we are and what we want from a relationship. Communication is how we establish boundaries, and share our values, needs and concerns. Communication is how we solve problems, make decisions and resolve conflicts. Communication is the vehicle through which nurturing relationships are developed and the message of love is given. Ineffective communication can leave us frustrated, with our needs unmet.

Effective communication is a particular challenge in remarriage, because it brings together individuals with little shared history and very different communication styles. You and a potential partner will likely have very different goals and agendas and communication is how those differences are expressed, understood and resolved.

The skills of communication, listening and problem solving

God made us relational beings. Every person has core emotional and relational needs. We enter key relationships in our life, such as marriage, to have these core needs met. In relationships, however, individuals can have competing needs. Communication and problem solving are the tools we use to articulate our own needs, understand the needs of our partner or children and resolve situations where those needs are competing. Whether our needs are met depends greatly on how effectively we use these tools. These tools or skills are especially critical in remarriage and stepfamily life, because there are so many needs, so many decisions to be made and so many opportunities for conflict and disagreement. If the individuals in your new family cannot effectively listen, communicate and solve problems, your new relationship will be in immediate peril.

The next several pages will address critical skills necessary for effective communication and problem solving in your relationships. Read through these pages and practice the skills. Identify your communication strengths and weaknesses. The absolute most important communication skill and the most basic need of any relationship is *mutual respect.* Above all else, respect others when you interact (Ephesians 4:29-31, James 1: 19 and I Corinthians 13:4-7).

<u>Note:</u> For a more complete and comprehensive look at communication and problem solving, please see our booklet, *Communication and Problem Solving Skills for Today's Relationships.*

Communication in Relationships

What is Communication?

Communication is a process of sharing information with another person or persons. Communication is almost anything you do or don't do. At any given moment during an interaction, you are simultaneously sending, receiving and decoding messages. Anything that causes some form of change (spiritual, emotional, physical or mental) in another person is communication. Non-verbal cues such as facial expression, silence or touch, for example, can convey as much meaning as spoken words. Effective communication happens when your message is accurately received by the other party and has the effects you desired. It is impossible to "not" communicate; effective communication is another story.

Characteristics of ineffective communication

What this adds up to, then, is this: no more lies, no more pretense. Tell your neighbor the truth. Watch the way you talk. Let nothing foul or dirty come out of your mouth. Say only what helps, each word a gift (Eph. 4:25, 29, *The Message*). Effective communication is intentional; if you really want to communicate, you will work hard to do so. You will genuinely care and make sure your child, friend or potential partner fully understands what you are trying to say. Behaviors that damage healthy communication are often used as weapons to defend ourselves or to attack another. Ineffective communication tends to be self-centered and self-protective. Below are examples of unhealthy communication.

Stonewalling—people stop communicating either because they don't know what to say, are too afraid to say anything, or they believe silence is a punishment. In any case, saying nothing abruptly stops communication. Communication is a "two-way street," not a monologue.

Grilling—the communication version of 20 questions or police interrogation. One person harasses and harangues the other into a "confession," or in other words, seeing it their way.

Blaming—is unhealthy for both parties, the "blamer" and the "blamee." The blamer merely feels weaker and more helpless because assigning power or responsibility to another through blame, undercuts one's own power and ability to respond. The blamee often feels guilty or inadequate and often simply quits communicating. The blamer and the blamee both lose.

Kitchen-sinking—is a scenario whereby a discussion of one issue ultimately opens the floodgates to a host of issues, most having little to do with the original topic.

Attacking: accusations, criticisms, and negative innuendo—tend to disrupt the communication process in a dramatic way. These are the tools of a frightened, defensive or angry person. When we feel attacked or accused, we want to defend ourselves.

When we feel criticized, we become fearful, hostile or ashamed. When we are accused or criticized by innuendo, we feel helpless (or crazy).

Needing to Win—will prevent the listener from really understanding what the speaker is saying. When the listener needs to win he or she is acting out of fear and low self-worth. Time will be spent on debating rather than solving the problem. Both parties lose.

Mind reading— is a common listening barrier. Mind reading is not only impossible, but also ill-advised. To attempt to do so will prevent you from paying attention to what is really said. Whatever your spouse says, you can check it out with the skills of paraphrasing or clarifying.

Placating— used repeatedly will end honest communication. A healthy partner wants to share information with you and wants genuine feedback. Placating or patronizing inhibits the growth of true intimacy.

Problem solving— interrupts the process of being heard for the speaker. If the listener enters into finding solutions before the speaker has asked, the speaker will not feel heard, the desired end of listening well.

Judging— what your partner is saying will also inhibit honest communication. The speaker will not feel safe to share him or herself in the future. It is up to the listener to be inviting and accepting of what the speaker is saying, then the speaker will want to share again.

Selective listening— is quite effective at frustrating the speaker. A selective listener will pick out only parts of a message and miss the true meaning in doing so. A selective listener does so to his or her advantage. Such a listener will hear only the parts that are desirable or will hear only the parts of a message that can be attacked.

Needing to be right— can make the listener preoccupied with proving his or her own point rather than listening carefully to the speaker.

The common theme of all these examples is a focus on self. All of these responses block the channels of communication. Effective communication is more than just words; it is the mechanism for growth and intimacy. Everyone communicates. The question is, "*What* are you communicating?" If you use any of the above, your communication is not only ineffective; it is destructive.

"I" messages

"I" messages are a basic communication tool and a healthy method for sharing your innermost experience and perceptions. It is healthy because it avoids using blame or shame. A well designed "I" message takes the focus (blame) off of the receiver and puts the focus (responsibility) on the sender (you) of the message. "I am beginning to take responsibility for myself when I can let you know what I am feeling in a particular situation."

The opposite of an "I" message is a "you" message." The "you" message is a message of blame. It communicates hostility and puts the focus on the other person. The natural reaction of the receiver to a "you" message is defensiveness. Healthy communication will be the casualty of such an interaction. Phrasing your message as an "I" message rather than a "you" message does not contribute to the escalation of a quarrel. An "I" message can be chosen whether the other person chooses to use such healthy communication or not. Below are some tips for creating "I" messages.

- Describe the behavior that is affecting you (without blame).
- State the feeling you have in response to this behavior.
- Describe the consequence this behavior might have for you (without blame).
- Stress the word *because,* in your message; it can help to connect the feeling and consequence elements of the message. This minimizes blame and keeps the focus on you.

Examples of "I" messages include:
"When you talk to me that way I feel hurt and discounted because I begin to think I do not matter to you." "When you did not kiss me good-bye this morning, I felt hurt because I wanted us to part on a more positive note." "When you called me from the office today, I really felt loved and important to you, because you thought about me." "When you forget to record the checks in the checkbook, I feel really irritated and concerned, because I have no way of knowing how much is left. We could overdraw."

Levels of communication
In *Why Am I Afraid to Tell You Who I Am*, John Powell suggests that you and I communicate on at least five different levels, from extremely superficial to deeply personal and honest. Emotional woundedness tends to keep us at the shallow end of communication. However, with personal growth and practice, we can move to deeper, more transformational levels of communicating. The reason this is so important is that intimacy occurs only at the deeper levels and intimacy is what holds relationships together. One of our deepest needs is to be fully known (flaws included) and fully loved.

- **Level five: Cliché.** This is the safest level of communication. There is no personal sharing. Everyone is comfortably behind his or her mask. At this level communication is never intentional and core personal or relational needs are never addressed. Examples of level five sharing include, "How's the weather?" "How's it going?" "I'm fine."

- **Level four: Reporting the facts.** The level involves minimal sharing. Facts about other people are reported with no personal commentary; much like the news on TV. Examples of level four sharing include, "The Mets are in town." "Looks like it may rain this weekend." "The neighbors are going on vacation next week."

- **Level three: Sharing my ideas and opinions**. This is where any real communication begins. Unfortunately, this is also where communication ends for the vast majority of couples. At this level a person is willing to give a little more of him or herself. Risk-taking increases slightly at this level. This level is where couples begin to find out if it is safe to be vulnerable with one another. Examples of level three sharing include, "I really don't like the new music at church." "I don't think we talk often enough."

- **Level two: Sharing my feelings, values and emotions**. At this level sharing of the personal self begins; "the real me is now peeking out to see if it is safe." If a person senses a safe response—shared feelings in return—then communication will progress and personal sharing will occur. Masks begin to come off. Examples of level two sharing include, "It really hurts my feelings when you forget our anniversary." "We don't have fun like we used to."

- **Level one: Complete emotional and personal truthful communication**. This is the level of confessional or transformational sharing that is only spoken in safe relationships. Here are the hopes and fears I may speak only with God. This is the place of deep speaking to deep, of truth-telling and vulnerability. The authentic self, with no mask, is finally present at this level. "I will share this only with someone I trust, someone with whom I have a "grace" relationship." Examples of level one sharing include, "I am struggling with my faith." "I have a need for more intimacy." "I don't have any real friends." "I am struggling with an addiction."

Action Step: Communication diagnostic.

- ❑ Do you have level one transformational conversations?
- ❑ Are you consistently saying, "tell me more" or are you avoidant or defensive?
- ❑ Are you able to actively listen for deeper levels of sharing?
- ❑ Do you encourage others to share by being attentive, accepting and trustworthy?
- ❑ Can you recognize superficial avoidance patterns (levels four and five) in your interactions?
- ❑ How many of the "ineffective communication" examples noted above do you use?
- ❑ Do you use more "I" messages or "you" messages?
- ❑ If you use more ineffective methods, "you" messages and superficial levels of sharing, what are you doing about it?

Why is good communication so important?

Good communication is about integrity: doing what you say and saying what you do. No matter what you say or how you say it, no one else will perfectly understand what you are trying to say. One of the biggest obstacles to communication is our tendency to evaluate, to pass judgment or to disagree with statements before we find out what is meant. Stephen Covey reminds us to "Seek first to understand before being understood." Another important obstacle is feeling that we have to defend our ego by defending what we have said. Our tendency to self-protect may be the single biggest hindrance to effective communication.

A client shares, "Jim never talks to me; he just stares at me and says nothing. I ask him how he's feeling about something and he tells me he doesn't know. It's frustrating. We never have conversations—I talk and he stares. Just one time I would like him to initiate a conversation or have an opinion or just talk to me—about anything. I don't know if he even cares about me." Bill has frozen emotions due to childhood wounds; communication is difficult for him.

Communication is *the way* we get our needs met in a relationship. If we cannot clearly articulate our needs or discuss them in a healthy, positive fashion, then our needs will largely go unmet. A persistent state of unmet needs can eventually destroy a relationship. Effective communication is so important in stepfamilies because remarriage, by its very nature, creates communication difficulties. This is true for several reasons.

- Stepfamilies feature the combining of mini-families, each with its own unique language.
- Most, if not all divorced individuals and their families have emotional wounds. One of the key traits of emotional woundedness is difficulty communicating and solving problems effectively.
- Wounded individuals have difficulty working through tough issues; they tend to get frustrated easily and give up.
- Individuals in the family may still be grieving past losses and therefore less available to be involved in family problem solving.
- Individuals adjusting to multiple changes tend to be self-focused.

A successful remarriage requires a great deal of flexibility, tolerance and acceptance because there are many differences to negotiate and these differences take a great deal of time to resolve. To survive, a new marriage and family must learn how to effectively listen, communicate, and solve problems and they must be able to tolerate and accept one another, especially when things do not go their way. Many of you reading this material have gone through a painful divorce because you, your partner, or both of you, were not getting your basic needs met in the marriage. Earlier we discussed emotional woundedness. We learned that most, if not all, divorced individuals have emotional wounds. One of the key traits of emotional woundedness is difficulty staying with the process long enough for effective communication and problem solving to occur. Effective communication is critical if a relationship is going to survive.

Creating better communication patterns

Good communication is honest, timely, accurate, and unifying. When we communicate honestly, the message we send clearly and accurately reflects the meaning we have in our heads about what we are communicating. Honest communication is necessary if we are to connect with others in an accurate and meaningful way. Communication that is not honest invites confusion, frustration, and separateness. Here are some suggestions for increasing the level of effectiveness in how you communicate.

Take responsibility for what you say. Good communicators are aware of their own ability to choose how they want to respond to another. They do not react to others, but rather express who they really are at the moment. Self-disclosure is their primary purpose for communicating. They know that their own thoughts, feelings and opinions are not controlled by someone else or by circumstances outside themselves. Therefore, they never blame others for their responses. They make "I" statements," (e.g. "I choose...," "I'd prefer...," "I need (want)...," or "I feel").

Utilize "leveling." In *A Couple's Guide to Communication*, Dr. John Gottman defines leveling as telling someone "what you are feeling by announcing your thoughts clearly and simply. It means that you should be transparent in communicating where you stand, and candid in signaling where you want to go" (p. 30). He states that leveling is difficult because it is far easier to tell what the other person is doing wrong than to state what we are feeling. Leveling is about saying what you feel; it is not an opportunity to criticize, punish or put-down your spouse

Wait and incorporate what others say. Listening patiently and actively rather than continuing with your own silent rehearsal of a reply or stream of thought triggered by the last sentence spoken. Most of us tend to ignore what others say and either override their talking with our own, or plan what we are going to say next. Don't interrupt. Wait and take in what the other is saying before choosing how you want to respond. They may be agreeing with you!

Focus on what is accurate. When we only focus on the disagreements or inaccuracies of what our communication partner is saying, we become confused, or respond to something entirely off the topic. If you have a question about what you hear, say, "I'm understanding you to say...is that accurate?"

Do not contradict. What the other is saying is always valid for him/her. Others always have a different frame of reference than you. The primary purpose of communication is to mutually understand each other's point of view. You may statc your disagreement, but avoid the phrase, "Yes, but..." when you contradict another, you invite defensiveness or justification rather than clarification.

Keep your voice pitch and volume at a comfortable level. Screaming may help relieve you of anger, but it rarely invites others to listen to what you have to say. You generate more heat than light, and you invite others to defend themselves or tune you out.

Summarize and validate. Regularly take the time to summarize what you have heard, what you have said, and what you both have accomplished in the conversation. Be sure and include your own understanding of what the other has said. Validation means communicating, that given the other person's perspective and beliefs, the way they feel makes perfect sense. Our willingness to consider the other person's point of view as valid is what builds intimacy in relationships.

Listen to yourself and others. Do you like what you are saying and how you are saying it? Are you responding in ways that accurately reflect your true thoughts and feelings? Listening to others is half of the communication process. By listening to yourself, you might learn something about yourself as well as about the topic you are discussing.

Persist in trying to understand vs. being understood. We often "go quiet" or leave the room when we feel frustrated, or want to use no response as a silent statement or communication weapon. If you both agree to a "cooling off period," then you both may want to leave or become silent. Otherwise, stay with the process until you are both satisfied and feel understood.

Be direct. Direct communication means you say what you mean and you mean what you say. Hinting, expecting the other to figure out what you are thinking or feeling, or wanting others to guess what you are trying to communicate, only confuses you and everybody else. The more concise and direct you are the better. Saying something like, "I like you and enjoy your companionship, will you go to the movies with me tonight?" is much more direct than, "I think I would like to go to the movies tonight. If you want, you could come along."

Stay in the present. Talk about how you feel right now, not how you felt last week, last month, or last year. The past and future are too abstract and dependent on one's own view. Since everyone's view is different, honesty is sacrificed when we talk about our view of past experience or anticipated future events. "I'm angry with you right now" is much more meaningful than "I was sure angry with you last week when..."

Ask for what you want. Others cannot read your mind, your heart, or your stomach. No one can know what you are thinking, feeling, or when you are hungry...unless you let them know by making statements about yourself and asking directly for what you want. If you expect the other person to anticipate and guess about what you want, the likelihood is you won't get it. The only way in the English language to ask directly for something is to use the words, "Will you...?" Every other phrasing is either not asking or indirect.

Plan ahead. Think about what you want to say before you start speaking. After the other person stops speaking, you usually have time to think a little ahead. However, too much planning and rehearsing in your mind allows the moment to pass, the topic to change, and the communication process to move on without your contribution. Planning ahead also means thinking about the other person. Is he or she more receptive to what you have to say before or after lunch? Is she or he having a good or bad day?

Avoid double messages. "I am not questioning your decision, I'm just wanting to know why you decided what you did" is an example of a double message. "Why didn't you take out the trash" said in an angry, commanding tone is a double message. Double messages breed confusion, and create barriers to communication. Since there are always at least two messages sent, honesty is lost somewhere between them. Be clear and straight with messages.

Tell the appropriate truth and tell it early. Even if the other person becomes angry or leaves the situation, tell the truth early in conversation. Refuse to let the other person's attempt at manipulating you or denying the importance of what you are saying, detour you from speaking the truth. Choose to be honest. Don't lie. Don't lie, even if you think it is going to get you what you want. It won't. And the price of discovery is always too high.

You nonverbal message should mirror your verbal message. Do you ever say one thing and do another, insisting that what you are saying is the only message? Perhaps you say one thing and your body language is showing something different? Picture yourself saying, "I love you" with clenched jaws. Keep in mind that actions speak louder than words, and so does body language.

Summary of key points

- Communication is anything we do that evokes a response in someone else.
- Communication is critical in a relationship and most of us are not good at it.
- Good communication is a learnable skill.
- Every person has a unique communication style, probably learned in childhood.
- Communication is how our needs are met.
- People do not usually stay in relationships where their needs are not met.
- You cannot get your needs met if you *do not* a) know what they are, b) tell your partner and c) work to meet your partner's needs.
- Wounded individuals have problems with the following:
  - Knowing their own needs
  - Expecting others to discover and meet their needs
  - Telling others directly what they need
  - Listening to others share their needs
  - Meeting the needs of their partner or family member

If you are having any difficulty knowing what your needs are or sharing those needs with someone, please contact a pastor or counselor.

Action Step: Are you sharing at level one or two? If not, why? Identify any obstacles, the ones inside you and those in your environment. (Examples: fear, insecurity, spouse does not listen or interact) What will it take for you and your partner to share level one or two conversations?

Listening

In *Saving Your Marriage Before It Starts,* Doctors Les and Leslie Parrott write, "Communication is the lifeblood of marriage. Having difficulties with communication does not bode well for marital satisfaction. In fact, one of the most important skills you can learn is how to talk so your mate will listen and how to listen so your mate will talk" (p. 73). Failure to listen has to be one of the primary reasons for miscommunication in relationships.

Sometimes honest listening can be enormously painful, but a willingness to listen with an open mind and heart can help trust and intimacy grow. You do not have to agree with everything you hear, but if you listen intentionally to your partner, you will be challenged to reconsider your attitudes and behavior. Listening opens every communication door. *The Message* rendering of James 1 says, *Lead with your ears, follow up with your tongue and let anger straggle along in the rear (v.19). Don't fool yourself into thinking you are a listener when you are anything but... (v. 22).*

By not listening intentionally, you are, in effect, saying you do not really want to know what another is thinking or feeling. An unwillingness to listen reflects a lack of respect. Listening is vital to the development of healthy relationships. We need to listen with our heart, head and hands. Listening should be motivated by our love for the other person (heart). Listening is a cognitive process of really trying to understand what our partner is communicating (head). Finally, listening should move us into action (hands). James 1: 19-25 reminds us that listening must lead to obedience—we must do something.

What is "active listening"?
"Active listening" can be defined many ways. For our purposes it means listening intentionally. To listen intentionally means to put the full weight of your attention and focus on what your partner is saying (not what you are going to say next). It means that the goal is to truly understand what your partner is communicating; not just the words but the meaning and feelings behind the words. Active listening builds intimacy because by it we convey that we really care about the person and what they have to say. There are several important "intentional" listening skills listed below. Which do you do well?

Paraphrasing is restating in your own words what you understand the other to say. Some suggestions of ways to lead into a paraphrase are "What I am hearing you say is...", "Do you mean....", or "In other words..." By paraphrasing, your partner will feel heard and miscommunications can be avoided.

Clarifying is when you ask more questions to get more information. Clarifying will give you the details and lets the other person know you are genuinely interested in what they are saying.

Feedback gives your spouse the information about what your reaction is to what has been said. It allows your spouse to know how the information has affected you. Feedback should be immediate, honest, and supportive.

Empathy in the listening process involves considering what the emotional experience of your spouse might be. What is your partner feeling? You do not have to agree, but you can listen and validate the feelings of your partner. An empathic response might be, "It sounds like you are really worried about this," or "It sounds like you have experienced a lot of pain over this." Name the feeling as you are listening to your spouse.

Being Open to what your partner is telling you. Do not jump to a judgment about the issue, but try to understand where your partner is coming from. Again, this does not mean you must agree.

Being Aware of the message you are hearing. Does it fit with information you already have? Listening well to your partner equals essential validation.

Guidelines for becoming a better listener
Listening, really hearing someone, is one of the greatest gifts you can give another person. Listening is powerful—it communicates that you are interested and that you care. Listening is a skill you can acquire. Below are several ways to improve your listening skills.

Put the other person at ease. Give them time, space and permission to speak. Let your body language communicate that you are prepared to listen.

Present a willingness to receive what the other person is saying. Look at them. Nod when you can agree, ask them to explain further if you do not understand. Listen for understanding.

Resist telling your story. Wait until they ask for your input before offering your story, and even then, be brief. Keep the emphasis on them.

Ask questions. People like to be very specific when prompted. It shows you are engaged and brings clarity to their situation.

Put yourself in their shoes. Do not criticize or give advice; see things from their perspective. Resist trying to fix things.

Reflect. Periodically summarize what they have said. This will clarify, keep you both on track and let them know you've understood. They will also be able to hear what they have said and take it deeper.

Remove distractions. Good listening means being willing to turn off the TV, close a door, or stop reading your mail or the paper. Give the speaker your full attention, and let them know they are getting your full attention.

Empathize with the other person. Especially if they are telling you something personal or painful, or something you intensely disagree with. Take a moment to stand in their shoes, to look at the situation from their point of view.

Be patient. Some people take longer to find the right word, to make a point or clarify an issue. Give the speaker time to get it all out before you jump in with your reply.

Be aware of your emotions. If what they are saying creates an emotional response in you, be especially aware of what they are saying and how you are feeling. Strong emotions tend to allow us to miss critical parts of what is being said to us.

Respond fully to the feelings that someone shares before responding with the facts. For example, when a child says, "I am afraid that there is a monster under the bed," few parents provide an empathetic response such as, "Sounds like you had a scary night." Most parents reassure the child prematurely by saying something like, "Don't worry, there are no monsters." This objective response can make the child feel alone and that their feelings are unimportant.

Use silence when the person is sharing feelings and you do not know what to say. Simply nod in understanding and allow yourself to be touched by what they are saying. Resist the temptation to say something just so that you are saying something. Make encouraging sounds when someone is sharing feelings and they seem to desire some acknowledgement from you.

Use short responses when the speaker is sharing something that is very important to them. Longer responses will make the speaker feel impatient because they may feel "derailed" by your intrusion. Choose them wisely, insert them carefully and don't just repeat them over and over. What you're really saying is: "I'm listening, carry on."

Remember that the attitude of your heart as a listener is always more important and more obvious than anything that you say in response to someone. Adopt a servant's heart. Make the choice that this conversation is about your friend or partner talking and you listening. Do not expect to get your point across or to teach him or her something; that will come with time. An attitude of respect and of trying to understand another person's world is much more important than learning how to formulate brilliant responses.

Master the group of skills we have just listed; they will serve you well in the months and years to come. Even tough issues, if broken down into manageable bits, can be resolved. Be aware of the blocks to effective listening. Resist shaming and blaming. Listen carefully to one another. Take responsibility for your part.

Solving Relationship Conflicts

Live out this God created identity the way our Father lives toward us, generously and graciously, even when we're at our worst. Our Father is kind; you be kind. Don't pick on people, jump on their failures, criticize their faults—unless, of course, you want the same treatment. (Luke 6: 36-37 The Message.)

Conflict is a natural part of all relationships. If you are going to have healthy relationships, you must learn how to resolve conflicts effectively. Conflicts occur because the needs, values or goals of one individual are not always compatible with those of another. Competing needs, situations where both sets of needs cannot be met simultaneously, are common in relationships. However, a tension is created when one or both parties feel that their needs may go unmet. If this tension continues without resolution, the relationship will be damaged. The solution is to find ways to meet each person's needs well enough so that each feels satisfied with the outcome. This is often referred to as compromise.

Healthy relationships are characterized by a willingness to address issues as they occur and the ability to resolve them in ways that enhance and affirm the relationship bond. Effective problem solving occurs when two people listen intentionally as each shares his or her needs and concerns and then respond to what is shared with understanding and acceptance as they search for possible win-win solutions. Anything less will create a backlog of unresolved issues, leading to bitterness, resentment and a breakdown of the relationship.

Problem solving styles

Your own approach to solving problems will greatly determine the success of any current or future relationships. If you are like most individuals, you probably avoid any form of conflict or confrontation. When conflict is unavoidable, you resort to an approach you have been using since childhood—you either freeze, fight or run. How effective is your problem solving style? In *From Conflict to Resolution*, Dr. Susan Heitler discusses five approaches to resolving conflict. The first four represent ineffective and blatantly unhealthy responses to conflict. If you use one of these, not only are you ineffective in dealing with relational conflicts, but you also risk becoming less and less healthy as a person.

The most common response to conflict is ***immobilization—doing nothing***. Some individuals view conflict as a red flag of danger. As they perceive the danger getting closer, their level of anxiety and fear rises. The anxiety they experience causes them to "freeze," leaving them literally unable to say or do anything, hoping that the threat will simply disappear. The tension or threat of conflict does subside over time even if an individual does nothing. However, the sense of relief experienced is false and short-lived. Avoiding issues makes one less adept at handling future problems. Unresolved issues never go away for long. In fact, unresolved issues build up, causing greater levels of anxiety, resulting in more avoidance. Anxiety and avoidant behavior are common problems in wounded individuals. Immobilization can manifest itself in many forms: low self-esteem, inferiority, inadequacy, insecurity, worry, fear, shame, guilt, tension, nervous habits, somatic symptoms, etc.

The second non-adaptive approach to conflict is ***submission—giving in***. For a variety of reasons, some individuals have learned to "give in" during conflicts. Whenever conflicts occur, they capitulate quickly to avoid being hurt and seldom directly express their needs or their position. This allows the other person to be in control. Giving in means that your needs will seldom, if ever, get met. Common expressions of giving in include depression, suicide, pleasing, helplessness, hopelessness, martyrdom, perfectionism, "walking on eggshells," passivity, and co-dependency.

The third approach to conflict is ***attack.*** Anger and a need to win or be right fuel this approach. Rage and anger are very energizing and action producing. Individuals who utilize attack always see the problem as "outside" them. They take little or no responsibility for the problem, only for the solution. Assuming that the problem will improve or be resolved only if they can get the other party to change, they resort to any means, no matter how destructive. This is classic "end justifies the means" thinking. Common attack methods include demands, manipulation, criticism, blame, sarcasm, accusations, "you" statements, coercion, threats, violence and intimidation.

The last type of unhealthy reaction to conflict is ***escape.*** Individuals who feel powerless or overwhelmed will flee from potential conflict situations. Escape can take many forms, both physical and emotional. Some individuals will flee the relationship entirely. Others will escape via addictions—drinking, smoking, drugs, gambling, shopping, pornography or food. Other common forms of escape include fantasy, suicide, work, exercise, traveling, excessive TV viewing, obsessive-compulsive behaviors, denial, social withdrawal, walking out of the room and refusing to talk. Below is a summary of popular alternatives to effective problem solving.

- fighting
- arguing
- hassling
- demanding
- blaming
- whining
- complaining
- avoiding
- hiding
- pouting
- obsessing
- worrying
- manipulating
- coercing
- denying
- rationalizing
- catastrophizing
- procrastinating
- yelling
- running away
- hitting

Does one of the above describe your problem-solving style? If so, you likely experience little satisfaction from or success in solving problems. Further, your relationships are likely turbulent, unfulfilling and short-lived. It does not have to be that way.

The final approach to conflict is to honestly and openly share your needs and concerns and search for mutually agreeable, "good enough" solutions. Successful problem solving requires listening, shared motivation, communication skills and practice. There is an implicit *promise* to keep talking and to keep exploring ways to meet one another's deep needs. To understand problem solving, you must understand core needs. Problem solving is about having our core needs met. Remarriage issues are often multi-layered, meaning that each person has one or more unmet core needs underneath their expressed needs. Core needs tend to be very basic needs that are usually out of our awareness. For example, a basic need in every conflict is the need for respect. When mutual respect does not exist, conflict resolution is extremely ineffective.

Understanding relational needs

Core needs are deeply held needs that often exist just below our level of awareness. Core needs are non-negotiable to our well being. Relational core needs are why we are drawn to others. Some needs can be met personally, for example, a need for achievement. The core needs listed below require the involvement of a partner. Having these core needs met is critical to the survival of a relationship. Resolving situations where these needs compete is also vital to relationship success. Having our needs met or resolving situations where needs compete cannot happen unless needs are known and articulated.

Most of us are unaware of our deep core needs. We may have a vague sense that our needs are not being met, but most often we cannot articulate what those needs actually are. A partner cannot meet needs you do not express. Conflicts cannot be resolved if each party is unaware of the unmet needs that are creating the discomfort and relational tension. Look at the list below; check the needs that you would identify as core for you. This list is not exhaustive. Add any needs not on this list.

Being heard when I vent
Help in clarifying my feelings
Being confronted respectfully
Encouragement
Feeling needed and valued
Comfort and reassurance
Respect
Supportive feedback
Emotional safety
Sexual intimacy
Companionship
Spiritual sharing
Reducing anxiety
Play
Reality checks
Acceptance
Appreciation
Love

List your three primary core needs

What makes these needs non-negotiable for you?

List the way you express these needs

List the reasons you do not express these needs

How do you want these needs to be met?

How do you react when your needs conflict with those of a close friend or partner?

Steps to effective problem solving:

- Honestly acknowledge that a conflict exists—one or both of us has unmet core needs
- Maintain an attitude of equality—your needs and values are just as important as mine
- Agree to problem solve together—we both agree to commit to the process
- Set aside quality time to talk—undistracted, uncommitted time
- Pray and invite God to be a partner—we commit to honor God
- Patently and non-judgmentally listen to the other person's concerns
- Clarify and simplify the issues—one subject at a time
- Dig beneath surface needs to find core needs
- Stay focused on current needs and the issue at hand
- Confirm that each person clearly understands their own true needs; their partners true needs and that each values the other's needs equally
- Generate possible solutions—creating a "pool" of possible solutions
- Mutually choose the best-fit option from the pool of possible solutions and determining if each partner is really satisfied enough
- Stay with the process long enough to see positive results (hanging in there)
- If problem solving works well enough, appreciate each other and celebrating the process
- Look back and re-evaluating if and when necessary

Attitudes that enhance problem solving (Read Philippians 2:1-5)

Problem solving is a promise. A promise to share, a promise to stay with the process, a promise to keep your word and a promise to meet the needs of a partner to the best of your ability. Your attitude can enhance or at the extreme, defeat the process. Below are some examples of thoughts and attitudes that can enhance the problem solving process.

- Realize that resolving conflicts is a process
- Take the long view—progress rather than perfection
- Share a commitment to personal self-examination
- Be clear about personal priorities
- Accept that personal changes will have to be made
- Keep a "partnership" mindset
- Focus on servanthood
- See God as a partner in the process
- Commit to solving (not avoiding) the problem
- Listen with your head and your heart

Part 3

Stepfamily Basics: Everything you need to know about stepfamilies before you join one

Successful stepfamily living does not mean surviving a year or two of predictable adjustments that then lead back to well-traveled nuclear family paths. Instead, remarriage is tightly bound to permanent changes in family and individual life cycles. Divorce loss and remarriage hope are interwoven into a lifelong tapestry where beginnings and endings meet by accident and where a cry of joy unerringly and without warning touches a moment of deeper sorrow. Loren Townsend

Stepfamilies come in all shapes and sizes, but they share some very specific and unique characteristics. Stepfamilies are born out of loss. They begin with a parent-child relationship that is stronger than the couple relationship. This is instantly confusing and perplexing to the couple and creates immediate conflict. Consciously unknown to the new couple, the parent-child alliance and numerous outside interfering relationships (e.g. an ex-spouse or ex-in-laws) actually have more influence on the family than they do. This is a surprise to the biological parent and a shock to the stepparent, who suddenly finds him or herself in an *outsider* position. The mini-family (a mom and her children, for example) is in charge, not the couple and certainly not the stepparent. Rules and routines originate from the mini-family, not from the couple. Those not a part of the mini-family (outsiders) feel excluded, even unwanted, and do not understand the rules or language of the insider family. The family will function this way for the first few years. Turbulence comes when stepparents and stepchildren struggle with the status quo and the biological parent gets caught in the crossfire.

Living in a stepfamily requires extending one's picture of "family" across at least two households; households to which children feel very loyal. In first time families, adults have equal history and shared traditions with their children. The adult team in a stepfamily begins with one member as an outsider and one an insider to each child in the family. As a matter of fact, someone outside the house (former spouse or relative) may be more of an insider than the stepparent. The result is that parents and stepparents feel fundamentally different about the same child: the biological parent feeling much more attached and engaged, and the stepparent feeling more excluded and ignored. Children also experience biological parents and stepparents differently. For them, the stepparent is not another caring, nurturing adult but an intruder who threatens to disrupt the close single parent-child relationship, which therefore represents yet another loss.

Stepfamilies develop through a series of stages, lasting from four to seven years. The first few years are extremely turbulent as family members try to adjust to one another. Stepfamily members do not even necessarily see one another as family, especially in the beginning. Every remarrying person brings with him or her many inaccurate stepfamily beliefs and some strongly held, yet extremely unrealistic expectations about how life in a stepfamily should be. To make matters worse, these beliefs and expectations are seldom disclosed before remarriage.

Remarriage creates a form of "instant family" with instant decisions to be made, instant relationships to be developed and an immediate sense of tension and frustration. Virtual strangers are now living under the same roof, with very different ways of doing almost everything. Remarriage has been likened to entering a movie set long after the filming has begun. The cast members have to adjust to a new person and to the fact that the script may have to be rewritten. You have to find a way to fit yourself into the existing story line. The adjustments are difficult for everyone.

If you are going to remarry and become a part of a stepfamily, you must understand these important stepfamily characteristics. Without a good understanding, you will fall into many traps common to stepfamilies—we call these landmines, and they are invisible. You may be wondering, why would anyone deny the realities of stepfamily life. The answers are shame or other emotional wounds and lack of awareness. Wounded individuals desperately want something normal in their lives. Since they often see stepfamilies as inferior or abnormal, their shame drives them to deny that stepfamilies are really different from first-time families. They do not want to know about the unique nature of stepfamilies; they want to recreate a nuclear family. This denial can have disastrous results.

So the remarriage scene is set—two people who love each other, who are ready to spend their lives together, and are willing to accept the fact that each perhaps has been married before, and each has children from a prior relationship yet, unaware that the beliefs and expectations each has, unknown to the other, will work to tear at the very fabric of the life they both want. A clear understanding of the realties of stepfamily life can radically change this outcome. Stepfamilies are different, but they are not inferior.

Note: For a more thorough understanding of stepfamilies, please see our book, *The Journey: A Travelguide for Christian Stepfamilies.*

What Makes Stepfamilies so Unique?

When stepfamilies look in the mirror what do they see? They see that being a stepparent is different from being a parent, that being a remarried parent is different from being a parent in a first marriage, and that growing up is a stepfamily can be even more complicated then growing up with only one set of parents. And it all looks hazy and confusing. John and Emily Visher, *How to Win as a Stepfamily.*

Nuclear families and stepfamilies have very little in common. Stepfamilies *never* become exactly like nuclear families. Stepfamilies are not inferior, but they are different. The above statements may seem obvious, but not for most remarrying individuals. Their goal is to recreate the nuclear family with a new marriage and a new partner, because that is the only picture of marriage and family that they have. They want their new stepfamily to look, feel and work just like a first-time family. Unfortunately, this just cannot and will not happen. If a person remarries with this goal, the results will be disastrous. Understanding the unique characteristics of stepfamilies is critical to the success of your remarriage.

Of course, there are similarities between stepfamilies and nuclear families. Both family types are composed of adults and children living together. In both, adults are in charge and their role is to guide, nurture, protect and prepare the children for adulthood. Family members have needs that the family attempts to meet. There are developmental issues and individual and family tasks to complete. Both family types have conflicts that must be resolved and decisions to be made. There are rules, values and beliefs that define the family and guide the members. Both families interact with the world around them, incorporating a larger sphere of interests and relationships. Finally, family members have hopes, dreams and goals for the future. The memories of a first-time family linger in the minds of many remarrying adults. While these memories and the hopes to restore what was broken are not wrong, they can create a blurred vision of the realities of stepfamily life. Below are some of the more salient of these differences, which characterize and set apart stepfamilies as unique from any other form of family.

Stepfamilies have a complex structure

Stepfamilies are the most complex form of family. Many different combinations of roles and relationships make stepfamilies quite distinct, not only from nuclear or one-parent families, but also from each other. Stepfamilies are composed of at least two previously separate systems, including children, multiple parental figures and a large extended family, with varying degrees of involvement. There are diverse custody and parenting time arrangements. The role of the stepparent may vary widely, from equal co-parent to benign spouse of the biological parent, with no stepchild involvement.

There is little or no legal relationship between stepparents and stepchildren

At present, the law affords stepparents only minimal rights. Ask a stepparent about the frustration of trying to get medical care or school records without written consent from a biological parent. Some families attempt to resolve this dilemma via adoption or name change. This seldom bypasses the real issues and has, at best, only limited success, typically with younger children. It is critical for the new stepparent to find a comfortable and realistic role with his/her new stepchildren. Part of the reality for stepparents is realizing that while they may play a major role in caring for a child, they have few if any legal rights in regards to that child.

There may be continual transitions
Children will be moving back and forth between households. These shifts can cause frequent schedule changes and extensive planning for transportation or other logistical considerations. This is especially true during holidays and vacation periods. Successful stepfamilies develop "permeable boundaries" to allow children to freely move back and forth without guilt or reprisal. Transitions work best when adults are flexible and keep children "out of the loop" and focus on the reality that children do best when they have access to all parent figures.

Boundaries are ambiguous
The concept of who is "in" the stepfamily can become confusing. Consequently, family boundaries are often unclear and permeable. This creates uncertainty around such issues as affiliation and togetherness and can become a source of stress and conflict. In nuclear families, there is a fairly clear sense of family—who the members are, where they live, how they relate. In stepfamilies it is not clear where the family "begins" or "ends." Children belong to at least two households, each with its own set of rules and roles. An important consequence of this is that individuals outside the family are involved in making decisions that affect the whole family. This serves to reduce the autonomy of the family, and often leads to jealousy and competition.

Role definitions are vague and ambiguous
Roles in stepfamilies have no clear names, definitions or expectations. The terms *stepparent* or *stepchild* for example, have no well-defined, universally agreed-upon job description or set of expectations. Neither society nor the church has normative definitions of step-roles. There is no consensus on how stepparents should behave in a given situation. Both adults and children bring largely unexpressed and unrealistic ideas of these roles into the family. In addition, there are no social channels through which to learn these roles and no agreed-upon model with which to identify.

Family members have very different individual, marital and family life cycles
In nuclear families, two adults become a couple at the same time and parents at the same time. This is not the case in stepfamilies, where adults and children come together from often markedly dissimilar marital and family experiences. They share no family history routines or traditions. Additionally, if children are of different ages, they likely have very different developmental needs or interests. Since remarriages typically occur later in life, there may be vast differences in career aspirations, finances, retirement, child-rearing practices and living styles.

Misbeliefs are common
The most common misbeliefs are that stepfamilies and nuclear families are the same or that love occurs instantly. Other popular misbeliefs are that children will be better off without the other parent, remarriage will solve all our problems, or that children will be

happy about a parent's remarriage. These myths are fueled by ignorance, by the media and by unrealistic expectations. The solution to myths is to deal with the reality of wounded adults and children, who can, with perseverance, become like family.

Stepfamilies have more stress than nuclear families

Stepfamily ambiguity, complexity and the lack of fit with societal norms for the "ideal" family cause much of the stress. The new stepfamily is in transition, and the necessary adjustments add to the stress. Most individuals are unsure of their roles and communication patterns have not been set. Problem solving is awkward and cumbersome. Virtual strangers are attempting to look, act and feel like a family. Few rules exist, and those that do exist are continually up for debate. One family member said, "It's like reinventing the wheel every time we talk."

Successful stepfamily integration generally takes years to achieve

The average is four years. This is an important point for families who are still holding on to the "instant family" myth. Stepfamilies do not "blend" instantly or easily. Generally, the first few years are turbulent and stressful as the new family seeks to break down barriers between individuals and between biological groups. Total strangers do not become intimate family members overnight. For example, in our experience, a stepparent should not assume a strong parenting role for at least one to two years.

There are "cut-off" relationships

Divorce or remarriage seldom occur without the tearing down of family structures. Some relationships get excluded, often by design. The family of the noncustodial parent typically experiences the biggest impact. Some new families purposely try to exclude other family members, including the former spouse. These "cut-off" relationships can create deep sadness and even acting-out behavior on the part of children. A critical stepfamily task is to provide children with opportunities to interact with important people in their lives, no matter how you may feel about them.

A biological parent lives in another household or in memory

The influence of another parent outside the home often creates ambiguity and feelings of helplessness and lack of control seldom seen in first marriages. Children usually have strong emotional ties to each of their biological parents, even if one of them has died. Adults often have difficulty accepting more than two parenting figures in a child's life, and often expect them to choose between three or four adults. This is unfortunate, since it represents a major adjustment difficulty for most children. If children are permitted the time to form good relationships with all the parenting adults in their lives, loyalty conflicts decrease and exposure to important adult relationships is ensured.

There are many loyalty conflicts

For most stepfamilies, biological loyalties never stop. These loyalties exist inside biological subgroups, for example a mom and her children, or toward a non-custodial biological parent. The most common loyalty conflict involves the stepparent. Children often feel the relationship with their custodial parent is threatened by the stepparent's efforts to join the family. Children also experience loyalty conflicts between same-sexed step- and biological parents. In fact, the nicer a stepparent is, the more conflict may arise. Loyalty conflicts also exist between siblings or biological subgroups. In many stepfamilies, individuals will always remain loyal to their biological subsystem. Loyalty conflicts exist for several reasons, the most significant being the extreme neediness of individuals in the stepfamily. A key task of stepfamilies is integrating the various subgroups into one whole. This may include grandparents and other relatives as well as the step and biological parents and children. Stepfamily cohesion, however, seldom reaches the same level as a nuclear family.

There is a widespread negative cultural connotation

Several cultural myths cast a negative shadow on stepfamilies. One such myth is that stepfamilies are inferior. Another is that stepparents are cruel or abusive, seldom providing adequate care or support for their stepchildren. These and other myths have been perpetuated over the years and have developed a strong stereotypic quality. We take pity, for example, on children raised in a stepfamily. We have almost archetypal images of cruel stepmothers or abusive, sadistic stepfathers. These negative images have strong implications for the stepfamily because they affect every aspect of stepfamily life. Adults, for example, may try too hard to overcome the negative stereotype, attempting to be" super-stepparents" and setting up impossible expectations. Children may shy away from a stepparent, diminishing any chance of a healthy, meaningful relationship developing. In this way, a self-perpetuating or self-fulfilling cycle is set into motion, maintaining negative perceptions and expectations.

There are power issues

The complexity of structure, ambiguity of roles and boundaries, and split loyalties create unique issues of power within stepfamilies. For example, the role of custodial parent carries with it considerable overt power, derived primarily from legal, social and emotional structures. At the same time, children from a previous marriage have considerable covert power over this parent. This power is derived from two sources. The first is the existence of another parent external to the stepfamily, which the child sees as an ally against the custodial parent. The second is the guilt of the custodial parent, over the breakup of the original family and any losses the children are perceived to have experienced. Power struggles are common in stepfamilies and often a consequence of the "insider-outsider" dilemma.

The stepfamily begins after many losses

Loss and grief are the trademarks of stepfamilies. Loss is how a stepfamily begins, either through death or divorce. Some of these losses can be invisible and therefore overlooked. Children experience the loss of family, parents, friends and security. They are forced to make changes over which they have little control, such as a new residence, new school, unfamiliar foods, rules and ways of doing things that may magnify the loss. Adults experience a host of losses. For some it is the loss of a dream, the loss of a familiar role in the family or the loss of daily contact with their children. Many lose the support of family, friends, community or the church. Many experience severe economic losses that prompt dramatic changes in lifestyle. These losses and changes create tremendous stress and stretch the coping skills of people already feeling overwhelmed. Sometimes the stresses of starting a stepfamily can quickly overtake any joy surrounding a new marriage. Several years after a remarriage, individuals may still be struggling with these losses. Allowing everyone in the family time to grieve is a critical task.

Stepfamilies experience many changes

Change is a normal part of all relationships. However, the changes experienced in new stepfamilies are far more numerous and intense than in nuclear families. Stepfamily members go through many transitions—from intact families to single parent families to remarriage. The changes surrounding each transition create periods of uncertainty, disorganization and disruption. Family members often resent and resist the numerous changes with which they are presented, changes over which they have no control and often did not want. Spouses do not have the luxury of an adjustment period that allows for gradual change. Instead they are thrust immediately into multiple roles. There is no time to gradually work through important issues such as power structure, decision-making, coping with extended family or making time for intimacy.

There is a complex past and no shared family history

Intimacy is somewhat dependent on time shared together. In stepfamilies, total strangers are living under the same roof. There are no common memories or traditions to draw people together. All families have a past. However, in stepfamilies the past is much more complex because a stepfamily's past includes baggage from the family of origin of each spouse, and "ghosts" from previous marriages. Parent-child relationships predate the couple relationship. This deprives the couple of the opportunity to develop an intimate relationship without children around. Developing a shared history is a major task. This task is often made difficult by the fact that many children, typically teenagers, are not interested in developing a shared history. For some children, making new memories in the stepfamily is a form of disloyalty to their former family. It is often helpful to begin a few new traditions that supplement rather than replace old ones.

Step relationships have no solid foundation of understanding, so the relationship is measured by what is happening at the moment

This is a real consequence of the insider/outsider dilemma. For a biological parent, the events of the moment are superimposed on a foundation of shared experiences and caring. A stepparent has no such knowledge of subtle cues or non-verbals and no established emotional ties. Most often, stepparent decisions are based on feelings often derived from being the excluded and/or unwanted "outsider." Family members need to learn one another's language. The older the child, the longer and more difficult this process becomes.

Dr. P Rule: Do not be overwhelmed by the above list, but please hear this message loud and clear: Stepfamilies are different from nuclear or first-time families. They are different, not worse or inferior. The problem is that most of us only know how to "do" marriage and family based on the "nuclear" family model. Take some time and review the factors we have just outlined. Which were a surprise? Why? How will these play a role in your new stepfamily?

New Beginnings: Starting a Stepfamily
Psalm 127: 1 "Unless the Lord builds the house..."

A new stepfamily is actually a collection of several already existing "mini-families." Understanding mini-families is critical to making a new stepfamily work. Mini-families are the intact groups that come together when adults remarry. The most common mini-family is a mom and her children, who have been functioning for some time as an intact single-parent family. The second most common mini-family is a dad and his children, even if he is not the custodial parent. Former spouses and their extended family constitute another mini-family. These biological groups often include other members: grandparents, aunts and uncles, even close friends. The salient point is that the *mini-family is the family, even after a remarriage.* The mini-family has its own traditions, rules, roles and ways of doing things, which are resistant to change. Much of the shared understanding in the mini-family is no longer in awareness; it cannot easily be explained or described, it just is. An important task of the new family is to transition from being a group of mini-families to becoming one integrated stepfamily.

Problems arise when an unsuspecting new family member violates an unspoken rule or way of doing something. Unusually intense emotions are unleashed that often surprise everyone. That family member (usually the stepparent or stepchild), however, finds little support. This is due to the fact that support and closeness lie more with the mini-family than with the new couple. This revelation comes as a shock to the stepparent or stepchild, who discovers that he or she is an "outsider" in the family. Later, the family as a whole will provide a safe place of support and understanding. Now, the mini-family holds that function, and this keeps couples and families from feeling truly united.

A ***hallmark*** of stepfamilies is the phenomenon of "insiders and outsiders." If you are part of a particular mini-family you are an insider. If you are not, you are an outsider. Insiders see and feel things very differently from outsiders. Insiders feel safe, understood, and possessive. Outsiders feel alienated, isolated and resentful. One stepparent put it this way, "Let me in or I'm out." The challenge is to acknowledge the mini-family, sort out the rules and roles and facilitate the creation of one integrated family. As you might have guessed, this takes time and patience. Most mini-family members do not want to lose their unique identity. They will resist any efforts to unify the family. Tolerance and flexibility will be important virtues if the family is to become inter-connected.

Do you ever get past mini-families?

It takes time for a new stepfamily to move from being a collection of mini-families to something that looks and feels like a family. Mini-families do not "blend" they combine. This combining process takes time and negotiation and can put tremendous strain on the couple and any decisions they must make. Things that can be done easily and with predictable results within the mini-family require much more effort and produce unreliable results when attempted by the new step-system—for example: planning holidays, playing a game, organizing a day, or choosing menus. So the couple, which must function as a strong team in order to bring the family together, begins stepfamily life vulnerable to being interrupted and pulled apart.

Yes, you do ultimately get past the mini-family stage. But stepfamilies never become exactly like nuclear families. To survive, the new couple must stay committed to the process long enough to develop a strong bond in the face of the pull of mini-families to remain intact. In the first two years, the new family is extremely fragile and vulnerable to break-up. This is a critical issue for the new couple. At first, there will be precious little time to spend together because they will find themselves embroiled in numerous child and family issues. Many new stepfamilies do not survive because the couple relationship is not adequately nourished.

How is a successful stepfamily supposed to look?
In her book *Making the Best of Second Best*, Kathleen Fox discusses how a successful stepfamily might look. She suggests the following characteristics:

- The new couple is emotionally finished with their former marriages, whether those marriages ended in death or divorce. They are not still actively grieving, filled with unresolved resentment toward a former spouse, or wishing the first marriage had not ended.
- The new couple is the strongest unit in the stepfamily—husband and wife come first for each other, support each other, and work together to parent the kids.
- Family members communicate. The communication may not always be sweetly reasonable, but it moves toward getting a problem solved instead of getting stuck in cycles of blaming or complaining. Problems and conflicts are addressed and dealt with as effectively as possible, instead of being ignored, covered up, or grimly endured.
- There is cooperation or at least polite communication with former spouses. Even if the relationship isn't friendly, it is primarily based on what is best for the children. If someone's former spouse is still hostile or bitter, that hostility isn't allowed to carry over into the present family.
- The adults in the family are willing to get help for themselves and the children when it is needed—whether that's a stepfamily support group, a 12-step group, a church, or individual or family counseling.
- The adults set an example of courtesy, flexibility, openness and tolerance over small matters. The family doesn't waste a lot of time and energy in power struggles over minor issues.
- All the kids are given clear boundaries and limits. No matter how parents and stepparents divide parenting duties or authority, it is clear that the adults are in charge. Kids aren't allowed to run wild or dominate the family because parent or stepparents feel guilty over past mistakes, try to compete with a former spouse for the kid's love, try too hard to be liked, or don't have the courage to make the tough choices that parenting demands.
- Things improve with time. Conflicts ease as family members get used to being part of a household and accept one another. Stepsiblings learn to like or at least tolerate each other while stepkids and stepparents develop bonds. The family

isn't rehashing the same problems after six years that it was struggling with at six months.
- Not every conflict, struggle, or difficulty is seen as a stepfamily issue. Some of them are recognized as part of the natural order of things in any family as people live together and kids grow up.
- Family members enjoy good times together—not everything is in conflict and tension all the time or even most of the time (pp.11-12).

We have never met a new stepfamily that even remotely resembled the above description. These characteristics represent an end point, a goal to work toward. The first goal of a new family is to hold on to one another and keep talking and working together even though it feels very uncomfortable and artificial. Loss and grief are a natural part of the first few years of stepfamily life. Successful stepfamilies give members permission to grieve.

Traits of a highly nurturing stepfamily

In *Who's Really Running Your Life*, Peter Gerlach explores the key traits of healthy families. The following list is taken in part from his work as well as the work of Rev. Ron Deal is his excellent book, *The Smart Stepfamily*. A common goal for all stepfamilies is to provide for the basic physical, spiritual, emotional and mental needs of all family members. This includes providing a place where each family member can feel consistently accepted, valued, appreciated, safe, supported, encouraged and loved and where children are prepared to become healthy, self-sufficient adults. Let's explore some common characteristics of nurturing families.

- The family is rooted in Christ.
- Family members are free to express their thoughts, feelings and opinions.
- Family problems are discussed openly and honestly and are usually resolved rather than denied or ignored.
- Every one is clear on who is running the family and everyone trusts the leader's decisions.
- The adult leaders take primary responsibility for the welfare and nurturing of the family.
- All family members feel valued, listened to and respected by one another.
- Children trust that their parental caregivers will demonstrate genuine concern for their hurts and fears.
- Mutual love and respect is freely shared among all family members
- Individual personalities are valued
- Love and affection are freely demonstrated
- There is a steady commitment to clear, shared, personal and family goals
- Mistakes and failures are handled with tolerance and compassion, and seen as growth and teaching opportunities
- Roles, rules and consequences are clearly defined
- Adults delight in and prize children as special, valuable and unique
- Each person is celebrated as unique and gifted
- Personal faith is shared and lived out

- Conflicts are resolved without shaming or blaming
- There is tolerance and openness to new ideas
- The family is a safe place to share emotions and work out issues
- Honesty and forgiveness are valued and modeled
- Family customs and traditions are shared and enjoyed
- Humor is enjoyed, but never used to shame or "put-down" someone
- Learning, asking questions and inquiry are valued
- Adults model and teach healthy sexual values and limits
- Servanthood to one another is encouraged
- Care and respect for others is modeled and encouraged

Merging mini-families

When you remarry, you will bring a host of things that must be merged. Unfortunately, as you might suspect, merging is very difficult. People are very attached to their stuff, their traditions and their way of doing everyday life. The merging process must be handled gently and gradually. What are some of the things families must merge?

- Material things: furniture, dishes, tools, clothing, books, pictures, cars, houses, time shares, bank accounts, camping gear, etc.
- Traditions and routines: food preferences, birthdays, saying grace, paying bills, time for dinner, celebrating holidays, weekends, privacy, sports, opening Christmas presents, vacations, visiting relatives, etc.
- Values and priorities: shopping, clothes, education, finances, honesty, church attendance, jobs, grades, accountability, curfews, etc.
- Communication and problem-solving: talk it all out vs. never talk; argue and yell vs. quiet and peaceful; right now vs. tomorrow; private talks vs. everyone involved; everyone talks at once vs. taking turns; etc.
- Family roles: oldest, youngest, tallest, only boy or girl, family clown, family hero, etc.
- Identity: names, residence, church, school, reputation, etc.
- Family rules: snacks, phone use, TV, chores, bedtimes, activities, curfews,
- Privacy: sharing a room, sharing a bathroom, car usage, sharing TV, game and sports equipment, etc.
- Family goals: retirement, college, vacations, etc.

The developing stepfamily

How does a new stepfamily develop? How does a group of virtual strangers with little in common and no shared history or traditions become something that resembles a family? Stepfamily expert Patricia Papernow has an answer. In *Becoming a Stepfamily*, Papernow explores in detail seven emotional stages she believes stepfamilies experience as they progress toward family identity and integration. During these stages, Papernow says that relationships, roles and alliances change. Each family member faces some unique challenges and has some key task to address.

In the first three stages, *Fantasy, Immersion* and *Awareness,* the family remains divided along biological lines, with the closest relationships, the "mini-families," represented by biological parents and their children. Relationships are stiff, often formal and seldom fluid. There tends to be a great deal of chaos and turbulence. Most divorces occur during these stages. In the middle stages, *Mobilization* and *Action,* the family structure begins to "thaw" and shift. Communication patterns become more open, rules for behavior begin to develop and the couple begins the process of becoming a team. In the later stages, *Contact* and *Resolution,* the new stepfamily solidifies with reliable, nourishing step-relationships. The average family takes about seven years to work through the complete cycle. Most of the time is spent working through the first three stages. We will examine these early stages in detail.

The Early Stages: Getting started without getting stuck

The stepfamily begins with family members biologically organized—most nourishment, agreement on rules, shared history and easy connections happen within the mini-families. This structure usually remains intact during the early stages and begins to shift in the middle stages, primarily through the efforts of the outsider (stepparent). The wish that remarriage will instantly create a new united family, and the gathering awareness that it will not, mark the progression through these stages. For most families, the key to starting the journey lies in letting go of some baggage—relinquishing enough of the fantasies, myths and "shoulds" to engage in the real work needed. Listening to one another and processing unrealistic expectations in an atmosphere of acceptance and encouragement is an important task of these early stages. It is critical that all family members be heard, because each will have a very different vantage point.

Stage One: *Fantasy—we are not in Kansas anymore!*
The journey begins with the adults in the family yearning to heal the pain created by divorce or death. Biological parents hope their new spouse will not only be a better partner, but a better parent as well. Stepparents hope to provide what had been missing (and be appreciated for it). Every new relationship comes with fantasies of how things will be. There are visions of everyone living happily ever after in an instant family filled with instant love. In most couples' fantasies, everyone in the stepfamily is an "insider." The stepparent believes, *"I love her so I'm bound to love her kids (and they'll love me)."* Or, "*They seem difficult now, but I'm sure things will be fine after we are all under one roof."* Biological parents are looking for someone to share the load of child rearing. Some individuals are looking for someone to rescue; others just want to do it right this time.

These wishes and fantasies come from several sources. Some are the result of previous losses and the legacy of hope inherent in becoming a new family. Other expectations come from unresolved childhood issues or past emotional wounds. Most couples bring an almost total lack of accurate information concerning stepfamily dynamics. Whatever the source, fantasies break down quickly in the face of the realization that stepchildren's loyalties remain with their biological parents, and stepparents often find themselves as outsiders in their spouse's old one-parent family. At this moment, stepparents are likely to feel disappointment, despair and loneliness more than love.

A plethora of emotions emerge. Some family members feel devastated, hopeless, and perhaps helpless; others feel betrayed or deceived; still others feel numb or drift into denial, as if ignoring or pretending will make the pain or confusion go away. The answer to the question, "*What has happened*?" is that stepfamily reality has just entered the picture. All the pre-conceived, mostly non-verbalized, even unrecognized myths and expectations carried into marriage have just crashed and burned before the family's very eyes. They know something is wrong, they just do not know exactly what it is or what to do about it.

The truth is, nothing will make the pain or frustration go away except hard work and a commitment to expose, evaluate and ultimately relinquish the myths that have been carried into the marriage. The key to survival during the fantasy stage of the journey is to keep talking and sharing, instead of getting stuck and blaming one another. The critical tasks are to understand and let go of myths and appreciate what is transpiring in the lives of the children. To accomplish this, each family member must bring to awareness and articulate their fantasies, wishes and shoulds. Only by "unpacking" the baggage—exposing these myths and expectations, especially those most unrecognized—can the family move to the next stage. Adults need to be patient with children, who may be acting out and having difficulty putting language to their feelings.

Stage Two: *Immersion-this seems overwhelming*

As the fantasies of the first stage turn into reality, the challenge of this stage is to "swim before you sink." The couple and family find themselves immersed in a host of problems, much like an army that is surrounded. The spouses are often so absorbed in their own feelings and so overwhelmed that they have difficulty listening to others, or even wanting to hear what others have to say. This is particularly true for the stepparent, who occupies an outsider position to the intensely connected biological parent and child and often ex-spouse. Stepparents find themselves assaulted by unexpectedly strong and negative feelings—jealousy, resentment, confusion and inadequacy—as they are subtly but consistently excluded. The biological parent, feeling less uncomfortable, may see these feelings as a lack of commitment to the new family—a frightening thought, as it signals another failure or loss.

Since stepfamily members lack knowledge of each other and do not share a common historical base, problem solving is extremely difficult. At this point, family members have no sense of a "family" perspective or a common agreed upon way to communicate or address problems, let alone solve them. The benchmark of this stage is a pervasive feeling that "something is wrong" but an inability to pinpoint or articulate the problems. The family has not yet jelled sufficiently to provide a safe place to openly share feelings or concerns. The family still remains split along biological lines, which means the insider family is experiencing less discomfort than the outsider family. There is still little clarity concerning the sources inherent in stepfamily structure that create predictable but sometimes intensely painful emotions (jealousy, feeling torn, lost or invaded, isolation, missing an absent parent, loyalty conflicts, etc.).

The key task of this stage is to "keep swimming" and to bear discomfort long enough to accurately name feelings and to hear other family members' experiences. A key danger comes from the unrealistic expectation that stepfamilies should function like first-time families. Problems can be seen as failures. Failure to negotiate this task often leads to shame (something's wrong with me) or blame (something's wrong with you). When shaming and blaming block effective communication, families become "mired in mud" and have difficulty moving to the next stage.

Dr. P. Note: The first two stages are where most stepfamilies get stuck.

Stage Three: ***Awareness-finally, we're making progress.***
This is the single most *critical stage* for the successful completion of stepfamily integration. Fading of the chaos and turbulence of stage two marks the beginning of this stage. Here the couple begins to develop a sense of what is happening in their lives and how it impacts the family as a whole. The family is ready to voice concerns with a reasonable expectation that they will be heard. An important goal of this stage is for couples to learn how to blame the situation and not each other and to name their concerns with the hope that they will be acknowledged and addressed. Clarity and self-acceptance begin to replace confusion and self-doubt. The key task of this stage is "mapping the territory," both for each individual and for the family. This means identifying one's own feelings and talking about personal needs that are not currently being met by the family. Family members must be able to bridge the gaps they have in their basic knowledge of one another to get a clearer picture of what each family member is feeling or needing.

During this stage, family members are beginning to piece together what is happening in their lives; they get a sense of where they are going as a family. During this stage, family members begin to understand and label sources of distress. The task is to maintain enough curiosity (tell me more) and empathy (it must be tough) in the face of differences and disappointments, so that each member's joys, pains, suggestions and requests can be voiced and heard.

Successful stepfamilies find a way to deal with confusion and disappointment and not give up. Family members are allowed to identify and articulate how stepfamily life "feels" for them. Fantasies and expectations are relinquished long enough to actively engage in the process of building a family out of virtual strangers.

Action Step: The challenges of beginning a stepfamily
Successful new stepfamilies find a way to bridge the gaps that separate family members. What are these gaps? They are the unique challenges found in every stepfamily—challenges that must be addressed.

- Gaps in empathy and understanding between family members
- Language gaps and communication issues
- Hostility, discomfort, or indifference that children often bring to their step relationships
- The struggles of being an outsider (jealousy, resentment, and inadequacy)

- The impact stepchildren have on the developing new couple relationship
- The challenge of negotiating even the most trivial of everyday family decisions
- The inappropriateness of the traditional parent role for the new stepparent
- The effect of unshared histories, and dissimilar traditions.
- Children's loyalty binds
- The lingering influence of an absent former-spouse
- Grieving the many, sometimes hidden, losses of the past. Allowing each person to grieve in his or her own way
- Expectations that now seem like impossible fantasies
- Dealing with children moving across households

How will you and your partner deal with these gaps? Successful stepfamilies discuss these issues and develop effective strategies *before* remarriage.

Dr. P. Rule: Successful stepfamilies start before the "I Do's" are ever said. They begin with prayerful consideration of all family members and a strong commitment to love, honor and respect each other. Successful stepfamilies begin when individuals take the first step to heal their wounds from the past. Finally, they begin when individuals see themselves as precious children of God, battered and bruised a little, experiencing the consequences of their choices, but forgiven and restored.

Partnering in a New Stepfamily

(I Peter 3:1-7)

Action Step: Write down what a healthy partnership looks like to you? What are your expectations? What are your negotiables? Your non-negotiables?

Partnership success

The success of your remarriage will rise and fall on the relationship you and your partner develop. When stepfamilies fail, it is because the couple relationship has failed. Yet, this relationship is often neglected and taken for granted. Why do you think this is true?

One reason is that parent-child relationships predate the marriage and put tremendous pressure on the new husband-wife team. Parents are torn between loyalty for their spouses and their children. For many remarrying adults, their children are still in chaos or at the very least, still need a good deal of care and nurturing. It is critical therefore, right from the beginning, to commit to building a marriage that works and lasts. Children of divorce and remarriage desperately need to see a marriage that works. Most remarrying couples know that building a new family will be hard work. Most know that remarriage will be much more complicated than a first-time remarriage.

Finding time to build a great relationship is a real challenge facing a new couple. The reality is that the relationship is in jeopardy almost instantly. Ask the average new couple about quality time and you will hear about parenting schedules, differences in child-rearing philosophies and handling stepsibling disputes. Most stepfamily couples spend their time putting out fires, negotiating complicated relationships and avoiding emotional land mines. If there are too many fires or too much intensity, the couple relationship will become strained, and the vital role of refreshing and sustaining one another will be damaged. Yet it is critical for a couple to build a relationship that works because the survival of a stepfamily depends on it.

Action Step: What is your plan to nurture the couple relationship?

The remarriage rule: marital satisfaction determines stepfamily stability.

If marriage satisfaction is high, tolerance of the normal conflicts of stepfamily life is correspondingly high. If satisfaction is low, tolerance for conflict is often so low that divorce occurs. Despite the importance of quality time together, most couples spend very little time working on "just" their relationship. In *How to Win as a Stepfamily*, Visher and Visher discuss some of the reasons for this: "Parent-child relationships have preceded the new couple relationship. Because of this, many parents feel that it is a betrayal of the earlier parent-child bond to form a primary relationship with their new partner. A primary couple relationship, however, is usually crucial for the continuing existence of the stepfamily. A strong adult bond can protect the children from another family loss, and it also can provide the children with a positive role model for their own eventual marriage relationship. The adults often need to arrange time alone to help nourish this important couple relationship" (p.77).

The stepparenting rule: finding a stepparent role that works for everyone
Finding a healthy role for the stepparent is a critical task for the couple. The stepparent-stepchild relationship is tentative and fragile in most stepfamilies and is a key determinant in marital success. The importance of finding a healthy stepparent role underlies a key difference between nuclear families and stepfamilies. In nuclear families, a troubled child has relatively little impact on a marriage, but a troubled marriage greatly affects the child. In a stepfamily, the marriage has little effect on the child because children generally have limited emotional investment in the new marriage. However, the child's emotional state has an enormous impact on the emotional wellbeing of the stepfamily marriage. This is because eventually the child's behavior will divide the stepparent, who is increasingly verbal and critical, and the biological parent, who becomes increasingly more defensive and annoyed with the stepparent's criticisms of his or her child.

This growing rift between parent and stepparent can easily sabotage the marriage. Both partners begin to feel misunderstood, threatened and unsupported by the other. Since the majority of couples spend little time thinking through the stepparent role, they are guided by pre-existing unrealistic expectations. Both experience shock when they realize the other does not share their views—as if love will make them see everything the same. Resolving this issue well will determine the future of the marriage and family. You and your partner must determine the roles the stepparent will play and when and how those roles will be implemented. What makes this task so difficult is that most couples normally do not cover this topic until they are in crisis—not the best time to solve problems.

Your marriage must become a safe place to share needs, requests, fears, hurts and disappointments. Can you love each other enough to work through these issues together? Can you focus on your partner's deep needs, even when you are upset and confused? Can you provide a safe place for your partner; a place where he or she is free to share while you listen non-judgmentally? Is it safe for your partner to share past failures or indiscretions? Can you re-think your expectations, placing them under the white-light of God's grace and mercy? God wants your marriage to be "rock-solid" and reflect his character.

Marriage types
In *For Better or For Worse*, Mavis Hetherington discusses the five types of marriages she has observed while conducting research fir the past forty years on divorce and

remarriage. According to Hetherington, the first three types have the highest risk of failure. She notes that marriage type seems to hold constant even in remarriage. That is, if you were in one type of marriage and divorced, your next marriage would likely be the same type. Which type fits you/your partner the best?

The pursuer-distancer marriage—the most common and the most divorce prone. One party, primarily the woman, confronts issues and initiates discussions. "Can't we talk more?" "Can't you turn off the TV for a while?" The other party, mostly men, avoids discussions and denies issues. "I need more space." "Get off my back." The wear and tear of this tug-of-war eventually exhausts the goodwill of the couple, leaving them empty and primed to split up. For couples locked into this pattern, change is impossible because balance and reinforce each other's position. Change takes both parties.

The disengaged marriage—the second most divorce-prone type features a couple who are self-sufficient and intimacy-avoidant. These couples share few things in common that keep relationships healthy and together. On the surface things may appear positive, but that appearance comes at the expense of talking about important subjects. The opposite of love is not anger but indifference. Indifference kills intimacy.

The operatic marriage—features two emotionally volatile individuals. These are extremists who do nothing in moderation. Even simple disagreements escalate into huge fights because both parties fuel the conflict and neither party "backs down." Volatility, however, soon takes a toll on these marriages.

The cohesive/individuated marriage—is the classic "baby boomer" marriage. These individuals are excellent at accommodating gender differences and display a strong sense of intimacy. They share responsibilities and grant each other a good deal of autonomy. Success in these marriages involves keeping a healthy balance between autonomy and togetherness.

The traditional marriage—has the lowest rate of divorce. This marriage works well if the couple shares a traditional interpretation of gender issues. The greatest challenge for this marriage type is change.

Building a solid marriage

How does a new couple build a healthy, solid marriage? In her book, *Becoming a Stepfamily*, Patricia Papernow talks about the qualities that make a marriage satisfying. Her list includes shared values and spiritual beliefs, shared rituals and gestures, a common problem-solving style, a similar way of looking at the world, and also small daily acts of self-sacrifice that signal an individual's willingness to put "we" above "me." Papernow refers to this as *middle ground.* It is her feeling that the balancing of differences and similarities leads to a successful remarriage. "All life with other people involves living with differences" (p. 40). She believes that finding the right blend of similarities and differences keeps a marriage fresh. "Stepfamilies often begin their lives together with deep cracks in their foundation, created by thin middle ground in the adult couple relationship. Fundamental and highly charged differences in understanding must be bridged for the new 'executive team' to succeed in the primary task of integrating step and biological subsystems" (p 41). Middle ground is a result; it comes from sharing life together, from placing more emphasis on positive than negative events and from continually looking for ways to nurture and serve one another.

A strong couple bond begins with several key ingredients: forgiveness, respect, love and acceptance. Strong healthy couples tend to make regular deposits into one another's "love bank." Deposits are made by spending quality time together and by acts of kindness and consideration. Healthy couples know a great deal of information about one another. They tell stories about their marriages that are positive and uplifting. Happy marriages are based on deep friendships. Committed partners listen to and are influenced by one another. Healthy relationships create an atmosphere where authentic sharing can happen. Needs are addressed openly and the couple can move fluidly *from my needs to your needs to our needs.* In strong marriages, couples share a deep sense of meaning and purpose. They search for ways to fulfill each other's hopes and dreams. Healthy couples are deeply aware of their flaws. They accept the fact that these flaws may, at times, create conflict, but they are committed to keeping the relationship strong. Building a strong couple bond follows the First Corinthian 13 model of agape love.

Why remarriages do not succeed

When remarrying couples consult me for premarital counseling, I share the statistics on remarriage success. Invariably they ask why so many remarriages fail. While there is no definitive answer to this question, there are some things I know. The ***number one*** cause of "remarriage death" is negativity. Couples who can stay positive, even when things are in chaos, seem to find a way to stay together. Couples that dwell on the negatives develop a viscous cycle of anger, blame and hurt that ultimately deals the marriage a mortal wound. The ***number two*** cause is unrealistic expectations and an inability or unwillingness to adjust these expectations after marriage. Impossible barriers are created when couples cannot accept one another or negotiate their expectations. Flexibility is a critical survival skill. The ***third*** leading cause of death is emotional wounds. Dealing with these wounds takes tremendous energy; energy that will render an individual emotionally unavailable to his or her new family. Emotional wounds make it difficult to objectively determine our source of pain; therefore we inevitably blame our partner or his or her children. A lifetime commitment to personal and spiritual health is another key survival skill. The ***fourth*** cause of death is unresolved guilt, anger or shame from prior relationships. Lack of closure means that any situation in your new relationship could trigger old feelings or wounds, making the new marriage look and feel like the old one. Completing the grieving process and letting go of the past is yet a third survival skill. The result of these causes of "remarriage death" is a lack of resilience, flexibility and effective problem solving. Unfinished business from the past makes it nearly impossible to give a new marriage, with all its challenges, the level of patience, commitment and tolerance it requires.

How will your remarriage look?

You have the ability to determine this. Take the time to review this chapter. Build your new marriage on the solid rock of respect, acceptance, tolerance and flexibility.

Understand that, just like you, your new partner is a flawed person who will try his or her best to be a good partner and parent. Anticipate (but do not catastrophize) the many ways that you and your partner will differ. Remember that "different" in a stepfamily usually translates as "wrong." Make your new marriage the primary relationship in your life. Today's children desperately need to see remarriages that work. Anticipate and confront some key remarriage "myths" such as, *Remarriage will give me an opportunity to correct earlier mistakes. Any one who loves me will instantly love my kids. My new partner will take over the parent role and do a better job than my last partner. Kids come first; the marriage will work itself out. My family will love my new spouse. We will be just like a first-time marriage.*

Parenting in a New Stepfamily
(Eph. 6:1-4)

Parenting is challenging in a stepfamily so it is critical to address as many issues as possible before remarriage. It is extremely likely that you and your partner will differ greatly in your parenting styles. This is because your style reflects your personality. Things you tolerate with ease will seem intolerable to your partner, and vice versa. Parenting in a stepfamily is "instant" parenting. There is no warm up period. Consequently, there are many issues to deal with immediately. The solution is to "walk in the door" with your eyes wide open. Be ready to let go of your pre-conceived notions of how things "ought" to be. Learn to take great care of yourself and keep your sense of humor. You cannot meet the growing emotional needs of your children if you have not taken care of your own needs.

Action Step: Many child-rearing disputes occur because parents have not developed clearly defined, agreed upon parenting goals. Without a clear vision of shared parenting, couples must "re-invent" the parenting wheel every time there is a dispute. When parents agree on goals and a definition of parenting, disagreements are reduced and limited to issues of methods (how do we achieve this in our child?).

What are your parenting goals?

How do you define effective parenting?

What values do you want to instill in your children?

Below are several important characteristics of effective parents. How many fit you?

- They learn what developing children need spiritually, physically, emotionally and cognitively.
- They work on their partner relationship.
- They dedicate significant effort to providing for their children's needs with love.
- They guide, nurture and protect their children.
- They develop themselves as healthy, growing individuals.
- They seek to understand what children need
- They teach children a healthy set of core values
- They love and value each child and thereby instills in each child a sense of being lovable and valuable
- They protect children from physical and emotional harm
- They provide firm, healthy boundaries
- They value each child's needs and teaches them how to articulate those needs

- They provide healthy nurturing and comfort
- They provide guidance, advice and support
- They teach life skills
- They teach the value of relationships
- They provide acceptance and approval
- They provide encouragement and appreciation
- They provide security
- They listen
- They model important character traits: forgiveness, tolerance, accepting responsibility, grieving, embracing change, accepting others, etc.
- They model a healthy reverence for God; help each child develop a personal, active faith

Healthy parenting exists in a healthy environment. Elements of this environment include: stability, good communication, forgiveness, personal boundaries, respect for privacy, clear rules and roles, fairness, acceptance of differences and social support. The normal challenges of parenting, however, are complicated in a stepfamily. Some of these stepfamily issues are listed below. These issues can subvert the real task of effective parenting. Discuss a plan for dealing with these issues.

- Custody issues
- Child support
- Children moving back and forth between households
- Jealousy among adults
- More adults to disagree on child-rearing philosophies
- Difficulty blending extra rules and roles
- Bonding issues
- Loyalty conflicts
- Less social support
- Emotional issues
- Finances
- Unresolved or ongoing legal issues

Common mistakes in stepfamily parenting

Trying to replace the absent parent. Many stepfamily parents wrongly assume that the way to create a healthy stepfamily is to eliminate the other parent from the child's life. Their reasoning is that the new family will be healthier for the children, who will be better of without the negative influence of the other parent. In this system, the stepparent immediately assumes a parental role and attempts to fill the role of the non-custodial parent. Children, however, never stop identifying with the absent parent. Family adjustment actually goes smoother if the child has access to the absent parent. Children will seldom see the absent parent the way the custodial parent does. Forcing a stepparent on the children too soon will cause undue emotional distress to children already overwhelmed with change and loss. Children do not immediately bond to total strangers, not matter how "nice" or well-intentioned.

Creating a false sense of togetherness. It is not uncommon for people to believe the myth that remarriage will give them an instant happy family. To make this dream come true, some couples engage in behaviors that attempt to force sameness on family members. Togetherness is a worthy goal and a process. Togetherness fosters a climate of healthy individualism coupled with care and concern for others. Sameness is fueled by fear, insecurity and control and discourages personal identity. Below are examples of ways couples force sameness in stepfamilies:

- Disagreements are not allowed.
- "Step" words are never used.
- No one knows they are a stepfamily.
- The stepparent must be called Mom or Dad.
- Family loyalty is highly emphasized.
- Stepsiblings are dressed alike to appear as though they belong together.
- Names are changed so that family members match.
- Children are pressured to play together.
- All family outings are together.
- Children are forced to choose one family.

These strategies are unrealistic, manipulative and dangerous. Jesus' teaching reminds us that identity comes from the inside, not from outward appearances. Forcing sameness perpetuates an untruth and forces the family to keep unhealthy secrets. Family members miss out on earning vital relationship skills and feel shame for being in the stepfamily. The solution is to celebrate differences while fostering togetherness and accept the fact that families integrate at their own pace. The lack of acceptance of the uniqueness of stepfamilies will fuel constant conflict and turmoil or the denial of reality.

Dramatically changing parent-child relationships. Many stepfamily parents are not aware of the stress that change and loss has on their children. Many try to implement changes that they feel will establish structure and consistency in their new home. Some dads look forward to the presence of a mom who will bring ordcr to thc family. When changes are introduced too quickly, children become stressed out, confused and disoriented, which leads to withdrawal or rebellion. Children tend to be one change "behind" their parents, which means that they are just getting comfortable with being in a single-parent home when their parents are preparing to remarry.

Denying problems and conflicts. Some stepfamily parents invest a great deal of energy denying that problems exist or that problems are minor and of no consequence. They subscribe to the unrealistic idea that in the "perfect family" problems do not exist, or that if they are ignored, they will go away. Problems are the norm in stepfamilies as family members learn to adjust to one another. Acknowledging problems and looking for healthy solutions is critical because children need to see adult role models handling conflict effectively.

The keys to effective stepfamily parenting are patience, tolerance and focus. Effective stepfamily parenting stays focused on the task—raising, healthy, Godly children.

Patience and tolerance will be needed, as this is a shared task. Set reasonable short-term parenting goals. Let the biological parent take the lead with his or her children. To the extent possible, seek to co-parent with the other adults involved with your children. Work as a team. Resolve petty disputes and tolerate annoying differences for the sake of the children. The most difficult reality of stepfamilies is that children need and want the involvement of all their parents. In Romans 12:18 Paul reminds us to be a peace with all. Your children are certainly worth it.

<u>Action Step:</u> Begin developing your parenting plan

- What do your children need from you?

- What changes do you need to make?

- What information do they need to have?

- How can you become more sensitive to their needs?

- How can you take better care of yourself?

- How will you co-parent with your partner? With your former spouse?

Developing a Healthy Stepparent Role

Mom to Sally, *Why don't you and Jerry* (Stepfather) *ever talk to each other?*
Sally to her Mom, *I can't talk to him, he doesn't listen or understand, besides he always says no or go ask your mother.*
Mom to Jerry, *Just try talking to her, she really wants your input. She's trying to reach out.*
Jerry to Linda (Mom), *I can't talk to her, I never understand what she wants. She doesn't listen to me anyhow. It's like I don't exist unless she needs something.*
Linda to Jerry, *Give her a chance to get to know you. I don't want to be the middleman here. Building a relationship takes time.*

Stepparenting is one of the toughest and most under-valued tasks a person can undertake. Our culture has not provided any positive models or guidelines for this important role. The media has given us the images of the wicked stepmother and the abusive, even incestuous stepfather. Unfortunately, stepparents sometimes fit this stereotype. The church has also struggled in this area. Most pastors have little understanding of the complexities of stepfamily life. Most churches focus on ministering to the nuclear family, which can leave stepfamily members feeling marginalized and even worse, like second-class citizens.

Stepparent challenges
In *Becoming Family,* Lauer and Lauer suggest that there are some unique reasons why the stepparenting role is so difficult to define.

Stepparents begin with expectations based on fantasy. All family members bring expectations about how the new stepfamily should be. Stepparents are no exception. Since the stepparent role is so ill-defined, many stepparents enter the stepfamily with a personal agenda, the most common being "the rescuer." The more unrealistic these expectations, the more likely the stepparent will be deeply disappointed and disillusioned. Examples of stepparent expectations include:

- Gratitude for accepting parental responsibilities
- Acceptance as an authority figure
- Instant acceptance as a family member
- Instant affection from the stepchildren
- Recognition and respect as a caring adult
- A settled, orderly life
- Exclusive one-on-one time with new spouse

These expectations are shattered almost instantly, as the stepparent discovers the realities of the "outsider" role. Instead of being hailed as the "White Knight" or finding themselves instantly loved and adored, stepparents find themselves embroiled in power struggles, ignored or looked at negatively, and feeling very disconnected from the other members of the family. Reactions resembling those below are more likely from stepparents.

- "I feel more like a maid than a mother."
- "My stepdaughter never seems to be grateful for anything I do."
- "After two years, I still feel like an outsider, like my wife and stepchildren are a group I will never be a part of."
- "I am beginning to wonder if my stepson will ever get over his hostility toward me."
- "I feel that every time I try to set some rules, it's like a declaration of war with my stepchildren."
- "I feel alone, unwanted and unappreciated."
- "I'm not sure my needs will ever matter."
- "If I would have known how hard this was…"

The term "stepparent" has negative connotations for most people. This is especially true of stepmothers. The original derivation of *step* is from the old English "steop" meaning orphaned or from death or loss. In the past, most "step" families were created due to the death of a parent. "Orphaned" children were taken in and raised by their new family. Today most stepfamilies are created by divorce and the term "step" has come to connote something inferior or undesirable. Stepparents are often not treated as "real" parents. Stepparents are seen as less likely to care for or be concerned about their stepchildren and more likely to be abusive. Consequently, children are assumed to be less loved or nurtured by a stepparent.

There is no consensus on the stepparent role. Roles such as son, daughter, worker, or student carry with them some fairly well defined and agreed upon parameters and expectations; not so with the role of stepparent. In most stepfamilies, there is absolutely no consensus on how this role will look, how much authority or control this role will have or how this role will be carried out. No one in the family, including the stepparent, is certain what this role should be. Even the person closest to the stepparent, the spouse who invited him or her into the family, is often uncertain about the stepparent role, and often the one most likely to feel in the middle or even change expectations when the stepparent and his or her children do not get along. The result is that stepparents often feel alone, without clear guidelines or expectations.

Without clear guidelines, most stepparents fall back on old roles, from childhood or previous relationships. Unfortunately, many stepparents become angry and defensive and lash out at family members, creating tremendous conflict in the family and especially between the spouses. The other common response is withdrawal. In this case, the stepparent pulls away from the family, and thus the family loses the benefits of a caring, concerned adult.

Children are also confused as to what their relationship to the stepparent should be. The stepparent is a virtual stranger, an unknown quantity. For them, the role of stepparent contains aspects of parent and non-parent. They realize the stepparent is an adult in their home, but certainly not one with whom they feel any closeness or safety. Most children will continue to look to their biological parent for support, nurturing and guidance. Some children never successfully bond with their stepparent.

You are required to engage in parenting behavior before you are emotionally bonded with the child. Bonding is the process of forming a secure, emotional attachment to another human being. In nuclear families, this process occurs over time, beginning with the birth of a child. Stepparents are rarely present at the birth of their stepchildren, yet they are often expected to respond with the same level of emotion and caring as if they were. Stepfamilies start with the stepparent and stepchild being virtual strangers. In addition, the spouse is extremely bonded to his or her children, leaving the stepparent feeling like an unwanted outsider. Since most stepfamilies are confused about the stepparent role, there is no sense of a timetable for relationship development between the stepparent and stepchild.

The dilemma of stepparenting is that stepparents enter the new stepfamily with no space designated for them, no parental roles open to them and no agreed-upon guidelines. Even if roles are available, most, if not all of them, are dependent on others for their performance. For example, a stepparent cannot lay claim to the role of parent unless the child's outside parent relinquishes that role. As long as the position of parent is not vacant, the stepparent cannot be a parent to his or her stepchildren. After examining the dilemma of the stepparent, Taube Kaufman, in her book *The Combined Family*, concluded that it seemed doubtful that stepparents could ever become effective parents to their stepchildren. To add to this confusion, we ask the stepparent to share a role with the previous parent in ways not clearly established or defined. Basically, we ask a stepparent and outside parent to share a role without telling them how this might be accomplished.

Questions that must be addressed

- Biological parent to prospective stepparent: "How will we integrate you into the life of my children?" "How soon should you begin playing a "parental" role?" "What role do you want to play?" "What obstacles or barriers do you see?" "Will you allow me to take the lead in parenting my children at first?" "Are we clear on household rules?"
- Prospective stepparent to biological parent: "What role(s) do you want me to play?" "Will you trust me with your children?" "What happens when we disagree?" "What do your children expect from me?" "If we agree on a role, will you support me?"

Clarifying the stepparent role

There really are a variety of roles a stepparent can play. The stepparent, the biological parent, the children, even the former spouse will contribute to what this role will be. Understanding and clarifying the stepparent role is a critical pre-remarriage task. This task involves several factors, such as, the roles the stepparent is willing and able to play, the needs of the children, the expectations of the biological parent and children and the level of involvement of the noncustodial parent. Everyone in the family needs to know what to expect and what is expected of them. Stepparents must understand that they enter the family as an outsider and that the role of parent belongs to the children's mother and father, whether they are gone forever or living down the street. Whatever role is chosen, relationships should progress slowly, with friendships developing long before discipline and other formal parental patterns are implemented.

Guidelines for becoming an effective stepparent

Carving out a healthy and acceptable role for the stepparent is critical to the survival of the stepfamily. Effective stepparents allow their role to develop gradually. Children and biological parents seem to adjust best when they are involved in the shaping of this role. Stepparents are most effective when the role they play is a natural one for them, utilizing their strengths and gifts in the family. Below are some guidelines for determining an effective stepparent role. Which will you struggle with?

Start small

Stepparents enter a new family with very little status compared to the biological parent. This status grows gradually as the child begins to view the stepparent as someone who can be trusted. The best initial approach is to be an observer—not the "new sheriff in town." The most effective first role should be that of monitor, someone who watches and listens but does not become too involved, too soon. Allow your stepchildren to relax and feel safe when you are there. Be present, but keep your agenda simple—"I'm here to be your friend."

Timing is everything

Resist the temptation to parent too soon, no matter what your spouse says or does. Your effectiveness as a parental figure is in direct proportion to the quality of the relationship you have developed with the child. Instant (step) parenting is a myth. Give yourself and your stepchildren time. Being patient and allowing a role to develop gradually is one of the hardest but most important things a stepparent will do. Generally speaking, the younger the child, the more readily the stepparent is accepted.

Respect the parental role of the same sex parent

Children need to have their relationship to the absent parent acknowledged and affirmed, whether that parent is dead or alive, loving or abusive. Pressure to abandon, to demean, or to ignore the existence of a parent places the child in an intense loyalty bind that will inhibit his or her ability to form a relationship with the new stepparent. The task of the stepparent is not to replace the non-custodial or absent parent, but to find a role that complements the role of the same-sex biological parent. As much as possible, seek to involve the other parent in important events in their child's life.

Get "buy-in" from the biological parent

Developing an effective stepparent role is not the individual task of the stepparent, but a task of the entire family. This is a key task for the biological parent, who must assume leadership in the development and implementation of the stepparent role. Effective stepparenting is not simply an extra activity that takes place in an unused corner of the family. It is critical for the new family's survival. The biological parent must pass on the parenting role to the stepparent in front of the children. Be sure your role has your spouse's blessing.

Support the role of the biological parent

Stepparents should find a role that compliments and supports the biological parent. A good example is that of a neutral sounding board for the spouse, someone who listens to his or her frustration about the children without criticism. Stepparents can also provide input and observation to the biological parent. Sometimes a stepparent will spot problems that the biological parent is not ready to acknowledge or deal with. In such cases, the stepparent must give the parent time to move through the issues. Forcing views on the biological parent or openly disagreeing with them will inevitably bring conflict. Mini-families do not change quickly.

Allow the role to reflect your unique strengths

The stepparent's role is an expression of his or her personal style, gifts and strengths and can complement the style of the other parent. It is not unusual for the strengths of a stepparent to be appreciated several years later; strengths that earlier may have been regarded as detrimental. Be patient, there will be opportunities where your strengths will be valued. Be yourself, stay with your strengths.

More than punishment

Parenting is far more than discipline or punishment. The purpose of discipline is to build character. Discipline and punishment are not identical. Unfortunately, some stepparents focus on punishment and thereby narrowly define their role. They wrongfully assume that their primary role is to immediately establish order and discipline in the new family. However, roles such as "new sheriff in town" can intimidate, confuse and alienate children. The stepparent should enter the area of discipline very slowly. Most children need 1-2 years before they are ready to accept discipline from a stepparent. At first, allow the biological parent to administer discipline. Co-parenting with the spouse allows the children to ultimately view the stepparent as a viable authority figure. In the meantime, develop other roles—friend, mentor or coach.

Find your niche

Every family is unique. Find a relationship with your stepchildren that fits your personality and reflects their needs and circumstances. Consider roles such as teacher, scout leader or coach. Approach the role of "parent" only after a genuine relationship with the stepchildren has been achieved. Choose a role that makes it easy for the children to move toward you.

The role should be mutually suitable

The best predictor of stepparent success seems to be the development of a mutually suitable role between the stepparent and the stepchild. The amount of closeness or distance, the content of the role, the amount of discipline and nurturance given by the stepparent must be a good fit for both. Involving the child in the development of the stepparent role increases the likelihood that a bond will develop. What kind of stepparent role is the child looking for?

Become an "'intimate outsider"

This is a term is used by Patricia Papernow I her book, *Becoming A Stepfamily*. She observes that even in the most intimate relationships, the ongoing presence of another same-sex biological parent (dead or alive) leaves the stepparent in a somewhat more distant position than the biological parent. At times this role can enable a stepparent to be a special resource. Because they have more emotional distance than biological parents, they may be more objective and much less likely to overreact on sensitive subjects. This role is so important to understand and become comfortable with. Some stepparents focus on the outsider part and become distant, both physically and emotionally. Some focus on the insider part and assume too much too soon in the relationship, often resulting in rejection from children and huge disappointment. With time and patience, you can make a real difference in the life of your stepchildren and play a valuable role that often the biological parent cannot play. Be yourself. Be an observer and a partner.

Take great care of yourself
Stepparenting cannot be all giving and no taking—that leads to burnout and resentment. Take time for yourself. Nourish and nurture the relationship with your spouse. Enjoy the journey. Do not create unnecessary stress by thinking you have to figure it all out the first month.

Let Christ be your role model
Jesus was a great friend. He was secure, kind and compassionate. He was generous with his love. He looked deep inside and saw the best in others. He came to serve not to be served. He never took advantage of others because of his status. He forgave completely. Love your stepchildren with a pure heart. Love from your fullness in Christ.

Dr. P. Rule: The key to developing a healthy, effective stepparent role is to discuss and define it *before* marriage. Even then, the role will need some fine-tuning after marriage. The ultimate goal is to become someone with an objective view, who cares deeply for the child and the family. Key traits of a great stepparent include patience, flexibility and adaptability. The bottom line however is the children—you do not have to love them like their biological parent does, but you must be willing to invest yourself in their lives. Agape love is a wonderful metaphor for stepparenting. Move into the stepparent role slowly and gently. Try to remember that this is just as tough for the child as it is for you. You will not always like them and they will not always like you. Take your cue from God's big heart; He has enough room for all of us. Find something special about each child. Be yourself and find a niche that works for you.

Action Step: What will your role look like? Take some time and think through the kind of stepparent role that fits you.

Part Four:

Remarriage Readiness

Are you ready to remarry? Are your children ready for remarriage? Are you and your partner ready to remarry? These are obviously very important questions. If you have worked through the issues we have presented in this workbook, you are now "ready" to address the issue of remarriage readiness. Take a moment and look back. You and your children (and perhaps your partner) started from a place of grief and loss. You negotiated a healthy "ending" and are now poised for a new beginning. You have taken a number of emotional and spiritual growth steps and you have partnered with God, and a few others, on your journey. Celebrate this achievement.

Remarriage readiness checklist
Below is a summary of personal steps we have challenged you to take. Each should be checked as you prepare for remarriage.

- ❑ I have explored the issues surrounding my divorce or the death of my spouse
- ❑ I can clearly articulate my "story" which focuses on taking responsibility for my actions and the lessons I have learned.
- ❑ I have examined God's Word relative to my situation
- ❑ I understand the need for grieving my losses and I have, in fact, grieved those losses.
- ❑ I am connected to and participating in a faith community
- ❑ I have learned to take great care of myself and my children
- ❑ I am clear about the baggage and expectations that what I bring to a new marriage
- ❑ I understand the challenges and realities of stepfamily life
- ❑ I am developing a personal stepparent role that is flexible and tolerant
- ❑ I have confronted my unrealistic expectations
- ❑ I relate to others based on my fullness in Christ
- ❑ I am clear about the distinctions between "real self" and "false self" dating
- ❑ I respect the boundaries of others
- ❑ I can articulate my needs, passions and values
- ❑ I have "let go" of my relationship with my former spouse
- ❑ I have addressed/resolved issues surrounding my sexuality
- ❑ I am working through any issues of abuse, neglect or abandonment
- ❑ I am addressing my emotional wounds

Were you able to place a check mark beside each statement? If so, you are ready to move to the last section of this workbook. If you left more than two blank, you may not be ready to move forward. It would be beneficial to review that section of the workbook or discuss the issues with a friend, pastor or counselor

Are My Children Ready for Remarriage?

Most children are not ready when we are

Remarriage can be tough on children; most children are not prepared for their parents to remarry. This is often difficult for remarrying adults to understand because they are so happy and so desperately want a better life for themselves and their children. The typical remarrying adult assumes his or her children will be as happy as they are. They reason that since they were unhappy in their prior marriage, the children were probably also unhappy. Or they believe that they have sheltered their children from the pain of a death or broken marriage. They further reason that since they are now happy with a new love and soon to be new spouse, their children must be equally happy. ***Nothing could be farther from the truth***. Children struggle with the losses and changes resulting from a death or divorce, even many years after the event. In addition, children do not adapt as quickly as adults. Most children are just getting over the loss of their family and settling in to the routine of single-parent life when they discover that mom or dad is getting remarried. Ask the average child and he or she will tell you about a desire to return to the original family, about missing the non-custodial parent, about spending less and less time with the custodial parent and about fears and uncertainties concerning the future. In the midst of their own personal changes, parents need to be sensitive to the adjustment needs of their children.

Helping children adjust to parental changes

When parents remarry, children can feel trapped by their feelings of love and identification with the absent biological parent and the growing, yet confusing attachment to the new stepparent. The absent parent may add to this distress by encouraging negative feelings about the stepparent. Children may harbor resentment against the absent parent for abandoning them or not visiting them, or most common, breaking promises. They may also show hostility toward the new stepparent as a defense mechanism against feelings of betrayal. The result is a very confusing state of affairs for children. Many children cope with all this by withdrawing or acting out. Below are ways you can help your children adjust to these changes:

- Let your children know that you understand how upsetting it is to have so many changes, about which they have no say, going on in their lives. Answer their questions and address any misperceptions.
- Help your children control the behavior they are displaying. Feelings and behavior are two separate things, and it is the behavior, not the feelings, that must be controlled.
- Help your children find nondestructive ways to express the physical and emotional energy caused by angry feelings.
- Give children as many choices as possible for different aspects of their lives. These choices help them feel they have more control, often leading to increased cooperation.
- Be patient with your children, give them reassurance, time to talk and straight answers to their questions.

- Remember that children live by feelings, not words, and are sensitive to subtle expressions and feelings to which grown-ups, dependent on words, have become dulled.

Understanding a child's transition from nuclear to stepfamily

There tends to be a common sequence of events and feelings that children experience in transitioning from a nuclear family to a stepfamily. Understanding this sequence of events can help you appreciate your children's grief and recovery issues.

Parents decide to separate and the father moves out; the children still love and want to see their father. They may secretly fear that he no longer loves them or that they may have caused him to leave. In part, this fear is due to the fact that most parents who leave begin withdrawing from their children months before. The children still want and love their mother, with whom they now reside. They typically become more dependent on the single parent in the home.

If the separation is caused by an affair, children can become extremely sensitized. Most children strongly identify with the "abandoned "parent. In many cases, the children are subtly encouraged not to be cooperative with the leaving parent's new living arrangements, especially if another person is involved. In *Second Chances,* Judith Wallerstein suggests that in cases of marital infidelity, children come to accept the parent's new partner less than 10% of the time.

When their mother remarries, the children may see the new stepfather as bringing either new security or a new threat. If they see him as a new sense of security, they may find it easier to let go of anger at their biological father. If the children continue to see their biological father, they may feel secure and willing to risk a relationship with their stepfather. On the other hand, the children may see their new stepfather as a threat to whatever security was established in the single-parent home. They may fear he will hurt their mother or them as their father did. They may feel that their mother has stopped loving them. If she loves them, they might reason, "Why does she want to get married?" To answer these questions, they may begin to test her to see how much she "really" loves them, and if she will really stay.

When the father remarries, the children experience another set of similar feelings. They may view remarriage as another desertion. Often, children are still dealing with the original loss of the father. They may fear their new stepmother will come between them and their father. This is especially true with female children. They may wonder if he will continue to love them. These fears and the sense of being abandoned are even greater if there are children in the new marriage. Acting out or extreme withdrawal are common coping strategies as children attempt to survey the new territory and see where (and if) they fit.

Children may regard the loss of a parent either by death or divorce as a betrayal. They will typically cling to the other parent for support. They believe they will be able to handle the loss with the other parent and that they will take care of one another. Remarriage after a death is seen as another major loss and a betrayal. The degree of the remaining parent's love is questioned, and the new stepparent is seen as coming between them and their biological parent. The result is fear, anxiety, insecurity and acting out.

A stepmother seems to be particularly suspect in remarriages after a death. She is perceived as coming between the children and their father or between the children and the memory of their mother. If the stepmother is gentle and kind, the children may think they are right in feeling annoyed because she is trying to replace their mother. If she is hostile, they may feel convinced that they have been wronged. If she steps in and tries to take the biological mother's place by providing love, guidance and nurturing, the children may respond by idealizing their mother and rejecting their stepmother.

Stepchildren often feel that if they have a good relationship with one parent, that the other parent will be angry or hurt and reject them. Children must constantly make decisions about whom to love and how much to love them, whom to give attention and affection to, and how much attention and affection to give. It is important to remember that divorce and remarriage have forced these children to make decisions they never wanted, and are ill equipped, to make. For most children it is a "lose-lose" proposition.

In general, children who are encouraged to have access to both biological parents are more able to relax and develop a relationship with the stepparent. They are not threatened with the loss of their biological parent, and therefore do not perceive their stepparent as taking the biological parent's place. Nor do they feel the stepparent is trying to usurp the position or role of their other parent. Children need to be constantly reminded of their place in the family, of their continued connection to both of their parents, and of the important part they play in being a member of the remarried family. Children need to be reassured that their parent does not care for or love stepsiblings or their stepparent more than them, only differently.

Children who visit part time represent a major challenge. This scenario almost always involves a father's children who may live in the next state, but probably live less than a few miles away. Often the father has a hard time deciding how much time he should spend with his children when they are with him. Generally it is best for him to spend some time alone with his children. Actually, time alone is important for each subsystem in the family: the couple, the mother and children, the father and children, and the stepparent and stepchildren. It is easier for a Dad to accept his stepchildren if he has alone time with his children. This tends to reduce his guilt and helps him feel he can be both a father and a stepfather without alienating or cheating anyone on time or attention.

The above description is fairly typical of the sequence of events in the life of a child of divorce and remarriage. A major question that arises for children after a remarriage is whether or not contact with the noncustodial parent will be reduced or even cut off. Children also wonder how and if they will fit into the scheme of the new family.

Remarriage struggles for children

Remarriage brings about many changes for children. Unfortunately, most children see things happening all around them over which they have absolutely no control. The result can be a great deal of stress. There are a number of situations that are particularly stressful to children, for example:

- Hearing their biological parents argue (over the phone, at the door, etc.) and say negative things. They may wonder if they are to blame.
- Not being able to see their noncustodial parent and resenting the stepparent for this.
- Feeling blamed for everything that goes wrong.
- Hearing their parent and stepparent fight, and feeling that it's always about them.
- Seeing their parents do more for stepsiblings than for them.
- Having stepsiblings get into their stuff and invade their privacy.
- Feeling unwanted and often testing those feelings via acting out.
- Fearing the noncustodial parent will love the stepsibling more than them.
- Feeling angry and depressed and wishing it could all be the way it was before the divorce or death.
- Having a stepparent tell them what to do and resenting it.
- Feeling that it's up to them to make the new household "work."
- Feeling like pawns or messengers between two biological parents who are still bitter.

Our experience is that children take at least a year longer to adjust to changes than adults. With the time between the death of a spouse or a divorce, and dating and remarriage getting shorter and shorter, children often have difficulty keeping up with the changes their parents are making. What this means is that long after your remarriage, your children may still be struggling with the prior divorce or death of a parent. Adolescents find it particularly difficult to adjust to a stepfamily arrangement. About one-third of adolescent boys and one-fourth of girls disengage from their stepfamilies, spending less and less time at home. Some adolescents leave the family altogether, either moving in with the other parent or with a friend or relative. For many, the energy to adjust to a new set of rules and people is just not worth the effort.

What children want to know

Children really want to know how their life will be affected. They are less interested in the emotional ups and downs of their parents than they are in practical issues, such as where they will live, where they will attend school, or how often they will be able to see their friends or absent parent. Children want to know which things will change and which will stay the same. They are uncertain if they will fit in or how they will be treated. The more time you spend answering your children's questions and addressing these critical issues, the better your children will adjust to remarriage and stepfamily life. Here are some basic guidelines:

- Make sure the new stepparent-to-be and the stepchild are not rushed into the first introduction.
- When the time is right, used relaxed gatherings of friends to make the introduction.
- Help your partner understand that you have no expectations with regard to his or her child.

- Do not allow the prefix “step” to be used until you are sure the child is comfortable with the new relationship.
- Involve the child as much as possible in plans that affect him or her.
- Help your partner maintain his or her normal routine with his or her child in the early stages, without interfering.
- Be honest, but do not burden the child unnecessarily with information about the new relationship.
- Do not involve a child in a relationship until you are both serious. In other words, there are men or women you will date that your child may never meet.

Steps to preparing your children for remarriage

Remarriage is another change in your child’s life and can re-create fear and uncertainty in your child. The steps outlined below can help allay your child’s fears and prepare them emotionally for remarriage.

- Tell your children about your pending remarriage long before it occurs.
- Arrange for your children to spend quality time with their future stepparent and stepsiblings.
- Reassure your children that your love for them will not change because of your pending remarriage.
- Reassure your children that their relationship with the non-custodial parent will remain intact and unchanged.
- Do not paint a rosy, bigger-than-life picture of the new family.
- Do not introduce the new stepparent as a replacement for the absent parent.
- Be candid about any obvious changes that will impact them.
- Answer their questions realistically.
- Do not minimize their feelings or concerns.
- Normalize their feelings and respond to their concerns with gentleness.
- Encourage your children to share their expectations about the new family.
- Be sensitive to their grieving and their hopes of re-uniting their nuclear family.
- Allow them to be involved in as many choices and decisions as is reasonable.
- Keep boundaries and rule clear; do not soften your rules or over-indulge your children because of guilt.
- Create opportunities for stepsiblings to have fun together and share their stories.
- Address resistance directly. If children oppose the marriage, do not allow them to believe they can control your choices. Discuss their concerns but stand firm.
- Read helpful books together
- Attend a stepfamily support group
- Consult a pastor or family counselor.

Things to understand about children and remarriage

Children have their own perceptions of the new situation and the role they may be playing. Understanding the viewpoint of the child can give a new couple an important perspective from which to assist the child in transitioning to a new home and family. Children see things from a very different point of view, for example:

- A child does not see his or her parents as divisible.
- A small child has no yardsticks by which to measure his or her parents.
- A child’s world is very small.

- A child wants conformity and uniformity.
- A child has no autonomy.
- A child almost always harbors the hope that his or her parents will eventually reconcile.
- A child craves parental approval.
- A child can sniff out a lie at twenty paces.
- A child sees and hears much more than most adults realize.
- A child does not require material compensation for emotional trauma.

Many children have anxieties and fears. Remarriage can heighten fears of being abandoned or losing love, and create high levels of stress. Before remarriage, it is helpful to discuss issues surrounding the divorce, even if these have been covered earlier. For example, children should be given concrete reasons why the marriage ended and why reconciliation will not occur. They need to be reassured that both parents love them and that they are in no way responsible for the divorce. They need as little change and as much consistency as possible. They need to know where they will live and with whom, when they will see each parent and any other important facts that may affect them.

Once a remarriage is planned, children will display a variety of emotions and reactions. Some are looking forward to new relationships; many are suspicious and tentative. Most children are not looking for a new parent; most are still grieving the loss of the biological parent. For many children, a double loss is experienced with remarriage. First, it is the end of the marriage of their parents and the loss of one parent. Second, with remarriage, comes the loss of the security of the single-parent home and the loss of attention from their one remaining parent. No matter how much in love the new couple is or how wonderful the stepparent, or how well off they will now be financially, very few children see the remarriage as anything but another loss over which they had no control. Be patient and supportive with your children.

It is difficult to know exactly how much a child is capable of understanding. It is safe to say that children have probably developed some ideas as to why Mom and Dad have separated and divorced. They might have trouble understanding why Mom or Dad might want to remarry. Remember that children are often one adjustment behind the adult. They may just be settling into the routine of a single-parent home while you are ready to remarry.

Discussing remarriage with your children

- Give children concrete reasons why your marriage ended and why reconciliation is impossible.
- Point out that the children are not responsible for the divorce and that they did not cause it; nor can they bring the marriage back again.
- Reassure the children that they are still loved and cared for by both parents.
- Allow your children an opportunity to express feelings of sadness, anger and fear that they may have about the remarriage.
- Explain and reinforce some basic facts: where they will live, who will take care of them, when they will see each parent, where they will attend school, etc.

- It is best if the children can maintain positive feelings toward both parents. Do not blame or demean the other parent.
- Try to maintain consistency in your children's lives. If possible, avoid simultaneous changes, such as schools, homes, babysitters, etc.

Below are some questions a future stepparent should think about and discuss with his or her new partner. These questions will help the two of you begin to formulate a healthy stepparent-stepchild relationship.

- How much does the child know about why the parental marriage broke down?
- How much does and should the child know about his or her parent's feelings for a new partner?
- How can a parent and his or her new partner know when the child is ready to meet the new partner?
- How much should a parent and his or her new partner inform a child about plans for the future?

Have your children talk about some of their concerns and questions. Give them an opportunity to voice their concerns in a safe, non-threatening environment. The following are possible questions for them to think about and discuss. Tailor these questions to your situation, for example, just beginning to date, introducing a serious partner or perhaps the prospective stepparent.

- What are some things you would like your Mom or Dad to know about their dating?
- If Mom or Dad has already introduced you to a person he or she is very serious about, share your feelings or concerns.
- How do you think it might be different, living with a stepparent?
- What language would you prefer using when referring to a "step" parent?
- What are some things you would like to know that would make it easier?
- If you could give advice to a new stepparent, what are the three most important things you would tell him or her?
- What advice would you give a kid who's getting a new stepparent?
- What actions can a stepparent and stepchild take to get along better?
- What's the best time you've ever had with _____ (the stepparent)?
- Do you like _________ (the stepparent) to go to the parent-teacher conferences?
- Do you like it when __________ (the stepparent) attends your games, plays, or other programs?
- What can you do to help ________ (the stepparent) like you?
- What can ________ (the stepparent) do to help you like him or her?

Children's readiness issues

There are some factors that clearly highlight a child's readiness (or not) for remarriage. How many of these statements are true for your children? If more than several factors are present, it is unlikely that you and your children are ready for remarriage at this time. Disrespectful to your partner

- Refuses to accept your partner as a stepparent

- Struggling with loyalty conflicts
- Acting out at school
- Depression/ mood swings
- Still grieving the loss of the nuclear family
- Unclear about the divorce
- Addictions/ self-destructive habits
- Failing grades in school
- Disobedient at home
- Opposes the remarriage
- Identity issues
- Feels guilty/responsible for the divorce

If more than three of these factors are present, please consider addressing them before you remarry. Talk to your pastor or a counselor about the issues raised. Do not make your child the scapegoat or focal point however. Deal with these issues in a family counseling environment that does not target one child as the "problem."

Action Step: Talk to your children. Do not assume they are okay. Develop a plan to help your children through the pre-remarriage process.

Am I Ready to Remarry?

"How do you really know when you are ready to get remarried?" is a question Jeff hears often in counseling. In many ways, that question started the process that ultimately became the book you are now reading. Actually, we have spent this entire workbook addressing various aspects of this question. Before you are ready to consider remarrying, you must have some areas of your life under control. This chapter will help you identify those areas and determine your personal remarriage readiness. The next few pages contain a number of questions that are designed to help you explore various aspects of remarriage readiness. Read this information carefully and answer the questions honestly. Less than 20 % of remarrying individuals go through this process, so congratulations. Before you begin, pause and ask God for courage and wisdom, wisdom to address these issues honestly and courage to act on your readiness decision (Eph. 3:20).

First, let us review some facts.

- Most individuals remarry before they are emotionally ready.
- Many individuals remarry with unfinished issues from their prior relationships.
- Most individuals do not fully appreciate or consider their children's needs before remarrying.
- Most individuals, and certainly their children, have not adequately grieved the losses caused by death or divorce.
- Most individuals do little or no divorce recovery work after a divorce or before remarriage.
- Most individuals are not as far along in their own divorce recovery as they think.
- Most individuals are *clueless* about the demands and challenges of stepfamily life.
- Most individuals do not take premarital counseling seriously.
- Most individuals do not consult their pastor or godly counsel before dating or getting engaged.
- Many individuals detach from their support groups when they begin dating seriously.
- Most individuals have no one in their life holding them accountable for their choices or spiritual development.
- Nearly 90% of divorced or widowed individuals eventually remarry.
- 1500 remarriages occur every day
- Over 60% of remarriages end in divorce.

The point is…

The point is we believe most people who remarry ***are not ready.*** If you are not convinced, just look at that last figure—over 60% of remarriages end in divorce. That is the bad news. The good news is that your remarriage can be successful if you are willing to honestly evaluate your personal remarriage readiness. We have explored many emotional and spiritual tasks and growth activities that must be addressed after a death or divorce. We have discussed some critical information about communication, problem solving and stepfamily life that you absolutely must know. What follows are twelve "success indicators." These indicators are guidelines or markers that you can use to objectively assess your remarriage readiness. One thing our culture has taught us: it is far easier to get married than to stay married.

The true source of remarriage success

The following twelve "indicators" have been developed from our personal experience, our work with singles and stepfamilies and from the writings of many experts in the fields of marriage, divorce and remarriage. The most important source, however, is God's Word, where He asks us to patiently and painstakingly apply His truths to our struggles and choices (Romans 12:1-2; Philippians 2:12-13; I Timothy 2:21-24; II Timothy 3:16-17). God knows that only obedience brings lasting peace and joy. The ultimate readiness factor is your answer to this question, "What is your first love?" If the answer is Christ, then you will remarry from your fullness. If your answer is a person or money, security, sex, power or anything else, then you will remarry, at least in part, to have those needs met. A spouse cannot fill the empty spaces— that is God's work.

Below is our list of success indicators. We will examine each of these in detail. As you read through these indicators, you must ask yourself honestly, "How well am I really doing in these areas?"

1. Adequate time has elapsed between divorce/death and contemplating remarriage.
2. Losses incurred through the divorce have been acknowledged and dealt with.
3. Legal issues from prior relationships are resolved.
4. Emotional issues with your prior spouse have been resolved; you are in a fairly healthy co-parenting relationship with your ex-spouse.
5. Your children's emotional issues concerning divorce and remarriage have been adequately addressed.
6. You recognize that a new stepfamily will be unique, not a remake of your old nuclear family.
7. You are able to embrace and involve your children's extended family.
8. Custody issues are resolved and in place.
9. Parenting time runs smoothly.
10. You are involved in a church and a small group.
11. You are growing spiritually and have at least one person to whom you are accountable.
12. Personal issues surrounding your divorce/death of spouse have been addressed.

Remarriage Success Indicators

1. Adequate time has elapsed between divorce/death and contemplating remarriage.

As a rule of thumb, it takes one to three years to grieve a serious loss, such as a death. A divorce is also a serious loss that is compounded by numerous life changes. These changes can be extremely stressful and emotional. Many of these changes have associated losses, often resulting in more stress and emotional upheaval. Among the changes that may occur include changes in friends, income, residence, church, neighborhood, school or support group. Emotions such as grief, anger, guilt, fear or abandonment are not uncommon. Many losses are involved, such as the loss of a dream, loss of financial security, loss of support, even the loss of children. Adjusting to these changes and losses can be very difficult. Taking the time to adequately deal with these changes, losses and adjustments is perhaps the greatest gift you can give yourself.

Point to Ponder: We recommend at least two years before you contemplate remarrying. We believe most couples remarry too quickly. For example, 60% of divorced individuals remarry within two years. This means many couples are remarrying long before the grieving process has ended.

Action Step: Take an inventory of the changes you have made

___Residence
___Income
___Church
___Friends
___Community
___Time with children
___ Job
___ Support group
___ Relatives
___ Social activities
___ Other

Think about the losses you have incurred (see Indicator #2):

___ Esteem
___ Financial
___ Security
___ Support
___ Lifestyle
___ Dreams
___Career
___Home
___Time with children
___Friendships
___Death
___Distance

Identify and place a check by the adjustments you have made

___Single-parent
___Moving to new a residence
___Starting a new job
___Working for the first time
___Living on less income
___New church
___ New school for children
___ Making new friends
___ Working with a limited budget
___ Obtaining credit in your own name
___ Moving to another city/state/country
___ Other

How long has it been since your divorce/the death of your spouse?

___ Less than one year
___ One year
___ Two years
___ Three or more years

Emotion Checklist (check all that apply)

- ❑ Abandoned
- ❑ Apathetic
- ❑ Anxious
- ❑ Ambivalent

- ❑ Apologetic
- ❑ Ashamed
- ❑ Bitter
- ❑ Bored
- ❑ Bitter
- ❑ Confident
- ❑ Confused
- ❑ Content
- ❑ Comforted
- ❑ Delighted
- ❑ Defeated
- ❑ Depressed
- ❑ Disappointed
- ❑ Discouraged
- ❑ Disgusted
- ❑ Enraged
- ❑ Envious
- ❑ Excited
- ❑ Exhausted
- ❑ Fearful
- ❑ Glad
- ❑ Grateful
- ❑ Guilty
- ❑ Happy
- ❑ Hateful
- ❑ Heart-broken
- ❑ Helpless
- ❑ Hopeful
- ❑ Hopeless
- ❑ Hysterical
- ❑ Independent
- ❑ Indifferent
- ❑ Inferior
- ❑ Insecure
- ❑ Inspired
- ❑ Impatient
- ❑ Irritated
- ❑ Jealous
- ❑ Joyful
- ❑ Joyless
- ❑ Judged
- ❑ Jubilant
- ❑ Lonely
- ❑ Loved
- ❑ Loyal
- ❑ Miserable
- ❑ Misunderstood
- ❑ Needy
- ❑ Neglected
- ❑ Nervous
- ❑ Optimistic
- ❑ Overjoyed
- ❑ Overwhelmed
- ❑ Peaceful
- ❑ Pessimistic
- ❑ Powerful
- ❑ Preoccupied
- ❑ Quiet
- ❑ Rejected
- ❑ Relieved
- ❑ Reluctant
- ❑ Resentful
- ❑ Resilient
- ❑ Restless
- ❑ Sad
- ❑ Secure
- ❑ Selfish
- ❑ Shocked
- ❑ Sorry
- ❑ Smart
- ❑ Supported
- ❑ Suicidal
- ❑ Surprised
- ❑ Tense
- ❑ Terrible
- ❑ Thankful
- ❑ Tired
- ❑ Trusting
- ❑ Ugly
- ❑ Unappreciated
- ❑ Unhappy
- ❑ Unlovable
- ❑ Unsure
- ❑ Unwanted
- ❑ Useful
- ❑ Useless
- ❑ Violent
- ❑ Weary
- ❑ Welcome
- ❑ Well
- ❑ Whole
- ❑ Withdrawn
- ❑ Worried

This list is from Burns and Whiteman's excellent book, *Fresh Start*. Look at the total number of emotions (adjectives) you checked. How many are positive? How many are negative? If the number of negatives far outweighs the positives, there is clearly some emotional recovery work yet to be done.

List any patterns in the adjectives you checked:

How many of the following are true for you?

- ❑ I have been living successfully and independently alone for several years.
- ❑ I am comfortable with solitude, normal socializing and with myself.
- ❑ I have addressed any emotional wounds from my divorce and am in recovery now for me, not for anyone else.

- ❑ I understand that a blended family is not a re-creation of the nuclear family.
- ❑ I understand that if I remarry, I will have to adjust to numerous individuals, some not living with me but related in some way to my new spouse or his or her children.
- ❑ I am not now addicted to or over-using any substance, activity or relationship.
- ❑ If I am struggling with abuse or an addiction, I am currently and will remain in active treatment.
- ❑ I am able to verbalize my needs without fear or dependency.
- ❑ I can handle conflicts without attacking, avoiding, denying, controlling or fleeing.

If most of these are true, great, you are emotionally healthy and growing. If many of these statements are not true for you, please consider talking to your pastor or a counselor.

<u>Rating Indicator #1:</u> Using a scale from one to five, rate your current level of readiness on this indicator. For example, a "1" would indicate that you have been divorced less than one year and have done little or no work on your situation. A "5" on the other hand, would indicate that you have been divorced over 3 years, and have addressed or are addressing the issues we have raised.

Nothing Addressed   **Fully Addressed**

1______2______3______4______5

2. Losses incurred through death/divorce have been acknowledged and dealt with. We recently spotted a bumper sticker that read, "Loss happens a lot. Get used to it." Anyone who has experienced the death of a spouse or a divorce can identify with these eight words. There are numerous personal losses associated with death or divorce. For many individuals these losses are overwhelming. For some, it is the loss of a dream, for others the loss of children, for still others the loss of a cherished partner. Many women experience a substantial loss of income, and a subsequent loss of life style. Many men suffer the loss of quality time with their children. One father talked about becoming a "paycheck dad" another referred to his new role as "Uncle Daddy." Many women who have felt abandoned by their husbands deal with the unenviable task of keeping a family together when they are falling apart. The emotional trauma associated with these losses does not heal quickly or easily.

Inadequate grieving is a major cause of remarriage failure. Most of us do not have the training or the motivation to adequately assess our divorce losses or the grieving process. This is especially true of those caught up in the excitement of a new love and possible remarriage. Our normal drive is to avoid pain at any cost. The result is that we block our own grief process and do not allow our children or ourselves an opportunity to mourn. However, blocked, frozen or denied grief can slow down or even stop personal growth and limit our ability to bond to others. It may be necessary to do some grief counseling or join a support group. The most common symptoms of inadequate grieving include:

- Depression
- Sleep or eating problems

- Denial
- Addictions
- Emotional reactivity
- Ritualizing the loss

Adults and children alike need clear permission and encouragement to grieve.

Forgiveness

Forgiveness is an important part of the grieving process. Forgiving others and ourselves is critical to our spiritual development. Below is a review of the six-step process we introduced in Chapter Three.

1. List the ways you have been hurt.
2. Surrender the right to get even.
3. Revise your picture of the one who has hurt you.
4. Move from hatred or bitterness to acceptance.
5. Get the freedom to wish that person well.
6. Be open to whatever God wants you to do.

Dr. P. Rule: Forgiveness means taking the initiative to extend grace to someone who has wronged you.

God desires to be intimately involved in your grief process. However, many individuals are angry with God, feeling that He has abandoned them or let them down. "How could you let this happen to us" is a familiar question for God. Sometimes we cannot ask God for forgiveness because we have not forgiven ourselves. Sometimes our hurt, anger or shame prevents us from forgiving others and we continue to hold on to the hurt, often resulting in bitterness.

Action Step: Losses I have experienced

Beside each loss, write down any related feelings and how this loss has affected you.

Example: Going to work for the first time: Afraid, insecure. I didn't know anything about the world of work. I had to buy new clothes, find day care for my kids, get up earlier, come home tired and fix dinner and try to spend quality time with the children. I'm exhausted, tired, scared and angry. I feel I have to do everything, with no help.

Loss of my home: ______________________________

Financial loss: ______________________________

Loss of friends: ______________________________

Loss of support: ______________________________

Loss of a dream: ____

Loss of esteem: ____

Loss of church: ____

Loss of lifestyle: ____

Loss of time with children: ____________________________________

Loss of ideals____

Loss of special furniture_______________________________________

Loss of a pet____

Loss of special relationships___________________________________

Loss of important roles____

Loss of social holidays or traditions_____________________________

Loss of emotional security______________________________________

How have you addressed the losses described above?

As you complete this section, how does it make you feel?

What new awareness do you have?

Is there something you need to do? If so, what?

Rating Indicator #2: Again, using a 1 to 5 rating scale, rate your progress on this indicator. A score of "1" would indicate that you have not acknowledged or addressed any areas of loss. A score of "5" indicates that you have acknowledged and addressed all the areas of loss associated with your divorce and that you have allowed yourself and your children to grieve. Circle the score that best applies to you at this time.

Nothing Addressed **Fully Addressed**

1_____2_____3_____4_____5

3. Legal issues from prior relationships are resolved.
Many divorces become adversarial in nature, often requiring attorneys and court appearances. We recently counseled a couple in which one partner was still involved in open litigation from a prior relationship. The other partner was soon drawn into the deliberations, mostly as a rescuer. The negative energy and consumption of time created by this situation soon broke this couple apart. It is critical to have all legal and financial issues as resolved as possible before contemplating remarriage. Far too many couples enter a new relationship with unhealthy motives. For some, it is the "rescuer" or "white knight" role; for others, it is the "rescue me" or "take care of me" role. These roles are only temporary and superficial and do not reflect the best reasons to remarry. Resolution in this area means there is currently no planned or pending litigation between you and your former spouse. Issues surrounding child support, spousal maintenance, and division of property have been completed. In addition, you are not looking to be rescued or rescue anyone from a perceived "bad" situation.

<u>Action Step:</u> **Check any planned or pending legal issues, including**:

- ❑ Custody arrangements?
- ❑ Division of property?
- ❑ Spousal maintenance?
- ❑ Child support?
- ❑ Houses or properties still unsold?
- ❑ College funds for a child?
- ❑ Retirement or investment funds?
- ❑ ______________________________

What emotional issues are you still wrestling with?

Are you at peace with the legal issues surrounding your divorce?

Do you continue to feel bitter or taken advantage of?

Do you foster thoughts of revenge or retaliation?

Do you fear that your ex-spouse will take you back to court to modify some aspect of the divorce settlement?

Do you consistently mention financial issues to your children, your friends?

Have these issues surface when dating?

<u>Rating Indicator</u> #3: Again, using a 1 to 5 scale, rate your status on this indicator. A "1" indicates that you are still unsettled about the legal issues surrounding your divorce and are contemplating some form of legal action. A "5" indicates that you are at peace with

the details of the divorce, that all arrangements have been settled and that you have no plans for future litigation.

Nothing Addressed — **Fully Addressed**

1_____2_____3_____4_____5

4. Emotional issues with your prior spouse have been resolved; you are in a fairly healthy co-parenting relationship with your ex-spouse.

Continuing attachment to a former spouse is a main cause of remarriage failure. Some marriages end with spouses remaining emotionally attached. Many marriages end with the couple being enemies. Perhaps there has been extensive litigation, or perhaps one party felt abandoned and devastated and then bitter. In many relationships, there has been a legal divorce but not an emotional one. Many former spouses hope and pray for reconciliation years after a divorce. To be sure, there is absolutely nothing wrong with this, except that if you remain psychological and emotional tied to your former spouse, you are clearly not ready for remarriage. Resolution in this area means that you and your former spouse are on fairly friendly terms (as much as it is up to you) and you are both endeavoring to co-parent your children. Any anger or resentment toward your former spouse has been acknowledged and resolved. You are no longer emotionally attached to or in love with your former spouse. The best interests of your children have been placed above your own personal feelings. You have come to understand that your former spouse will be involved in your life at some level as long as your children are.

Types of former spouses—which are you?

In *The Good Divorce*, Constance Ahrons discusses several roles former spouses can play. The bases for her "roles" are two factors, ability to interact and ability to communicate. Let's look at these different roles. Which one describes your situation? Is that okay?

Perfect Pals. These rank high on interaction and communication. For them, the disappointment of a failed marriage did not overshadow the positive elements of a long-standing relationship. They still considered themselves good friends and spoke to each other once or twice a week. Ahrons reports that, even after five years, most of the individuals in this group had not remarried. She believes this group comprises about 10% of divorced couples.

Cooperative Colleagues. These rank moderate on interaction and communication. While they did not consider themselves best friends, they did cooperate on issues concerning their children. They were able to compromise and solve problems fairly well. A common factor among this group was their ability to compartmentalize their relationship; they could separate marital and parenting issues. Ahrons reports that 38% of her sample fell into this category.

Angry Associates. These rank moderate on interaction and low on communication. This group felt angry every time they communicated—which they did infrequently and only to make arrangements for their children. Conflict was the major issue for these couples.

They were generally unable to compartmentalize their anger. This group comprised 25% of Ahrons' sample.

Fiery Foes. This group ranked low on both interaction and communication. They rarely interacted. When they did, they fought. Most of this group had highly contested divorces with ongoing legal battles. A third party was often required to make arrangements for the children. Nearly 25% of her sample was in this group.

Dissolved Duos. This group had no contact. Typically one partner left the area altogether. Many children in this group never heard from the other parent. Fortunately, this group comprised less than 2% of Ahrons' sample

Based on Ahrons' categories, describe the relationship with your ex-spouse (check any that apply)

- ❑ Cordial
- ❑ Adversarial
- ❑ We can't talk
- ❑ I dislike him/her
- ❑ He/she dislikes me
- ❑ We are still enmeshed
- ❑ I am still in love with him/her
- ❑ He/she is still in love with me

Developing a parenting plan with your former spouse and maintaining a cordial relationship with him/her is a wonderful gift you can give your children and yourself (Romans 12: 9-18; Philippians 2:3-5). Which of the following describes the parenting plan between you and your ex-spouse? If you do not have one, work to get one as soon as possible. A parenting plan outlines how the two of you (plus new spouses) will cooperate to co-parent your children.

- ❑ We cannot agree on anything concerning the children.
- ❑ We cannot talk to one another.
- ❑ We fight and argue in front of the children.
- ❑ I totally disagree with his or her rules when the children are with him or her.
- ❑ I speak negatively about by former spouse in front of my children.
- ❑ He or she does not respect my rules, values or beliefs.
- ❑ At times we can talk about the kids.
- ❑ There are a few areas of agreement.
- ❑ There are many areas of agreement.
- ❑ We are not openly hostile to one another.
- ❑ We work hard to respect one another's parenting style.
- ❑ We actually have a "co-parenting plan" that we have discussed and both try to follow. If so, describe your "co-parenting plan."

<u>Rating indicator # 4:</u> A "1" suggests you do not have a parenting plan or a cordial relationship with your ex-spouse. A "5" suggests you have developed a healthy working relationship with your ex-spouse.

Nothing Addressed				**Fully Addressed**
1	2	3	4	5

5. Your children's emotional issues concerning divorce and remarriage have been adequately addressed.

Children are often adversely affected by divorce, even years later. In fact, research reviewed by Pam and Pearson in *Splitting Up* suggests that when divorces are particularly adversarial and the conflict between parents is prolonged, the emotional damage to a child can be quite severe and long lasting. In our experience, the adage, "the parting parent left the spouse but not the children," is not accurate. Children feel that they have lost a parent as well as the stability of their biological family.

Children process issues much more slowly than adults, which means that even though you may be ready to remarry, your children may not. Provide an opportunity for your children to process their own grief and loss. Do not assume they will be fine. When parents are locked into blaming one another for a marital breakup, it is often the child who readily takes the blame. In these instances, children may adopt a scapegoat role in an effort to reduce pressure and conflict between parents. Look for signs of poor adjustment, such as withdrawal, acting out, or other changes in conduct and behavior. If such signs become evident, consult a counselor. One child Jeff counseled began getting poor grades in school in an effort to bring her parents together.

Most children do not abandon the idea of their parents' reuniting, which is one reason why a pending remarriage may create conflict for children. In a study conducted by Judith Wallerstein and Joan Kelly, the authors reported that after five years, over one-half of the children did not regard their new family as an improvement over their previous family. Even though their family failed prior to the divorce, the children said that if they had a choice, they would return to it.

Which of the characteristics mentioned above describe your child?

<u>**Dr. J. Rule:**</u> Your children must be absolutely settled emotionally, academically, socially and spiritually before you should consider remarriage. Children who are unsettled need your time, attention and focus.

<u>Action Step:</u> **Your children need your watchful care. How many of these are you doing?**

- ❑ I have taken my children to counseling.
- ❑ I do not see their struggles as an indictment of my parenting or me.
- ❑ I regularly observe my children for signs of poor adjustment.
- ❑ I have observed new behavior in my children that may signal a problem.
- ❑ I am reading books on children and divorce.
- ❑ I have been to a support group.
- ❑ I provide opportunities for my children to talk to me and I listen.
- ❑ I understand my children need to grieve.
- ❑ I do not "put down" my ex-spouse in front of the children.
- ❑ I do not use my children as a support or crutch.

- I talk regularly to adults responsible for the care of my child (relatives, day care workers, teachers, babysitters, Sunday School leaders, etc.)
- I do not share details of my dating or personal struggles with them.

Children in trauma may exhibit new behaviors or intensify normal behaviors. Below are a few behaviors to look for:

- Bedwetting
- Crying
- Losing or gaining weight
- Hiding food
- Depression
- Anxious habits
- Fear or panic
- Dependency

If you observe any of these behaviors, consult a counselor. Be careful to avoid becoming dependent on your children for emotional support. This is a common problem when we feel alone and abandoned and have no one to talk to except our children. Please be a good observer of your child's behavior and do not hesitate to contact your pastor or counselor if these behaviors become evident. Most children do not welcome a remarriage, so bring them along slowly and be sensitive to their feelings and needs. Taking a child to a counselor does not mean you are a bad parent.

Rating indicator # 5: A rating of "1" indicates that you did not know your kids needed any attention. A number "5" indicates that you fully addressed their needs. For example, you may have read books, took them to counseling, been aware of their needs and emotions, sensitive to subtle messages in their behavior, and were very clear on being OK to take care of them. A rating of "5" also means that, "I am not dependent on my children."

Nothing Addressed — **Fully Addressed**

1_____2_____3_____4_____5

6. You recognize that a new stepfamily will be unique, not a remake of your old nuclear family.

Stepfamilies are not the same as nuclear families. They are born of loss, with roles that are very ambiguous. Stepfamilies take several years to successfully integrate. During those years, there is a good deal of turbulence and stress as virtual strangers, with few shared traditions, attempt to become a family. Many individuals seek to recreate the biological family model in their next marriage, which is seldom successful. The reasons for wanting to recreate a nuclear family vary, but the most common include a need to "do it right this time," or to "prove that my ex- was wrong about me," or to "do the best for my children." We mistakenly think we can turn a stepfamily into a nuclear family by having the children call our new spouse "Mommy" or "Daddy" as if they do not know the difference. Resolution in this area means that you understand the differences between a nuclear family and a stepfamily.

Key differences between a nuclear and stepfamily

Nuclear Family	Stepfamily
Everyone starts together	Parent-child first
Roles are well defined	Roles poorly defined
Boundaries are firm	Boundaries are vague, permeable
Family members all stay in one household	People come and go.
History and traditions are made together	History and traditions are separate
Life cycles are all in sync	Life cycles are out of sync

Successful stepfamilies exist when individuals are committed to working through the blending process together, with no illusions and with a strong faith in the God of second chances.

It is far more difficult to create a second marriage than a first marriage when children are involved, and it is more important to succeed. The risks are higher and everybody knows it. Judith Wallerstein.

Rating Indicator #6: A "1" means you intend to have your new stepfamily look just like a nuclear family. "5" means you understand a stepfamily can never be just like a nuclear family.

Not Understood ... **Fully Understood**

1______2______3______4______5

7. You are able to embrace and involve your children's extended family.

After a divorce, it is not uncommon to feel uncomfortable around your former spouse's family. Resolution in this area means that your children have access to all family members, even your ex-spouse's family. To the best of your ability, you are maintaining a cordial relationship with them for the sake of your children. This may take some work, since families tend to take sides. There is no better opportunity for grace and forgiveness than to embrace your child's extended family for that child's sake.

Dr. J. Rule: Unresolved anger and selfishness often keep family members away.

An emotionally healthy response to your former spouse's family means that you are able to do the following:

- ❑ I recognize that my child needs, and will benefit from, time with his extended family.
- ❑ I am able to put my own feelings aside for the good of my child.
- ❑ I am working to create and/or maintain a cordial relationship with my child's extended family.
- ❑ I can extend grace and forgiveness to those who have hurt me.
- ❑ I intend to be at peace with my former spouse's family, as far as it is up to me.
- ❑ I will not use my child to punish my former spouse or his or her family.

- I will endeavor to be flexible and adaptable in order to facilitate my child having contact with his or her extended family.
- I will find healthy things to do when my child is gone.

Rating Indicator # 7: Rating yourself a "1" suggests you have no interest in a cordial relationship with your ex-in-laws. A rating of a "5" means either you have a good relationship or are working very hard to create one for your child's sake.

Poor Relationship — **Good Relationship**

1______2______3______4______5

8. Custody issues are resolved and in place.

Sometimes after a divorce, custody arrangements change, as when a teenage boy chooses to live with his father. Resolution in this area means that there is no current pending litigation concerning custody and there have been no recent custody changes. Some changes are sudden or traumatic, and take some time for adjustment. Readiness means your children are settled in terms of school, residence and visitation schedules. This is important for remarriage readiness because custody changes are extremely traumatic and could place an extreme hardship on a new marriage. If you and your prospective spouse are considering changing custody arraignments after your marriage, please be very careful. The stress of litigation can also be devastating to a new marriage.

How many of these statements are true for you?

- My ex-spouse and I communicate regularly about our children.
- We both are committed to the welfare of our children.
- We have discussed custody issues in a healthy, forthright manner.
- The children are settled in terms of residence, school, etc.
- I have no thoughts of changing custody arrangements as soon as I am remarried

Rating indicator # 8: A "1" suggests that custody arrangements are not in place or that I am planning future litigation in this area. A "5" suggests that custody is a settled issue and that you and your ex-spouse are committed to the welfare of your children.

Custody Unsettled — **Custody Settled**

1______2______3______4______5

9. Parenting time runs smoothly, for the most part.

Children are often used as a weapon between adversarial spouses. Jeff once had a case where visitation pick-ups were so difficult due to ugly yelling matches between the parents that a neutral agency had to be retained just to pick up and return the visiting children. Resolution in this area means that children have easy and equal access to both households. Visitation pick-ups and drop-offs are trouble-free. Neither parent says negative, hurtful things about the other in front of the children. Both homes provide adequate space for the children and are reasonably similar in terms of rules, such as bedtimes, fast food or TV. The spiritual needs of the children are taken seriously by both parents. One divorced couple Jeff counseled made it a priority that their children attended Sunday School regularly, no matter whose weekend it was. Being positive and friendly with a former spouse during parenting cycles and being flexible and considerate during holidays and vacations, is a good readiness sign.

How many of these statements are true for you?

- ❑ I am able to be composed and cordial during exchanges.
- ❑ Co-parenting is a shared experience
- ❑ I do not use my children as "go betweens" with my former spouse.
- ❑ I am cooperative and flexible about parenting schedules.
- ❑ I would never personally sabotage my former spouse seeing his or her children.
- ❑ I believe it is important for my child's welfare to maintain a healthy relationship with his or her parent.
- ❑ I value the input of my co-parent

<u>Rating Indicator # 9:</u> A "1" suggests my ex-spouse and I either do not communicate about our children or we do so in a destructive manner. A "5" suggests we are able to put aside any differences and cooperate for the sake of the children.

Uncooperative **Cooperative**

1_____2_____3_____4_____5

10. You are involved in a church and a small group.

We are grieved over how many divorcing couples stop going to church or pull away from fellowship. For many, the choice to stop attending church is about guilt. For some it symbolizes a new, freer lifestyle. For still others it represents the result of feeling disconnected, or even unwanted. We are also grieved when divorcing couples are abandoned or avoided by their friends. We believe the church should be a place of grace and forgiveness. Regular attendance and involvement should not stop because of a divorce. Singles are whole people, with much to offer.

Resolution on this factor means that you and your children are attending a church on a regular basis and involved in some ministry, such as a small group or your church's singles ministry. Resolution also means you have resolved with God your role in the divorce. For some, this may entail forgiving a former spouse. For others it may involve asking for forgiveness. God never intended for us to harm one another or break our oaths. I John 2:1 tells us that when we do, however, we have an advocate, Jesus Christ. God's solution for our hurt, pain and fallenness is repentance, followed by reconciliation and restoration. Make no mistake, no matter what your role in the divorce, God is waiting to embrace you with open arms of love.

How many of the following statements are true for you?

- ❑ I am attending church regularly. (If you left your own church after the divorce, you are willing to talk to the pastor and explore returning.)

- ❑ I am involved as much as my schedule allows.
- ❑ I am plugged into a small group or support group and I am sharing my needs.
- ❑ My children are involved in church with me.
- ❑ I have reconciled my role in the divorce.

Rating Indicator # 10: A "1" means you are not attending church regularly and have not gotten plugged into a small group. A "5" means you are attending church and small group regularly and are developing relationships in your group.

Nothing Addressed				**Fully Addressed**
1______	2______	3______	4______	5

11. You are growing spiritually and have at least one person to whom you are accountable.

You cannot grow spiritually in a vacuum. An accountability partner is someone with whom you can share your spiritual journey. Take the time necessary to find someone you can trust, someone who will listen and provide Godly feedback. Success on this indicator means that you have an accountability partner and you are actively developing your faith. You are reading your Bible regularly and practicing your faith in the real world. God's precepts and principles are your guide in life. There is at least one person to whom you are spiritually accountable. Growing in your faith and active involvement in a local church is an important way to avoid a serious mistake: dating someone who is not a believer or with whom you are unequally yoked. There is a very clear difference between a nominal church attendee and a committed believer. Dating someone who promises to start going to church or promises to become a Christian after you are married is a huge red flag. Resolution means that you are committed to dating only solid believers, who are working through their own issues.

Action Step: Check all that are true:

- ❑ I have an accountability partner, his/her name is ____________________
- ❑ We meet regularly. (If you don't have an accountability partner, get one.)
- ❑ I am open and disclosing with my accountability partner
- ❑ I attend a small group Bible study
- ❑ I share my issues in my small group
- ❑ I have a personal relationship with God
- ❑ I am connected with other believers
- ❑ I have my own spiritual practice—prayer, study, quiet time
- ❑ I am detached from my own sense of timing, in favor of God's

Rating Indicator #11: A "1" suggests you have not found an accountability partner and that you are not regularly in God's word. A "5" reflects that you meet regularly with an accountability partner, with whom you are open and honest.

No Accountability	Good Accountability

1______2______3______4______5

12. Personal issues surrounding your divorce have been addressed.
Some people believe that signing a piece of paper (Marriage license) will help them live happily ever after. We know that is not true. Signing a divorce paper will not make all your pain go away either. You want a new life for yourself and your family. For most, especially right after a divorce, that seems a million miles away. There are actually two divorces, a legal one and an emotional one. As you might have guessed, the emotional one is a little trickier to work through. Some individuals are emotionally divorced long before the separation. Others take years before they feel emotionally disconnected from their ex-spouse. A few never achieve emotional divorce.

To say that a divorce raises personal issues is a vast understatement. In many ways, a divorce is like a funnel, where every weakness, insecurity and unresolved issue from our life seems to gather. And like a funnel, if your pour in too fast, things will spill over. We have listened to the stories of many who have experienced depression, anxiety, hopelessness, abandonment, stifling fear, guilt and panic as they were faced with the challenges of being alone and raising a family alone. Divorce is always devastating, even if you were the one who wanted it. No wonder God says he hates divorce, because He hates broken promises and He sees how it affects His people. A mistake many divorced individuals make is to deny the negative effects the divorce has had on them. Take the time to resolve these issues. We have never seen an individual unaffected by divorce.

<u>**Action Step:**</u> **How many of the following are true?** (Check all that apply).

- ❑ I have dealt with the woundedness of my past
- ❑ I am developing a healthy single lifestyle.
- ❑ I am working through any sexuality issues.
- ❑ I am not overwhelmed by loneliness.
- ❑ I have a support group of friends and family to whom I am honest about my life and circumstances.
- ❑ I have attended counseling and/or divorce recovery
- ❑ I am not currently struggling with any harmful habits or addictions: alcohol, drugs, workaholism, gambling, rage, violence, sex addiction, etc.
- ❑ I have learned how to express my feelings in a healthy manner
- ❑ My finances are stable
- ❑ I have resolved (am resolving) any career issues
- ❑ I have identified and corrected any harmful dating patterns
- ❑ I have forgiven myself and anyone else who may have harmed me in any way
- ❑ I know that someone I just met cannot meet my needs
- ❑ I know what my needs are and can articulate them to others
- ❑ I recognize what makes me needy
- ❑ I consistently take good care of myself
- ❑ I do not need a relationship to meet my needs

- I am able to say "no" and mean it
- I know clearly what my boundaries are
- I gently but effectively educate people about my boundaries
- I respect and honor the boundaries of others
- I have defined what I value in a relationship
- I have defined what I absolutely will not tolerate
- I do not place demands on others that I do not demand of myself
- I am willing to be in the process of growth with a partner
- I no longer engage in activities hoping to meet a partner
- I am my "real self" in relationships
- I never use sexuality, power or money as a way to attract partners
- I do not compare myself to others
- I readily participate in activities rather than sitting at home
- I see and appreciate people for who they are
- I have numerous role models of good relationships around me
- I am living my life to the fullest
- I stay away from verbal foreplay early in a relationship
- I am comfortable ethic my sexuality; I hold to my sexual boundaries and respect those of others
- I limit my together time in the beginning of a relationship; I get to know the person slowly
- I spend much more time courting in person that I do by phone or email
- I am clear about how I want and do not want to be treated and I communicate those desires to my partner
- I have lived alone successfully for some time
- My finances are under control
- I am comfortable with solitude
- I have a good support network
- I understand the role of grieving
- I possess adequate social skills
- I am not addicted to any substance or activity
- I have above average listening skills
- I am a good communicator
- I do not keep secrets from my partner
- I have no problems with anger or violence
- I would never hesitate to seek professional help for an issue
- I am growing in my walk with God
- I am able to show affection without inhibition
- I have worked through any issues from my past
- I can tell my story without extreme emotionality
- I have a good relationship with my children
- I have a healthy, working relationship with my former spouse
- I harbor no resentment toward my partner's former spouse
- Issues around child support and parenting time are in good order
- My children are adjusting well; there are no serious academic or behavioral issues

- ❑ If/when serious issues with my child become evident, I will not hesitate to consult a professional
- ❑ I wish to remarry for healthy reasons; I am not desperate, lonely or afraid of growing old all alone. I am not looking for someone to help with finances or the kids
- ❑ I have no illusions of changing my spouse or his or her children after remarriage
- ❑ I am able so share my needs without hesitation
- ❑ I understand that the first few years of remarriage will be challenging

How did you fare?

Rating Indicator # 12: A rating of "1" suggests that most of the above statements are not true for you at this time. A rating of "5" suggests that a majority of the above statements are true.

Not True				**Mostly all True**
1	2	3	4	5

Rating: points are possible; add your scores from each of the twelve indicators.

45-60—probably ready to remarry (address any low scores)
30-45—questionable, look at areas of struggle (1's or 2's).
Below 30—definitely not ready to remarry, we recommend pastoral or professional help with your particular areas of struggle.

Action Step: You have just read through the twelve success indicators. You now have some sense about your readiness for remarriage. If more than three areas need major attention, you are probably not ready for remarriage at this time. If you are already in a relationship, talk about slowing down the process and working on these areas. Commit to not remarry until the unresolved areas have been addressed. If you are not currently in a relationship, address these issues before you begin or resume serious dating.

Dr. P. Rule: Success in remarriage is more about *being* a good partner than *finding* a good partner.

Things to Talk about Before You Remarry

There's an opportune time to do things; a right time for everything on earth.
Ecclesiastes 3:1 The Message

One of the most important ways you can raise your chances of remarriage success is through honesty and openness with a potential partner. The more you know about yourself, one another and the realities of remarriage and stepfamily life, the more likely that your marriage will survive. This is especially important since most remarriages fail in the first two years. Few couples think through critical issues before remarrying.

In *Stepfamilies*, Dr, James Bray reports some of his research observations. In one instance, he interviewed several stepfamily couples whose marriages had not lasted through the end of his research. He asked them, looking back, what kind of things might have helped them? Compiling all their responses, three common themes emerged. *First,* they reported that it would have been helpful to know that the intense stress and turmoil would eventually end. Couples reported that they just could not handle the stress and conflict any longer. *Second*, it would have been helpful to know what to realistically expect from stepfamily life, especially the stepparent-stepchild relationship. And *third,* it would have been helpful to have some form of stepfamily "road map," which included information about how to form a successful stepfamily. Dr. Bray then asked several remarried couples who had done well what kept them together. The consistent answer was commitment: commitment to build a life together no matter what; to keep communicating about issues; to share feelings; to accept and to learn from each other.

The point is to keep talking and keep listening. Most remarriages fail because of unexpressed, unrealistic expectations and an inability to solve problems effectively. Some of the topics listed below have already been addressed. This worksheet provides an opportunity to explore several key issues in depth. By examining these issues you are increasing your chances of success immeasurably and you are doing something few other remarrying couples ever do.

Family-of-Origin Issues (your birth family)

Describe your family growing up.
What was your father/mother like?
What did you like/dislike about your childhood?
What are ways your parents related to one another that you admired? Disliked?
How did you spend holidays as a child?
Was there any physical or sexual abuse?
How were you praised? Disciplined?
In what ways are you like your same-sex parent?
In what ways are you like your opposite-sex parent?

Couple Issues

Discuss why you want to remarry.
What do you want from this relationship?
Do you like the same activities?
How are your lifestyles similar? Different?

How do you feel about the past, present?
What are your priorities, dreams and goals?
What are your career aspirations? Are you settled vocationally?
Where do you want to live? (Now and in the future)
Are we spiritually compatible?
Do you laugh at the same things?
What's your idea of a fun evening, a fun vacation?
What do you like to do in your spare time?
Do you enjoy your job?
How are you at expressing feelings?
Would you describe yourself as outgoing? Shy?
How do you express anger?
How do "we" express anger?
What do you want your partner to know/do when you are angry?
Is there violence in your past?
Have you discussed in-law issues?
Do you prefer a clean or messy house?
How should chores be split up?
What are your hobbies?
Do we enjoy the same activities, topics, and music?
Do we trust each other with confidences?
Have we shared dreams and goals? Do we feel understood? Supported?
Are my ideas valued and acknowledged?
How will this marriage change our lives?
Have you discussed having children of your own?

Prior Marriage Issues

Have you discussed why your marriage failed?
Have you both successfully worked through your anger and grief?
Are there things you are still angry about?
Are there other "leftover" emotions?
What did you learn from your prior experience?
How is this relationship similar to and different from the last?
What is your current relationship with your ex-spouse?
How will you handle contacts from ex-spouses?
Is there any jealousy or insecurity about your partner's ex-spouse?
If moving into a home where an ex-spouse lived, talk about those feelings.
How will you communicate with your ex-spouse?
How much contact with an ex-spouse is appropriate?

Conflict, Problem-Solving and Decision-Making

How do you solve problems?
How did your parents solve problems?
Did either set of parents have problems with anger?
How do you react when angry? Attack or withdraw?
How have you resolved arguments?
How have "we" resolved arguments? Is it satisfactory for both or unfinished business?
How do you argue?
Do you view arguing as "bad"?
How well do we argue or resolve conflict?
Do we discuss issues well?

Who was the decision-maker when you were a child?
How were decisions made in your last marriage?
How will we make major decisions?

Bonding Issues

When did you begin to say to each other, "You're for me"?
What were you looking for in a partner?
When did you begin discussing marriage?
How did you "know" he/she was "the one"?

Parenting Issues

How should children be disciplined?
How were you disciplined as a child? Was it okay?
Have you discussed child-rearing issues?
Do you have different views on discipline? What are they?
Have you spent time observing one another's child-rearing styles?
What role should children play in your home?
How will our remarriage affect the children?
How will our remarriage affect our children's relationship with their other biological parent?

Co-Parenting Issues

How often will your children be visiting?
How often will children be visiting your home?
How will we make them feel welcome?
What rules should we develop? What will you do when your rules differ?
How will visitation happen?
What about summers and holidays?
How often do you want your children to visit? Is that okay for both of you?
What possible areas of conflict might we encounter?
Will visiting kids do chores?
What are your expectations of me when your/my children come to visit?
What are my expectations of you when your/my children come to visit?
Will they want lots of one-on-one time with you?
Will there be space for each child?

Stepparenting Issues

What role do you want to play as a stepparent?
What are your expectations as a stepparent?
What will your stepchildren call you?
Will you be able to follow the lead of the biological parent at first?
Who will discipline my children, your children?
How shall we handle differences in child rearing?
What happens if our kids don't get along?
How will we handle family vacations?
How will household responsibilities be shared?

Financial Issues

Who will manage the finances?
Are you a spender or a saver?
How much and what kind of debt did we each bring into the relationship?

What about tithing and giving to the church?
How will child support be paid? Who will pay it?
Will we have separate or joint checking accounts?
How will we pay bills? (Together, it's a man thing, etc.)
How were bills paid in your last marriage?
How will financial decisions be made?
What are your long-term financial goals?
How will retirement be paid?
How will college for children be paid?
How do we feel about indebtedness?
Is there a will or trust?
Who will be responsible for health insurance?

Spiritual Issues

Where will we go to church?
How involved in church activities will we be?
Do we agree on spiritual issues?
Will we support the church financially?
How shall we handle children attending church?
Should visiting children be made to attend our church?
Do we understand each other's personal relationship with God?

Addiction Issues

Are there any addictions you struggle with? (These include but are not limited to: drugs, alcohol, sex, gambling, food, work, caffeine, nicotine, or adrenaline)
If you do struggle with one of the above, are you in active recovery? (Do you attend a support or recovery group? Are you in treatment?)

Sexuality

Are there sexual issues that must be addressed?
Do you have clear boundaries around your sexuality?
What are your sexual expectations?
Are there events from your past (abuse, rape, incest) that impact your sexuality? If so, are you actively working on those issues?
Is sexuality a shaming subject?
Is there past teaching that sex is wrong?
Are you comfortable talking about sex?
Can the two of your discuss sexual expectations freely?
Have you discussed co-habitating?
If the two of you are sexually active, does this square with your faith? If not, what will the two of you do?

Action Step: Highlight any areas of concern. Are there any red flags? Be sure to keep talking and listening. If necessary, involve your support group, pastor or counselor.

Are We Ready to Remarry?

To a large extent, success in a marriage depends of the goodness of fit between the expectations, needs and behaviors of a husband and wife. It also depends on how they go about solving their problems, healing emotional rifts when they do occur, and supporting each other in difficult times. Mavis Hetherington, *For Better or For Worse*

Psychologist Robert Sternberg says that love has three faces: passion, intimacy and commitment. *Passion* is the motivational component that fuels romantic feelings and physical attraction. Passion instills a deep desire to be united with that person. *Intimacy* is the emotional component that encompasses the sense of being bonded with another person. It includes feelings of warmth, sharing and emotional closeness. *Commitment* is the cognitive component. It refers to the conscious decision to live with each other and to maintain a relationship over time in spite of the difficulties that may arise. Sternberg suggests that passion tends to develop rapidly and intensely and then declines as the relationship progresses. In contrast, intimacy and commitment continue to build gradually over time. Long term relationships are those that can nurture and maintain intimacy and commitment over an extended period of time. Understanding these dimensions of love is critical as you begin to answer the important question, "Are we ready for remarriage".

Well, are we ready?

In his excellent material on stepfamilies (*StepfamilyinFormation* website), Peter Gerlach suggests that the critical remarriage question should be, "Am I remarrying the right people, at the right time, for the right reasons? "People" involve all the individuals (adults and children) that will make up the extended stepfamily. The "right people" means that all these potential relationships are acceptable to the two spouses, even if these people or their circumstances never change. The "right time" means that all legal, logistical, personal and relational issues that could detract from giving full attention to remarrying and building a stepfamily are completely resolved and under control. The "right reasons" means that the remarriage is happening between two healthy people who draw their fullness from Christ, not one another.

<u>Action Step:</u> Couple worksheet. This is a time to get clear on the beliefs and expectations you bring to your relationship. There will be areas of total agreement and perhaps a few areas of disagreement. In our experience it is the "unknowns" rather than the "knowns" that most often create conflict in relationships.

List any potential problems in dealing with the reality of an "extended stepfamily" (the fact that former spouses and in-laws will be involved in your lives).

Review the key points about stepfamilies stated below and discuss how they relate to your situation:

- Stepfamilies begin due to loss.
- No matter what you do, the first years of stepfamily life will be turbulent.
- A critical task is to find an effective role for the stepparent.
- The couple relationship is the most important yet most neglected relationship in the family.
- Parent will experience intense loyalty binds between their spouse and their children.
- Children are members of two households
- Rules and roles are ambiguous.
- There are no common traditions or ways of doing things.
- The stepparent starts out as an outsider.
- Remarriage stands squarely on the shoulders of faith.

Discuss the fact that it takes four to five years to successfully integrate a stepfamily. List the issues that might create conflict? What are some strategies for staying committed during troubled times?

Identify and discuss your parenting styles.

- Are they similar or vastly different?
- If you both have children, who's parenting style will be applied when all the children are together?
- What are your goals for the children?
- What have you noticed about each other's children that you are reluctant to talk about?
- Will you try to change each other or each other's children?
- Who will handle discipline? How will it be handled?

Determine your personal problem-solving styles.

- How do they differ?
- How will the two of you arrive at win-win solutions?

- What method did your parents use?

Examine compatibility issues: where are you most/least compatible?

Discuss sexual compatibility. Are the two of you comfortable talking about sex? Are there any unresolved personal or relational issues?

Discuss stepparenting issues.

- What role do you want to play as a stepparent?
- What stepparent roles have you observed or experienced?
- How did the roles you observed and/or experienced impact you?
- What role does your partner want you to play?
- What role do you want them to play?

Discuss unresolved issues from prior relationships.

- Are you more jealous or suspicious than before?
- Are you determined this time to try harder to prove you can be a good spouse?
- Do you have unresolved shame from the past?
- Are there issues from past relationships that will impact your spouse? Examples might include a prior spouse that was unfaithful, or mismanaged money or failed to care for your needs.

Examine your personal communication styles.

- How will the two of you make sure that open lines of communication exist?
- Will you communicate like your parents did?

Write your definition of a healthy, Godly marriage.

Examine misbeliefs, such as:

- We will be a family, not a stepfamily
- Stepparenting is just like parenting your own kids
- We can handle our own problems
- Stepfamilies are just like any other family
- We'll change everyone's name to be the same.
- We have been living together and doing okay, so remarriage should be easy.
- The past is in the past.
- Former spouses will never be a part of our family
- I will never choose my kids over you
- I will not treat your kids any differently than I treat my own

Share you marriage goals and priorities.

Discuss how you will carve out "special times" to talk and share.

How will you tell each other if there is a problem or if a need is going unmet?

Together you will build a model for how your new marriage and family will look and operate. The key is to be flexible and knowledgeable as you design your family together. Pray for wisdom. Allow the Holy Spirit to give you peace, patience and understanding as you share your hopes, fears and dreams.

Premarital education

In *Preparing to Marry Again*, Dick Dunn discusses three mistakes people make when contemplating remarriage—eloping, not telling friends about the marriage until the wedding, and not getting adequate premarital counseling. Premarital counseling is critical before remarriage; yet most remarrying couples skip this vital remarriage step. This is unfortunate, because remarriage and stepfamily life require enormous adjustments on the part of the couple. Anticipating and normalizing these adjustments will allow you and your future spouse to be prepared for the inevitable conflicts that stepfamily life can create. Some individuals avoid counseling because they are reluctant to admit that they have any problems or because they have difficulty sharing their thoughts and feelings. Refusal to do any form of premarital counseling or education is a "red flag." Please consider contacting a pastor in your area. Commit to attending a pre-remarriage education class or to premarital counseling with a pastor or counselor.

What do I expect from remarriage?

- What do I really want from a committed, long-term relationship?
- What changes do I need to make to achieve that type of relationship?
- What am I looking for in a partner?
- What are my negotiable expectations? My non-negotiables?
- Am I remarrying because of loneliness, financial need, or assistance in raising my children?
- Have I resolved any lingering issues from my divorce or the death of my spouse?
- Am I clear about the role I played in my divorce?
- Have I successfully mastered being single?
- Do I have a strong support base of friends, church and/or family?
- Have I worked through the key divorce recovery issues?

List your expectations

Each of us brings expectations into our marriage. Most of these expectations come from our family-of-origin. Many want a family just like the one they grew up with; others want one that is just the opposite. For those who have come through a divorce, expectations are often colored by a sense of failure in a prior marriage that did not live up to expectations. The key is communication. Below is a sample list of the expectations of a remarrying couple.

Jill's List	John's List
I want to keep working. I want John to help around the house. I want John to take me out once a week. When John's kids are with us, I expect them to help out around the house.	I will do the yard work. I will pay the bills. I want to go away with Jill for the weekend without her children. I expect Jill's kids to do chores.

My expectations for our marriage and family are:

What emotional needs do I expect to be met in this relationship?

Marriage is most effective when our needs are met. What are some of your personal and relational needs? Review the following list. It is likely you are expressing most of these needs. An important question you must answer is, "How well will my partner be at meeting these needs?" Below are some common needs.

The need to feel loved and cherished
The need to give love
The need to feel understood
The need to feel appreciated
The need to be listened to
The need to be challenged
The need for adventure
The need to give and receive comfort
The need to conceive children
The need for encouragement
The need to trust and be trusted
The need for security
The need to be respected and validated
The need to share experiences with someone
The need to share the wonder of God with someone
The need for acceptance
The need for approval

The need to feel sexually and physically desirable and fulfilled

The need for tolerance

The need to be forgiven when we are wrong

Action Step: Review the above needs. List any we may have missed.

- How well does your partner articulate his or her needs to you?
- How well does your partner respond to your needs?
- How well do you respond to your partner's needs
- How are you at identifying and articulating your own needs?
- Which needs are hardest to articulate?
- Which of your partner's needs is hardest to meet?
- How well do the two of you handle competing needs?

Dr. P. Rule: We must give our partner permission to meet our needs. Some of us struggle with this. It is not wrong to share your needs with a partner or expect that he or she will attempt to meet them. Keep in mind that our partners are not mind readers. Express your needs clearly and listen carefully as his or her needs are expressed to you.

How do I view our relationship?

- How do I picture our relationship? (God's picture of marriage is found in Genesis 2; Song of Solomon 4:9-10; Ephesians 5: 21-33).
- What is the greatest strength of our relationship?
- What are the deep personal needs inside of me that I believe this marriage will meet?
- How well does my current partner fit my ideal?
- Am I spiritually compatible with my partner?
- Are we good friends?
- What do I appreciate most about my partner?
- What is my partner's greatest strength?
- What is my partner's greatest weakness? How will I respond to this weakness?
- What changes will I have to make for this marriage to be successful?
- What changes will my partner have to make?
- How willing am I to make changes?
- Can I accept my partner just the way he or she is?
- Do I have any issues with my partner's family?
- Are our children compatible? Will there be extraordinary stress blending them together because of wide age differences or special needs? Are there sexual or modesty issues that must be addressed?
- Do my partner and I have similar goals and dreams?
- Are there issues between us that we have difficulty discussing?
- Am I ready to make a commitment?

Point to Ponder: Commitment is critical to a successful marriage. As our friend, Pastor Tim Coop, is fond of saying, successful marriages have "closed and locked the back door."

- What wounds or hurts do I still have from my previous relationship?
- Have I resolved any guilt or shame from my divorce?
- Am I free of anger and bitterness?
- Am I ready to spend the rest of my life with this person?
- Have I been in prayer about my decision?
- Am I feeling pressured to make a commitment?
- Am I able to see myself as a redeemed, fully forgiven child of God?
- Can I see myself living the rest of my life with this person?

Have we spent an adequate amount of time together?

- Have we seen each other at our best and worst?
- Have we observed one another around our children?
- Are there questions about how we interact with one another's children?
- Am I at ease around my partner's children? Are they at ease with me?
- Can I live with my partner's children just the way they are? If I could change one thing about my partner's children, what would it be?
- Do the children get along? How will we help them get along?
- Have any former spouse issues surfaced?
- Have we handled conflicts or disagreements well?
- How do outings go with each other's extended family?
- Does the relationship have our families' blessing?
- Has premarital counseling been initiated?
- Have we shared our pasts honestly?
- Are there any "red flags?"
- Are we comfortable praying together?

Defining effective parenting

Parenting is such an important topic in remarriage and stepfamilies. It is critical that the two of you develop a definition of effective parenting. Write down the key elements of effective parenting. We have included some examples below.

- Teach life skills
- Protect children from physical and emotional harm
- Provide healthy nurturance and comfort
- Provide healthy boundaries and guidance
- Come from a place of love not obligation
- Seek to understand what children need
- Provide acceptance and approval
- Provide encouragement and appreciation
- Model a healthy reverence for God
- Discipline with love
- Provide security
- Listen

Our definition of effective parenting includes:

Effective parenting is a choice; it must be intentional. Few parents intend to harm or neglect their children; however, most parents do not have a "purpose" or "goal" in raising their children. Our intent must be to provide our children with a safe, nurturing environment where they can grow and learn healthy life skills and develop a mature Christian lifestyle. Design a plan to intentionally become effective parents.

Telling the children

When do we tell our children we are getting engaged?

If the relationship is getting serious, of course, the children should be involved. Your children should be the first to hear of your plans to remarry and they should hear it from you. Once an engagement is planned, the children should be informed and any questions answered. In some cases, it is best to tell each child separately. This allows each child to respond independently.

What details do children need to know about our marriage plans?

Children will have many questions; be candid.

- How will things change?
- Will I be able to see my mom or dad as much after the wedding?
- What will they do at the wedding?
- Does this mean my mom and dad will never get back together?
- Will I be able to live at the same house with a bunch of new people?
- Will I get my own room?
- Will we be moving?
- If we are moving, where will I go to school?
- Where will I stay?
- How will I get to school, piano lessons, scouts, or ball practice?
- What will you do with my cat, dog, turtle, etc.?
- What about my friends?
- What about grandma and grandpa?

Children need a great deal of reassurance during this time. Our advice is to change as few things as possible. If some things have to change, tell your children well in advance. Be very clear about the changes and how they will impact their lives. When appropriate, let your children have input about some of these decisions.

Where will we live?

- Is either of our homes or apartments suitable?
- Is it feasible to find a neutral new home?
- What impact will moving have on the children?
- Will there be enough space for everyone?
- Do we keep open rooms for children who are not there full-time?

It is difficult to have a new person or persons move into your space, and it is equally difficult to be that new person. The following are guidelines from Visher and Visher's book, *How to Win as a Stepfamily*.

- Consider it money well spent and the easing of many unpleasant hours if you can find a new living place to start your life together.
- Include your children and stepchildren in your search. From the beginning make it a family project.
- When it comes time to decide who gets what space, have a family conference.
- When you move in, have all stepfamily members take part.

Discussing wedding arrangements

- What kind of wedding do we want?
- Are their wedding "issues" from the past?
- Where will we get married?
- Are there issues around the wedding and who will be involved?
- Who will be invited? Not invited?
- How will we pay for the wedding?
- How will our wedding be sensitive to stepfamily issues?
- Will our children be involved? How will they be involved?
  Not all of your children will want to be involved in your wedding, but they do want to know that you care. Therefore, invite them to be participants and let them choose. Forcing them will create needless barriers and resentments and ignoring them will cause deep hurt. How will you involve your children in the wedding? Will the pastor address your children during the ceremony?
- Family Medallion
  Dr Roger Coleman has developed a medallion that can be given to children during the wedding ceremony. This act reassures children of their place in the new family and symbolically represents the commitment that stepparents make to the care of their stepchildren. You can learn more about this wonderful resource via his website: *www.familymedallion.com.*

In *Promising Again,* Herbert Anderson and his co-authors suggest that remarriage involves ten important "markers" to be successful. These markers are critical issues to which a new couple must be alert.

1. **Former relationships have been grieved**. Remarriage is born in grief. Past relationship losses must be mourned and forgiven to establish a healthy environment for a new beginning.
2. **Newly formed couples develop openness to the reality of the former relationships.** Healthy boundaries must be set. Closure of past relationships allows the new couple to interact freely about the past, present and future without defensiveness. Without closure, past relationships can become unwelcome ghosts in new relationships.
3. **A new marital relationship has a developmental cycle of its own.** New life stories evolve from new relationships. Closure allows a new relationship to develop its own identity.

4. **Increasingly, a new community is being formed around the new couple.** A new relationship is a blend of the old and the new. Supportive relationships must be both developed and maintained.
5. **Members of the new family become realistic about the differences between this family and former families**. Families cannot be replicated. A new family will blend old and new traditions and integrate different histories, values and preferences. In the process, something unique will be created.
6. **Children are free to develop and maintain full relationships with both biological parents.** Children are healthiest when they have access to all family members, including the extended families.
7. **A body of new rituals is formed.** Family rituals create identity and enhance bonding between members. Healthy stepfamilies preserve old traditions while they develop new ones.
8. **There is allowance for the time it takes to form a new family**. The average stepfamily requires four to seven years to become stable and provide a place of safety and nurturing for its members.
9. **An openness to experimentation and a sense of humor are critical.** Healthy stepfamilies do not take themselves too seriously. Important growth qualities are tolerance, patience and flexibility.
10. **Couples who marry again may decide to have children of their own.** While this forms the most complex family form, many couples decide to include *yours, mine and ours.* It is, however, best to wait until the family is stable before having children.

The structure of your new family

As a couple, begin to think about the topics you want to discuss with your children. The more they know about stepfamilies in general and the kind of family you want in particular, the more likely that your new family will survive and thrive. Stepfamilies do best when all individuals (children and adults) are able to talk about their issues in a warm, accepting environment.

> **Dr. P. Rule:** James 1:1 tells us to consider it pure joy when we encounter trials, because trials forge our character. Consider the time you spend together, wrestling with the type of family you both want to be a time of bonding and growth. God wants our families to reflect His character. A stepfamily by its very nature resembles the Body of Christ, in that we have all been adopted in and there is unity in our diversity.

Healthy partnership checklist

Remarriage is clearly a challenging adventure. The most successful remarriages feature two emotionally and spiritually healthy individuals who can articulate what they want and what they have to offer and are in touch with reality in terms of their own limits as well as the challenges of remarriage and stepfamily life. Healthy partners have healthy lifestyles and are clear about their expectations, values and needs. Great remarriages and stepfamilies start with a couple who have a strong bond. They embrace the truth that they are flawed human beings, imperfect, but redeemed and made whole by the grace of God. ***They understand that although they will do their best as partners and parents,***

there will, at times, be conflicts for which there are no easy or immediately observable solutions. They commit to resolve these conflicts with patience and gentleness, finding win-win solutions based on the model of servanthood and mutual submission (Eph. 5:21). Finally, they understand that they can only love well if that love comes from their fullness in Christ. Anything less leads to control, manipulation or codependency. Share the following list together. Respond to each statement. A positive response to the majority of these statements means that the two of you are well on your way to having a great remarriage.

- ❑ We are absolutely committed to putting each other first in our marriage.
- ❑ We address and solve problems effectively.
- ❑ We communicate well.
- ❑ We understand the realities of stepfamily life.
- ❑ We are not ashamed of the term stepfamily; in fact, we use this word to describe our future family.
- ❑ We have discussed and developed a stepparent role; we are content to let that role develop gradually.
- ❑ We accept that each of us is a flawed person; we accept each other exactly as she or he is.
- ❑ We are clear on the ongoing role of former spouses in our remarriage.
- ❑ We avoid making disparaging comments about former spouses in the presence of our children.
- ❑ There is nothing we cannot discuss. There are no "taboo" subjects.
- ❑ We have been absolutely honest with one another. There are no secrets.
- ❑ We have deep love and respect for one another.
- ❑ We share many interest and values.
- ❑ We seem to handle conflict well.
- ❑ We can be ourselves around each other.
- ❑ We are both completely emotionally detached from any past relationships.
- ❑ We would never hesitate to consult a counselor or our pastor if the need arose.
- ❑ We freely discuss spiritual issues and are spiritually compatible.
- ❑ We enjoy each others friends and family.
- ❑ We support each other and provide useful feedback when asked.
- ❑ We openly discuss sexual issues; we respect each other's sexual boundaries; our goal is to honor God and one another.
- ❑ There is a strong sense of mutual trust.
- ❑ We are committed to share life together.
- ❑ We have a solid church relationship.
- ❑ We have been candid about our emotional wounds; we support each other's counseling, recovery or growth activities.
- ❑ We have thoroughly discussed finances, including giving, savings, debt, education and retirement.
- ❑ We are committed to parenting our children/stepchildren well.
- ❑ We are committed to co-parenting our children with all other parenting adults.
- ❑ We have thoroughly discussed our different parenting styles and have come to a successful resolution.
- ❑ We understand that discipline is about building character, not about punishment.

- ❑ Our children have been allowed to grieve their losses.
- ❑ Our children have free access to the other parent and extended family.
- ❑ Our children are free to ask any question about the past, present or future.
- ❑ Our children are in a stable place socially and emotionally.
- ❑ Remarriage issues have been thoroughly discussed with the children.
- ❑ We enjoy each other's children and harbor no fantasies about changing them after marriage.
- ❑ We have discussed having/not having children together.
- ❑ We have a home planned that will accommodate our unique family needs; we understand that the best case scenario is starting out in a home new to everyone.
- ❑ We are sensitive to the adjustment issues our kids will experience.
- ❑ We have spent adequate time getting to know one another.
- ❑ We pray together regularly and seek God's guidance for our lives.
- ❑ We have involved our support group in our decision to remarry.
- ❑ We have attended several pre-marital counseling/education sessions.
- ❑ We understand that no matter what we do, the first two years of remarriage and stepfamily life will be turbulent.
- ❑ We have disclosed our past to one another.
- ❑ We have interviewed successful stepfamily couples.

A new beginning

As we come to the end of this workbook, we want to congratulate you for doing something very few remarrying adults actually do—going through the process of remarriage preparation. Your journey has taken you from endings to new beginnings. The hidden landmines of a new marriage are unspoken expectations and unresolved issues from the past. The keys to a great remarriage are commitment, respect, flexibility, tolerance and acceptance. The model for marriage is the incredible grace of God. The key Bible passage is I Corinthians 13. Great remarriages as made up of individuals who have chosen to do life together—flaws and all. Great remarriages reflect the character of the creator of marriage. God stands for remarriages and stepfamilies. Jesus grew up in a stepfamily. We are reminded of Paul's words to the Church at Philippi. *There has never been the slightest doubt in my mind that the God who started this great work in you would keep at it and bring it to a flourishing finish on the very day Christ Jesus appears (Phil 1: 6* The Message*)*. Paul was talking ultimately about the day of Christ's return. This is your day—celebrate. Thanks for letting us share in your adventure. God bless you on your journey

Developing a Vision for a New Stepfamily

The following study can be helpful as you explore God's principles for relationships. The key to developing a unique identity for your new stepfamily is sharing your feelings and expectations and listening to God's heart for the family.

A. Our vision of the family

Explore the following questions and discuss them with your spouse.

- What was your image of a family while you were growing up?
- If you were married before, what was your image of family in your first marriage?
- What is your image of a stepfamily?
- How are these images the same? Different?

B. Biblical structure of the family

Read Genesis 2:24; Ephesians 5:21-6:4; Colossians 3:16-21; I Corinthians 7:3-4 and I Peter 3:1-9. What do these passages have to say about the following?

- The role of the husband?
- The role of the wife?
- The relationship of husband and wife?
- Relationships with children?

C. **Identify expectations** (Galatians 5:13; Philippians 4:10-13; Ephesians 4:15)

The following is a list of expectations you may have about stepfamilies. Circle the number of each one that applies to you. Perhaps there are others that are not listed. Discuss them with your prospective partner, children and stepchildren.

1. Expecting your stepchildren to love you and their stepsiblings quickly.
2. Assuming that children or stepchildren who do not live with you will not affect your marriage.
3. Assuming you will not have to deal with your new partner's former spouse or memories of a partner who has passed away.
4. Expecting a woman to be instantly maternal because she is a woman.
5. Expecting a man to step in instantly and take over the role of disciplinarian.
6. Expecting your partner to take care of the stepchildren so you will not have to do much with them.
7. Expecting grown children and stepchildren to have no effect on your marriage.
8. Expecting to quickly fix irritating habits in your stepchildren.
9. Expecting your former spouse to "go away" and not interfere in your new family.
10. Expecting "smooth sailing" as you start your stepfamily.

If you have not already guessed it, these are unrealistic and potentially damaging expectations. What expectations does God have as you enter into a stepfamily? Write down your answers and compare them with your partner's.

D. Biblical exploration for a new stepfamily

Below are several biblical concepts that have great relevance to remarriage and stepfamily life. Review the following scriptures together and discuss how to apply these principles in your life and family.

Servant model of leadership (Mark 10: 42-45; Luke 14: 8-11; John 13: 2-17)

The model for leadership in a stepfamily is that of servant or shepherd. God calls us to lead through example and with integrity. A shepherd knows his sheep and the sheep know his voice intimately. A servant is humble and not filled with self-importance. Leading a stepfamily is not an easy task. Some family members will resist being led. The servant or shepherding model suggests that leadership be relational, personal and based on example, not coercive or authoritarian.

- How can I apply this leadership style to my family?
- How can we as family members support this leadership style?
- What areas of my personality will resist leading like a servant?

Acceptance and forgiveness (Matthew 6:14-15; Matthew 7:1-4; Mark 11:25; Luke 17:3-3; Matthew 18:21-35; Galatians 6:1-5)

Forgiveness means we are giving up the right for payback or revenge and leaving it in God's hands. Issues from the past have a way of reappearing in stepfamilies. Walking away from these old issues is difficult, but important to the success of a new family and the spiritual health of the family members. The result of unforgiveness is often bitterness, which becomes a poison in our souls. The fruit of acceptance and forgiveness is an atmosphere of trust that is created in the home, where individuals can draw closer to one another, embrace their differences and find ways to connect.

- In what ways can I show acceptance for a family member with whom I disagree?
- Are there forgiveness issues I am not willing to acknowledge? Toward a former spouse? A stepchild? My current partner? Myself?
- In what areas of my life do I struggle with acceptance?
- What wounds still hurt me and make me vulnerable?

Love (I Corinthians 13; I John 4:19-21; Matthew 10:29-31; Ephesians 3:17-20; Luke 10:27-37; I Thessalonians 5:11)

Often adults and children in stepfamilies see love as a glass of water—holding only so much. Many of us remarry and enter stepfamilies having experienced a loss of love, so the fear is real and present. In truth, because of God's infinite love, we are able to extend love to new members of our stepfamily. It is only when we truly embrace how much God loves us that we are free to love others. Love is so important in a stepfamily. The family is often so stressed and fragmented. Family members need love, encouragement and patience, especially when they seem unlovable.

- Is there someone in the family I will have difficulty loving?

- Am I experiencing a deep-rooted joy from knowing how profoundly my Father loves me?
- Do I struggle with receiving love?

Our unique personhood in God (John 14:27; Luke 12:4-7; Matthew 11:28-30; Romans 8:15-17; Luke 15:11-31; II Corinthians 5:17; Ephesians 1:5-6; James 1:1-4).
At times when our self-worth is nearly depleted, it's important to remember that God loves and values us and will never give up on us. The struggles of a stepfamily can take us to the brink of feeling like a total failure. We may be tempted to give up. God holds us in such esteem. He encourages us to persevere because he knows it will not only build our character but will also yield fruit such as peace and joy.

- Do I believe and live by who the Father says I am?
- Am I relaxed and peaceful in my lifestyle?
- How does this translate into my "at home" behavior?
- Do I have regular "quiet times" with God?

God's guiding hand in times of uncertainty (Matthew 6:33; Psalm 25:9; James 3:17; John 16:13; Joshua 1:5-9; Psalm 23:4; Isaiah 41:10; John 16:33; Romans 8:31; Hebrews 13:5)
Adults in a stepfamily are dealing with numerous changes happening all at once. It's easy to feel overwhelmed, depleted and distant from God's promises. It's important to know God is present and that He will never leave you or forsake you.

- Do I feel secure in my Father's protective care?
- Do I genuinely believe that what God promises, He will do?
- Do I trust God with our family circumstances?
- Do I experience the peace that comes from knowing God is in control?

The value of community (Act 2: 42-47; Romans 12; I Corinthians 12)
God calls us to community with other believers. Inside that community we experience support, encouragement, accountability and guidance. We will not grow as individuals or as a family without healthy community. Transformation occurs within a community of believers who allow God's spirit to change them from the inside out. Sharing with others in a community of fellow strugglers is both encouraging and insightful. Community is a safe place where we can learn new lessons, try out new behaviors and understand that we are not alone. Join a small group that encourages sharing and caring for one another.

- Am I able to freely share with others
- Can I trust others with my fears and struggles?

Bibliography and Suggested Readings

Ahrons, Constance. *The Good Divorce*. New York: Harper Collins, 1994.

Anderson, H. Hogue, D. and M. McCarthy. *Promising Again.* Louisville, KY: Westminster John Knox Press, 1995.

Barnes, Bob. *Winning the Heart of Your Stepchild.* Grand Rapids: Zondervan, 1992.

Barnes, M. Craig. *When God Interrupts*. Downers Grove, IL: InterVarsity Press, 1996.

Bienfield, Florence. *Helping Your Child Through a Divorce*. Alameda: Hunter House, 1995.

Bonhoeffer, Dietrich. Life Together. New York: Harper and Row, 1954.

Bray, James. *Stepfamilies.* New York: Broadway Books, 1998.

Bridges, William. *Personal Transition.* Booklet. Mill Valley, CA: Bridges and Associates, 1998.

Bridges, William. *Transitions.* New York: Addison-Wesley, 1980

Burkett, Larry. *The Financial Guide for the Single Parent.* Chicago: Moody Press, 1997

Burns, Robert & Tom Whiteman. *The Fresh Start Divorce Recovery Workbook.* Nashville: Thomas Nelson, 1998.

Deal, Ron. Building a Successful Stepfamily. Little Rock, AR: Family Life, 2001.

Deal, Ron. The Smart Stepfamily. Bloomington, MN: Bethany House, 2002.

Dunn, R. *Willing to Try Again*. Valley Forge: Judson Press, 1993

Dunn, Dick. *Preparing to Marry Again*. Nashville: Discipleship Resources, 1999.

Einstein, Elizabeth. *The Stepfamily*. New York: Macmillan, 1994.

Evans, Marla. *This is Me and My Two Families*. New York: Magination Press, 1996

Everett C. and S. Volgy. *The Healthy Divorce*. San Francisco: Jossey-Bass, 1994.

Ferguson, David, Theresa Ferguson, Bruce Walker and Joyce Walker. *Discovering Intimacy.* Austin: Intimacy Press, 2000.

Fox, Kathleen. *Making the Best of Second Best*. Rapid City, SD, 1998.

Gerlach, Peter. "Stepfamily inFormation." http//www.stepfamilyinfo.org, Stepfamily Association of Illinois.

Gerlach, Peter. *Who's Really Running Your Life*? Xlibris Corp., 2000.

Gottman, John. *A Couples Guide to Communication*. Champaign, IL: Research Press, 1976.

Hansel, Tim. *The Hidden Adventure*. New York: Guideposts, 1987.

Heitler, Susan. *From Conflict to Resolution*. New York: Norton, 1990.

Hendrix, Harville. *Keeping the Love You Find.* New York: Pocket Books, 1992.

Hetherington, E. Mavis and John Kelly. *For Better or for Worse*. New York: Norton, 2002.

Jones, Thomas. *The Single Again Handbook*. Nashville: Thomas Nelson, 1993.

Johnson, Laurene. *Divorced Kids*. Nashville: Thomas Nelson, 1990.

Kaufman, Taube. *The Combined Family*. New York: Plenum Press, 1993.

Keen, Sam. *Beginnings Without End.* New York: Harper and Row, 1975.

Kubler-Ross, Elisabeth. *Handbook for the Soul*. New York: Little, Brown and Company, 1995.

Kubler-Ross, Elizabeth. *On Death and Dying*. New York: Collier Books, 1969.

Lauer and Lauer. *Becoming Family.* Augsburg Press, Minneapolis. 1999.

Leman, Kevin. *Living in a Stepfamily without Getting Stepped On*. Thomas Nelson, Nashville. 1994
Lofas, Jeanette. *Family Rules*. New York: Kensington Books, 1998.
McCullough, Michael, Steven Sandage and Everett Worthington. *To Forgive is Human.* Downers Grove, IL: InterVarsity Press, 1997.
Monroe, Robin. *I Have a New Family Now*. St. Louis: Concordia, 1998.
Henri Nouwen, *Reaching Out*. New York: Doubleday, 1975.
Nouwen, Henri. *The Wounded Healer*. New York: Image Books, 1972.
Nowell, David Z. *Stepparent is not a Bad Word*. Thomas Nelson, Nashville, 1994
Olson, David. *Building Relationships: Developing Skills for Life*. Minneapolis: Life Innovations, 1998..
Ortberg, John. *The Life You've Always Wanted.* Grand Rapids, Zondervan 1997.
Ortberg, John. *Everybody's Normal Till You Get To Know Them.* Grand Rapids, Zondervan 2003.
Papernow, Patricia. Becoming a Stepfamily. San Francisco: Jossey-Bass, 1993.
Parke, Ross & Armin Brott. *Throwaway Dads*. Houghton Mifflin, New York. 1999.
Parrott Les and Leslie. *Saving You Marriage Before It Starts.* Grand Rapids: Zondervan, 1995
Parrott, Les and Leslie. *Saving Your Second Marriage Before it Starts*. Grand Rapids: Zondervan. 2001.
Parziale, Jeff. *Developing Healthy Relationships.* Tucson: InStep, 2002.
Parziale, Jeff and Judi. *The Journey: A Travelgiude for Christian Stepfamilies.* Tucson: Fenestra, 2002.
Powell, John. *Why Am I Afraid to Tell You Who I Am?* Valencia, CA: Tabor Press, 1974.
Reed, Bobbie. *Merging Families*. St. Louis: Concordia, 1992.
Robbins, Harvey and Michael Finely. *Why Change Doesn't Work*. Princeton: Pacesetter, 1996.
Rosenberg, Maxine B. *Talking about Stepfamilies.* New York: Bradbury Press, 1990.
Savage, Karen. *The Good Stepmother*. New York: Avon, 1988.
Seibold, Myrla. "When the Wounding Runs Deep" in Mark McMinn and Timothy Phillips, eds. *Care for the Soul*. Downers Grove IL: InterVarsity Press, 2001.
Smith, M. Blaine. *Should I Get Married?* Downers Grove IL: InterVarsity, 1990.
Smith-Broersma, Margaret. *Devotions for Couples in Blended Families,* Grand Rapids: Kregel, 1996.
Sternberg, R. Triangulating Love, In R. Sternberg and M. Barnes, *The Psychology of Love.* New haven Ct: Yale University Press, 1988
Visher J. and Visher E. *How to Win as a Stepfamily*. New York: Brunner-Mazel, 1991.
Wallerstein, L and S. Blakeslee. *Second Chances*. New York: Tichnor and Fields, 1990.
Wallerstein, J., Lewis S. and S. Blakeslee. *The Unexpected Legacy of Divorce,* New York: Hyperion, 2000.
Whiteman, Thomas. *A Fresh Start for Single Parents*. Colorado Springs: David C. Cook, 1997.
Willard, Dallas. *The Spirit of the Disciplines.* New York: Harper, 1988.
Williams, Frank, *Leaders Guide for Divorce Recovery*, Family Counseling Agency, Tucson, Arizona. 1980.